DOING TEXT
MEDIA AFTER THE SUBJECT

DOING TEXT
MEDIA AFTER THE SUBJECT
EDITED BY PETE BENNETT AND JULIAN MCDOUGALL

DEDICATION

Dedicated to David Bowie, for 'Being Text'.

ACKNOWLEDGEMENTS

Our thanks go to John Atkinson at Auteur for taking this on and to the inspirational teachers writing here who responded to such a challenging invitation and the subsequent pestering and hectoring. Julian would also like to acknowledge Stephen Jukes for support. Pete would like to thank Ofqual and the Department of Education for saving Media Studies, albeit without any obvious relish.

First published in 2016 by
Auteur
24 Hartwell Crescent, Leighton Buzzard LU7 1NP
www.auteur.co.uk

Copyright © Auteur Publishing 2016
Typeset by SmartScrolls.
Printed and bound by Printondemand-worldwide.com
Cover: *Vitreosity* by Bedwyr Williams, reproduced by the kind permission of the artist and Limoncello Gallery.

All rights reserved. No part of this publication may be reproduced in any material form (including photocopying or storing in any medium by electronic means and whether or not transiently or incidentally to some other use of this publication) without the permission of the copyright owner.

British Library Cataloguing-in-Publication Data
A catalogue record for this book is available from the British Library.

ISBN: paperback 978-1-911325-02-4
ISBN: cloth 978-1-911325-03-1
ISBN: ebook 978-1-911325-04-8

CONTENTS

Preface ix
Nick Peim

1 Doing Text 1
Julian McDougall

2 Reading Text 17
Steph Hendry

3 Wearing Text 37
Claire Pollard

4 Writing Text 59
Pritpal Singh Sembi

5 Playing Text 73
Barney Oram

6 Making Text 93
Emma Walters

7 Performing Text 113
Mark Parsons

8 Connecting Text 131
Chris Waugh

9 Eating Text 145
Gill Burbridge

10 After the Subject 163
Pete Bennett

Index 181

DIGITAL TOOLS

Each chapter is accompanied by a set of digital resources to help teachers 'do text' in the classroom.

The resources are freely available at http://www.cemp.ac.uk/projects/doingText.php

CONTRIBUTORS

Gill Burbridge is Vice Principal for Teaching, Learning and Achievement at Leyton Sixth Form College in north-east London and a teacher of Communication and Culture. Previous incarnations have included Drama and English teacher, wine bar manager and head of fictions for a renowned bookseller. She has worked as a senior examiner for AQA on a number of specifications and is currently Principal Moderator for AS Communication and Culture.

Steph Hendry began her teaching career as an English teacher and moved into Media Studies within a year of qualifying. She has now been teaching Media for over twenty years, running a high achieving Media Studies course in a successful Lancashire College. She has also worked for a leading Awarding Body as Principal Moderator and has been at the forefront of Teacher Support and CPD delivery for ten years, writing and delivering training for Media teachers. She is a freelance writer and author of a range of A Level Media resources including a forthcoming A Level Media Studies textbook.

Barney Oram is a teacher of Applied Media at Long Road Sixth Form College, Cambridge. He is a principal moderator of Film Studies for an awarding body and co-author of *Teaching Digital Video Production* (2003) with Pete Fraser and *Teaching Videogames* (2008) with James Newman.

Mark Parsons is a Media and Film Studies teacher and is currently working at Wellington International School in the United Arab Emirates. He undertook his PGCE at Edge Hill University and has since gained an MA in Creative Media Education from CEMP at Bournemouth University. Although originally from Liverpool, his teaching career began in south-east and then south-west London, where he was Head of Department.

Claire Pollard has been a Head of Media Studies in Tower Hamlets schools since 2006 and has a Master of Arts in Creative and Media Education from CEMP. She has taught sessions for students and teachers on behalf of Oxford, Cambridge and RSA exam board, the British Film Institute and the Media Education Association. She lives in Hackney, East London where, despite being a responsible mother of two, she wastes far too much time obsessing over the nineties.

Pritpal Singh Sembi is Head of the School of Media at the University of Wolverhampton, as well as a veteran gamer since the days of the Sinclair Spectrum 16K. He currently teaches Film Studies and pursues an eclectic mix of wider research interests in gaming, film, philosophy and pedagogy. He is nearing completion of his doctoral research but is all too frequently afflicted by debilitating bouts of gaming obsession

Emma Walters has taught media in Further Education since 2003, prior to which she worked in the media industry (Live TV! / Mirror Group, Red Productions, Lime Pictures, Rapture TV and Granada Studios). At the time of writing (2016), Emma is in her fourth year of a Professional Doctorate of Education (Creative and Media) in CEMP at Bournemouth University whilst continuing to teach Media, as well as being a mum to two wonderful, clever and very stoical daughters (Annie-Blue & Violet Florence).

Christopher Waugh teaches Secondary English at the London Nautical School. After forays into radio broadcasting and some time in the fitness industry, Chris took up teaching English in an outdoor education school in the Southern Alps of New Zealand. Remaining in the classroom, but switching hemispheres to London in 2009, Chris has gradually shifted more of his and his students' work online – all of which can be seen at www.edutronic.net.

PREFACE

Nick Peim

During the late 1970s and early 1980s something happened to what at that time could only obscurely be identified as textual studies. Then the very idea of such a field, although long ago presaged in de Saussure's imagining of a general semiotics, was only beginning to emerge. Even in the historically relatively conservative field of literary studies, it soon became clear that there was an explosion of ideas becoming available from a wide array of forms of knowledge: anthropology, linguistics, psychoanalysis, philosophy, sociolinguistics. These ideas were energized by a new wave of intellectual superstars whose works slowly filtered through the various barriers that had kept the Anglophone world mostly free of their dangerous influence. Derrida, Foucault, Lacan declared variously that language and text were ontologically fundamental. It was language that shaped subjectivity, discourse that organized the categories of our thinking and the objects they produced, and the language of western metaphysics was to be found not only in philosophy from Plato to Heidegger, but also, and demonstrably, was at work in the most ordinary, everyday instances of language in use. Textuality enfolded both being and experience: '*il n'y a pas de hors texte*', Derrida had scandalously declared. What's more language, it was revealed, was intricated with both the most intimate private experiences and the most contested public categories. The world was a vast intertext of meanings in flow and in conflict. Language and textuality had become political. Almost any point of entry would provide access to socially, culturally significant meanings. The subject that would take on this new way of looking at and understanding things would have to challenge the most cherished assumptions of well-established forms of knowledge. But it would hold out the promise of a vast textual playground to engage in now that Barthes and others had provided 'the key to all mythologies' and had declared the legitimacy of 'the pleasure of the text'.

A big question hovered over the possible arrival of some new highly charged field of textual, linguistic study: Where would it find a 'home', or at least a recognized, authorized space, to reside? Within the already strongly classified discourses of education this was not a straightforward matter. As the eighties moved on, Media Studies and something then proposed as 'cultural studies' both seemed to offer a possible resting place for some new form of textual studies, some newly emerging field of knowledge engaging with language and textuality. In addition, the very core of liberal humanities curricula, English, in some quarters in Higher Education was proving alarmingly hospitable to the new and often strange and strangely productive continental ideas. 'Literary theory' was stirring up new possibilities especially in urban Polytechnics that were to become the so-called 'new universities' of the early 1990s. Literature was joining hands with history. English had discovered its own dubious origins not so as much an essential national linguistic and cultural project as an experiment in colonial cultural hegemony. Feminism had dared to take on the most sacred textual domains, suggesting that what had been hallowed Literature was often more compromised in terms of sexual politics than more lowly forms of lower-case literature or even the hitherto despised modes and products of popular culture. And then came the bombshell as watching Dallas was discovered to be an act of politico-cultural defiance and audience studies put all the emphasis that had been given to specific texts and their meanings into a new perspective.

Neither media studies nor cultural studies had uniformly taken hold across the various contexts of education, but had emerged as apparent forces to be reckoned with. English in HE had in some quarters, and not only in the so-called 'new universities' where there was more likely to be the kind of vaguely leftist energies and more open intellectual climate that would entertain the new textual world order. Even the bastions of elite education housed some so-called radicals of English. Eagleton's *Literary Theory: An Introduction* had been seminal in introducing a range of continental thinkers in accessible form while also challenging the claims of English to a necessary centrality in the humanities. Some of the imported ideas and their implications especially those concerned with the historical politics of literary culture and with the ordering of language in education as symbolic violence threatened to be deeply problematic if not catastrophic for English. Having turned against itself, English was ready, it seemed, or almost ready, to commit a noble suicide. And with the new upstart would-be disciplines waiting in the wings it felt as though a new world order was on the immediate horizon and new possibilities for a new educational constituency were in the process of being born.

In 1989 I attended a NATE (National Association for the Teaching of English) conference in Swansea when such conferences were held over several days in the Easter vacation and were attended by several hundred delegates. Many of the commissions were taking on big, fundamental ideas concerning subject identity. The commission I contributed to was called 'The Dream Syllabus'. It was about a new Cultural Studies A Level and was attended by a key figure in the then AEB one of the main bodies authorized to provide A Level examinations. We discussed the possibility, still novel in those days, that a pair of jeans might constitute a text and considered a scheme of work on the iconography of power tools. It was proposed that the new syllabus we devised would be called 'English and Cultural Studies' by way of indicating that English could never again be that canonically oriented literary form of study that had no method but that relied on time-honoured reverences and that appealed to sensibility rather than knowledge or technique. English would be displaced by the clearly more interesting, more relevant and more politically canny textual studies.

The great transformation never happened, of course. The dream syllabus never materialized. The risk was too great to compromise a subject as widespread and as well-respected, in its traditional form, as English. The brief experiment of GCSE English 100% coursework schemes that had allowed enormous freedom to aspiring radical English teachers was likewise displaced by the predictable banalities of the National Curriculum. In 1993, *Critical Theory and the English Teacher*, the book I had written that sought to demonstrate how new ideas and energies could deconstruct English and open up new practices in language and textuality in the secondary school, was published. It arrived just in time to confront the new pedestrian curriculum that would be unable to accommodate its recommendations. In Higher Education English had found a way to manage the contradictions that had seemed to threaten the subject with dissolution. The new textual order and the old textual order could live side by side. Modularity absolved English from having to construct any kind of internal coherence and consistency. You might deconstruct the appalling sexism of *Othello* in one module while attending to the genius of the tragic spirit in *King Lear* in another. 'Semiotics' and 'the Romantics' might appear as module titles in the same unproblematized field of study. Eagleton took up a Chair in English at Oxford and wrote books about Shakespeare and Irish Literature. I became, briefly, a Media Studies teacher.

It was perhaps most of all in Media Studies that the new textual order found some space for actually becoming embedded in pedagogic practices that were in some significant ways able to enact its deconstruction of textual pieties. It was not so much in the theoretical content that Media Studies kept faith with the principles of semiotics and textual theory, but in its modes of engagement with commonly shared cultural practices, practices that corresponded more nearly with actual cultural lives of contemporary people. Audience studies made pedagogical sense in Media Studies where there was no necessary canon and where there could be some explicit recognition that popular culture speaks to us all – and not as a debased textual form crying out for exposure to derision nor demanding knowing ideology critique. As the present volume shows decisively, Media Studies holds out some hope of textual engagements in educational settings that are aligned with lived experiences but that can also engender critical, reflective knowledge about those engagements.

We might ponder on the fact that Media Studies has become that space. But let's not forget the continuing differences in the statuses of academic subjects. That the more restricted forms of textual engagement that English offers remain at the core of the National Curriculum and that English retains a relatively elevated academic status are testament to the strange but powerful grip of an educational order that has been and remains difficult to shake off. The so-called 'long revolution' has indeed been 'long' as the young people say. We don't know if the happy playground of Media Studies might in the very long run have some serious impact on the established academic order and might seriously challenge what Derrida has called the 'violence' that attends 'the legitimization of canons'. At present – and from a certain detached perspective – it doesn't look like it. My own inclination is to be grimly pessimistic on the matter. Fortunately, the authors of the present volume don't share my gloom and have illustrated vividly in it how theoretically informed, contextually sensitive textual teaching practices can keep significant new pedagogic energies and ideals alive.

Nick Peim
July 2015

I: DOING TEXT

Julian McDougall

Imagine there's no subject, it's easy if you try (ish).

This collection provides teachers of Media, English and other textual curricular with a set of interdisciplinary learning and teaching strategies for what we might call 'new pedagogies'.

These are written *by* current practicing classroom teachers *for* teachers. For application in readers' classrooms, a 'digital tool' works alongside the collection, offering the kinds of online resources that cannot be offered in the book format.

At the same time, we hope this collection is of interest to a capacious readership, everyone concerned with the cultural politics of teaching and learning about and with popular culture, digital media and the mediation of everyday life.

Imagine 'doing text' after the subject.

These chapters are written by teachers working in a highly particular and politically situated environment – the secondary and further education curriculum in England in 2016.

Fifty years ago, Richard Hoggart established the Centre for Contemporary Cultural Studies in Birmingham as a space for the serious study of 'mass culture', as weaved into the fabric of everyday life by Raymond Williams in *The Long Revolution* (1961, 2016).

In the aftermath of the recent passing of both Hoggart and Stuart Hall, culture has never been more visibly a 'site of struggle' in education as it is today. Progressive teachers of Media (and English), the products of the CCCS legacy, would now seem, perhaps more than ever, to lack a space for inter-disciplinary thinking and subsequent pedagogic work, about the ever-increasing textualised essence of everyday life, just when, in the 'always connected' social media zeitgeist, they need it the most, we would argue. At the same time, a curious 'double think' pervades. The same policy-makers who deride the study of media in education call for media literacy as a panacea for all 'cyber-ills' and call upon ICT teachers to equip their students with the functional tools to furnish the 'digital economy'. In short digital media is to be used but media culture is not to be the cynosure of critical thinking. To paraphrase Frau-Meigs (2014), we are in the age of 'coding without decoding'.

In the context of these contradictions, and specifically the current reformation of the secondary / further curriculum in England (impacting on 14–19 year olds, but with a knock-on effect on both primary and higher education), this book offers a resistance to such 'epistemological violence' in order to recondition teaching with and about media 'after the subject'.

The teachers writing for this collection do so in order to reclaim their subjects in a flattened textual hierarchy. For decades, 'Subject English' (Peim, 1993) has grappled with an awkward inclusion of media, film and digital texts of all kinds, but always with recourse to literature as 'standard', thus situating all other reading practices as 'other'. Equally, 'Subject Media' has struggled to distance itself from English. The current threats to more progressive pedagogy in both fields, and between them, critiqued by Pete Bennett in the book's final piece, makes this collection all the more timely.

Only by allowing English and Media teachers – often the same people – to work with texts of all kinds in an equal relationship, as our authors do here, can the emancipatory energy of both disciplines be adequately harnessed for their aspirational goals – for active, critical literacy – to be realised.

A vital framing for the approach we take here, informed by the CCCS practice of producing collaborative 'working papers', rather than 'finished' monographs, is provided by the late Stuart Hall:

> We wanted to explore the 'common sense' that provided a basis for moral and social as well as literary and visual judgements.... We were attempting to make up, on almost a week to week basis, something that today has become widely known as 'cultural studies'. (Hall, 2014: 3, foreword to CCCS: 50 Years On. Birmingham: UoB / Midland Arts Centre)

Hall and his colleagues were concerned with shifts in / to 'post-war capitalism'. We are working in a more 'neo-liberal', but perhaps no less (or even more) hegemonic 'common sense', within which new digital media are discursively framed as economically vital, at the same time dangerous, but not worthy of 'serious study', for educational critique for its own sake. In this sense, nothing has changed, and the 50-year anniversary of the CCCS, and the tributes paid in 2015 to Hall and Hoggart, further the need to reimagine this project. As Hall concludes in that last piece, there is an 'ongoing necessity for serious engagement with contemporary culture, in all its complex and changing forms As Bob Marley once put it "don't give up the fight"' (ibid.).

AFTER THE MEDIA?

This collection is a logical 'next step' from, and application of, the key arguments we developed in *After the Media: Culture and Identity in the 21st Century* (Bennett, Kendall and McDougall, 2011). The reviews of that text received some critical recognition:

> The principal contribution of the book is what the authors call 'the pedagogy of the inexpert'. They argue that teaching Media should not imply that the teacher has to

adopt a position of expertise where the students are expected to build defences for a safer consumption of media. Instead, the authors suggest, the teacher should adopt a more horizontal position and read and practice media and culture with the students who are asked to engage actively and to participate by contributing in the course. (International Journal of Media & Cultural Politics)

One could sprinkle words like provocative and challenging throughout this review, but what is most impressive is the mix of erudition and enthusiasm, the view of change as opportunity, as liberation not threat, the focus on people and students. That is what makes *After the Media* an inspirational book. (Media Education Journal)

But at the same time, questions were asked about practical implementation, about how this would work in the classroom – a fair charge against books written about teaching by University researchers, having fled the 'chalkface'. Specifically addressing questions about the book by Mark Readman in his 'CEMP conversation' interview (2011), *Doing Text* replies with examples provided by 'real teachers' responding to the provocation to imagine a new curriculum, reclaiming both Subject English and Subject Media in response to the conservative reformation of education and the marginalisation of textual learning.

We asked our authors to start out from a textual practice – reading, eating, wearing, playing, performing, writing, connecting, making – and go on a circular journey through the following text-types and back to the starting point:

- Aspect of everyday life
- 'Mass media' text considered 'popular'
- DIY home creativity – text(s) produced by students outside of school
- Literary text (play, poem, novel or film acknowledged as 'literary')
- Art work
- Videogame
- Online media exchange / social media event.

Crucially, each author weaves these text types together without imposing a hierarchy by affording greater prominence to the literary text, or to any other. This is a truly flattened textual landscape, entirely relativist, in other words. Across these chapters, then, our authors present applicable learning and teaching strategies that weave together art works, films, social practices, creativity, 'viral' media, theatre, TV, social media, videogames and literature. The culmination of this range of strategies is a reclaimed 'blue skies' approach to progressive textual education, free from constraining shackles of outdated ideas about textual categories and value that have hitherto alienated generations of students and both English and Media from themselves. The results re-imagine English and Media teaching in order to resist the self-regarding model of studying texts in terms of their supposedly generic – and bounded – qualities (e.g. romantic poetry or *film noir*) or media formats / platforms (e.g. broadcast media/new media). Instead, the contributors work across boundaries in meaningful thematic contexts that reflect the ways in which we *really* engage with reading, watching, making and listening in our textual lives. The project recasts both subjects as combined in a more reflexive, critical space for the study of our everyday social and cultural interactions. The ways in which teachers and students 'bring and buy' degrees of expertise and media experiences might be thought of as a kind of textual 'bric a brac' store.

Fig 1.1 Bring and buy pedagogy.

After the subject *or* travels down the epistemological cul-de-sac with a talking dog?

Media education after the media, we have argued, would be formed out of a flattened cultural hierarchy combined with a relativist pedagogy. This would arise out of the death of Media Studies as we know it but also the death of English, Art, Drama and all other 'subjects of text'. We'd replace this with a more reflexive pedagogy of the texture of mediated life.

There is no doubt that media education has failed to be any kind of radical project. Considering our lofty intentions to both critical emancipation and industry supply, we've failed to either change media for the better, politically, from the outside or the inside. The centre has held for the industry – our 'real' media is not generally produced by media graduates from less privileged backgrounds, so there has been no redistributive success with attendant progressive outcomes within media institutions. Neither do we seem to have a more critically reflexive mass media audience as a result of equipping a generation of students with the required new literacies. Things are, the nuances of new online and social media dynamics aside, pretty much as they always were. The reason seems obvious to us – we've taught new stuff in the same old ways. We've needed, but for the most part haven't had, a more negotiated pedagogy whereby degrees of cultural capital are negotiated and exchanged in a 'porous expertise' between students and between students and teachers – closer to Rancière's 'indiscipline' (Bowman, 2012).

The political aspect to this is obvious – Media Studies has failed to work as the redistributive public intervention Natalie Fenton calls for because, whilst the habitus has changed, our pedagogic approaches have done little to redistribute the ownership of 'fluency' between and among social class stratification, as Papacharissi and Easton (2015) observe:

> Digital fluency, like the preference for haute cuisine or the ability to chat at a cocktail party, comes from the deeply ingrained worlds produced in class and education.
> (2015: 181)

Doing Text means we remove 'the media' from our field of reference and work instead on the mediated storytelling of the self and our students' performative textual interactions across spaces and places.

For years I have shared my ideas about media teaching at conferences with a talking dog video to exemplify the issues I have tried to raise. The video, a YouTube upload with many millions of views, is very funny, so I can be comforted in the certainty that the audience will enjoy seeing it, regardless of what they take from my presentation. The dog appears to be pleading with its owner for a particular kind of bacon – '*The Maple Kind, Huh?*' When I show the video, I generally ask media teachers to wear their everyday life hat first and their teacher hat second and to plot their responses on a 'relativist continuum'. At one end of this spectrum is the 'Peim provocation' – a relativist position on textual value, at the other end is 'Laughey's Canon' – from his notable 'Back to Basics' essay (2011) calling for a hierarchy of media texts to enrich our students and in the middle the 'Readman dilemma', questioning my use of such a hugely popular piece of 'DIY media' and implying that a 'canon of prominence' might be emerging – in other words, in choosing the 'best' talking dog video (in terms of online 'audience share'), am I reproducing the notion of 'what counts' I am seeking to dismantle? Teachers attending the workshop are asked to put themselves somewhere on this line – from the position that any textual event is of interest to media education to the view that citizen media is of interest as a phenomenon but on the basis of mass impact and on to a more conservative perspective on quality media. The most interesting discussion is around what happens when one hat is replaced by the other – how do our teacher identities merge with our lifeworld thinking? Are we confusing taste for expertise, or through Bourdieu's lens still imposing various criteria of 'distinction' (1986) to re-construct and affirm our own collective identity as media teachers? Such an identity is fraught with inner contradiction, media teachers feeling they are at once radically 'other' (say, to English teachers) but at the same time craving legitimation, at the same time more 'down' with the students' culture, maybe, but clinging to authority through a loose Vygotskian sense of scaffolding the prior media knowledge of our students.

Fight the Power? Read (Media), Write (Make or Play), Curate, Argue ... (Double) Mediadapt, then Act (we hope): what counts for (digital) media education, how do we know and what do we do?

Media Studies in England sits at an obtuse angle to the international community of media *literacy* educators. This field sees our situation – with the formal, institutionalised 'Subject

Media' in its fourth decade, as a gold standard. Other countries don't have a subject, but they do tend to have far more policy legitimation for teaching about and with media as literacy. There are, though, crazy ambitions for this kind of work, as the heading above describes. Young people receiving this media literacy education will, it is hoped, be critical, creative, aware of more or less hegemonic corporate practices at work behind their social media activities, come to be reflexive about the mediated curation of their lives in third spaces, use media to change the world for the better, contribute to the global economy with their twenty-first century literacies *and* participate in a new digital public sphere. And more than anything else, their advanced new media literacy will keep them safe online. This, to say the least, far reaching ambition is evident in the recent Unesco declaration on Media and Information Literacy which, among many other objectives, calls upon those charged with enabling it to 'enhance intercultural and interreligious dialogue, gender equality and a culture of peace and respect in the participative and democratic public sphere' (Unesco, 2015).

And yet there is no *pedagogic* rationale for how this might all come about. If we had one, what would it be like?

For media educators the concept of the 'third space' (Gutierrez, 2008; Potter and McDougall, 2016) referred to above is important. This might be, literally, an area between official curriculum and informal knowledge, with skills and dispositions brought in from home. Or it could be a metaphor for a new way of thinking about the way we generate 'new knowledge' about textual lives within our classrooms. This kind of third space is where we can negotiate textual meaning through dialogue. To do this we need pedagogical strategies designed to mediate expertise, subvert traditional roles and create a space where we can 'do text' across epistemological fault-lines. There are models for this already, closer than we might think. We could purposefully take the lead from aspects of art teaching practice to draw a parallel between the making of 'the work' and the design of learning (Orr and McDougall, 2013), arguing that doing text is a kind of 'third studio space' – theory gets 'made' here. Such a (more) radical pedagogy for media education cannot maintain 'stupefying distance' that can 'only be bridged by an expert':

> The ignorant schoolmaster is named thus… because he has uncoupled his mastery from his knowledge… he does not teach his knowledge, but orders them to venture into the forest of things and signs. (Rancière, 1991: 11)

Deleuze and Guattari's (1987) metaphor of the rhizome offers this kind of contrasting 'take' on knowledge, our textual agency being potentially the intersection, always in flux, of a 'thousand plateaus', so any engagement with media is at the same time production, theoretical working and (medi)adapation, an event in time and space, highly specific and situated by being always-already indebted to historical contingency and present contexts. Crucial is our pedagogic attunement to this, and we can adapt Lines' (2013) application to music education to suggest 'the rhizomatic (media) educator identifies particularities and becomings in a [media] learning happening and acts accordingly. This requires a certain kind of "active" ethical disposition' (Lines, 2013: 28). Note we have replaced the word 'music' with 'media'.

From *Levinas and The Rockford Files* to Ways of Being in the Occulus Rift to (Just) Doing Text

In *After the Media*, we started out by arguing that Media Studies has started from the wrong place, and that the problem has been our belief in the idea of 'the media' and its separation from ourselves, just as the category of literature imposes an alienating model of reading. We went on to show how Media Studies in particular and text conscious subjects in general have rarely been concerned with the social practices of all textual activity but have instead mistakenly focused on the illusion of *the text*. The current project hinges on an understanding of text as fluid and as much about the reader as the read, therefore there is no contradiction in our following up this call to 'de-text' the subject with 'Doing Text'. Doing text, being text, and all the other active, social markers in our chapter titles, can move us away from the hegemonic process of 'textualisation' (Hills, 2005: 27) through which 'a mediated and symbolically bounded entity is rendered recognisably discrete'. By giving prominence to teaching young people to deconstruct texts using handed down textual analysis techniques and to make texts as both applications of 'theory' and demonstrations of received professional practices in the form of 'conventions', we have been complicit in the alienating function of education as it 'promotes a deliberately narrowed attention to the skill as such to be enjoyed in its mere existence rather than in any full sense of the human purposes it is serving or the societal effects it may be having' (Williams, 2015: 198).

The practice of doing theory on popular culture is no less politically essential. We must continue the dialectical work of pointing a critical theory lens on 'mass culture'. Žižek's body of work partly sustains this legacy. The more apparently indulgent and perhaps obscure close reading we might exemplify by putting Levinas to work on *The Rockford Files* is valid and important. Essential, too, is the 'mediaptation' facilitated by students' interrogating their experiences in 'hyper-real' games with the help of sociocultural frameworks of virtuality, immersive literacy and performative identity – how does Girl number 20 perform ideology in *Assassin's Creed* in Occulus Rift? (see Williamson, 1981).

Whether we work on such 'cartographies of becoming' (Masny, 2013) in Cultural Studies, Media Studies, English, all or none of them or some conception of Digital Humanities is by the by if the pedagogic approach is consistently one of negotiation and porosity. But we must be acutely aware that neither unraveling the re-staged flawed hero figure of 'Maverick' in Jim Rockford's narratives as a hermeneutics of lived experience nor pausing the acceleration of 'new media dynamics' (Hartley, Burgess & Bruns, 2015) momentarily to do ethnography on virtual community are of any political value, in Williams' sense of the Long Revolution, if teachers teach and students don't work equally reflexively to constantly re-negotiate how 'the very essence of textuality slips through our fingers' (Merchant et al, 2013: 253). Back at the 'chalkface', an anecdote from Shaun Hides, reflecting on the shift to teaching 'disruptive media' adds more pragmatic weight to our project of decoupling media practice from 'the media':

> Some students didn't want to be involved in activist media making, as they worried it might hamper their chances of eventually getting a job in the mainstream media. What it meant was that we weren't articulating clearly enough that they needed to understand their futures in new ways, not that we want to make you into activists, but into the kinds of people that could be activists. (Qtd. in McDougall, 2015: 5)

Debates over the ideal subject identity of media education and more recently media literacy have been overly and unhelpfully polarised in recent years, as we've mapped out elsewhere (Berger and McDougall, 2012). The 'great and the good' in their various manifestos and polemics agree on much. William Merrin suggests *'If we all become media producers, we need to know how that production may be used against us* (2014: 160) and proposes the new 'usersphere', where, *'the user differs from the audience, therefore, in being personally responsible'* (2015: 161). Antonio Lopez (2015) has shared an alternative form of 'ecomedia pedagogy', consisting of scenario work, working with media gadgets as boundary objects within an ecotonal approach, slow media work and various community and grassroots media initatives. In his most recent 'Making Media Studies', David Gauntlett (2015) observes the contemporary subject as a 'diminished blob of the old themes, but with two new peaks of exciting and vital activity, everyday making and data exploitation and surveillance'. In taking forward his pedagogic rationale, he draws a parallel with research *through* design as opposed to *for* design, similar to our own conception of learning as curated 'studio work'. Helen Keegan (in Fraser & Wardle (eds), 2013) draws on Jenkins' transmedia learning principles to emphasise the need for media education to embrace technology as 'a post-disciplinary.... epistemological reboot' where we work with students to design culture, not observe it or re-make it. David Buckingham, often situated as both the 'father' of the subject and a sober voice against 'the optimistic aspirations that surround debates about young people's internet culture' (2015) is equally clear that the textual centre cannot hold, nor could it ever. Writing about the importance of enabling young people to take a reflexive stance on their own engagement with celebrity culture, Buckingham uses this contemporary example to resist the over-celebration of participatory culture by observing the 'vanilla' flavour of this culture. He shows how the 'classic' key concepts of media education, pedagogically framed for 'powerful knowledge' (Young, 2008) can enable students to reflect on celebrity as both/ neither real and/or constructed, an approach which 'directly challenges seemingly obvious distinctions between "media texts" (on the one hand) and "the world" or "reality" on the other' (in Fraser & Wardle (eds), 2013: 38).

Burnett and Merchant (2014) offer perhaps the most readily poignant articulation of what we are trying to get at when we talk about 'Doing Text':

> The focus of analysis is not the singular event that occurs around the text but the way that this interconnecting mesh of emotions, materialities, activities and intentionalites inflect and interfere with one another. (2014: 11)

One perspective is shared by all here, the 'fiction' of the singular, bound text. We've gone further to observe the fiction of 'the media' as part of the same problem, as Peim has for the construction of 'literature' and we could say the same about art, taking a lead from Grayson Perry, drama and most definitely the idea that 'technology' is any longer an entity separable from the rest of life. But there's a consensus emerging that the precepts of these simple models of culture and knowledge must give way to something akin to a more ethnographic pedagogy, along these lines:

Ethnography (Pole and Morrison 2003:3)	Pedagogy
Focus on discrete location, setting or event(s).	Every media education encounter is unique.
Concerned with full range of social behaviour.	Media literacy practices of each students are specific and can be both habitual and idiosyncratic – 'it's complicated'.
Range of research methods.	Mixed method teaching/differentiation, resisting theory/practice boundaries.
Thick description to identification of concepts and theories grounded in the data.	Curational approach – co-making 'the work' as both media production and media learning.
Complexities more important than trends.	Student reflexivity – meta-literacy of the self in textual culture/voice privileged over student 'competence'.

Fig 1.2 Curation Pedagogy

We concluded *After the Media* with a set of questions to work with when trying to do text in this way:

> *What is a text? What is the difference between a text and an event?*
>
> *How would you describe your textual experience? What does it look and sound and/or feel like?*
>
> *What different kinds of spaces and places are there for consuming and producing textual meaning?*
>
> *What does it mean to be a producer or consumer in these spaces and places?*
>
> *What different kinds of associations and affiliations do you make? Who with? What for?*
>
> *How do you understand the idea of authoring? What is being creative?*
>
> *How do you represent yourself in different spaces and places?*
>
> *How might we need to think the traditional categories of learning: reading and writing, speaking and listening?*

This was our starting point for an implementation in the 'third space' notion of the extended classroom. The chapters that follow work with these questions. They share approaches to teaching with, and about, media after the media, after the subject and, possibly sometime soon in England, quite literally without the subject we currently call Media Studies – the 'concept formally know as', perhaps.

So, this book is a collaboration between two editors, eight teacher-authors and their students, and, to paraphrase and adapt Deleuze and Guattari further, since each of us is several, this is quite a crowd-source. The teachers writing here, and sharing their resources through the digital tool that accompanies the book, each weave together a collection of textual events and practices, across existing cultural and epistemological boundaries. If we open them up across and between each chapter, we can imagine a 'scheme of work' going something like this.

REALLY DOING TEXT

It is impossible to 'map' this kind of 'distributed cartography' as an actual scheme of work in the way we currently understand such a document. But as these chapters are each lines of flight, within which it is possible for students to start with any 'text-point' and return to it via all the others, the same is true across the chapters. In other words, a reader wishing to implement this approach can pick a page at random, start with one of the text events cited (or choose their own alternative in a similar vein) and work through the entire book as a 'rhizomatic scheme' in any order, returning to the source text eventually. Here is an idea of how that might shape up.

Starting out with *Game of Thrones*, students are working with fragmented, 'pulled down' contexts for reading, but not in contrast to some notion of traditional literacy, instead emphasizing the significance of reading habits (*associations and affiliations*) and the idiosyncracy of 'staggered' narratives and spoiler protocols. Then onto *Benefits Street* and the secondary encodings of paratextual hashtag reception (*what is a text, what is an event?*). Here, the experiences of multi-screen reading – spaces and places – connect us to the immersive, promenade theatre of Punchdrunk, in contrast to the apparently dark, silent reading practices (*categories*) at work around the National Theatre's *A Streetcar Named Desire*. The (perhaps) Brechtian masking/unmasking utilised by Punchdrunk informs student curation, as we move through travelogue TV (*Italy Unpacked*) to the photography of Rankin via Grayson Perry, with students vlogging the construction of meaning (*of being producer and consumer*) through engagement with the experiences of artists as well as of their art. The Punchdrunk masks offer another link, now to the Occulus Rift and how the ways textual experiences *look, sound and feel* are subject to various 'degrees of separation' between ideas about text and about reality. Next, student and teacher selfies are connected via WhatsApp and Pinterest (*representing in spaces and places*) for some reflexive identity work, with the selfie understood as an everyday life practice and a media text, indistinguishable. At this point our 'textual traffic' (Kell, 2011) takes in the *Grand Theft Auto* 'I'm not a Hipster update', the postmodern stock text, *The Simpsons* and a Kermit meme, all put to work with Stuart Hall, and all in an intertextual relation with the teacher's Doc Marten boots but with a hefty disclaimer: '*They will not thank me for increasing their textual agency if they write something wacky in their exam and get a poor grade.*' This reminder is akin to coming out of an immersive game, back into the reality of Williams' 'deliberate narrowing' – the *traditional categories of learning*.

Skyrim comes next, treated as a convergent text crossing all the forms given to our teachers in their brief. This project was an experiment and in some chapters our authors map out their students' navigation across the textual plateaus as a circular route, others walk us through a more embedded approach to a particular text or curriculum area. *Skyrim* is used as 'source text' for an array of activities that bring to the surface the blurring of *what it means to be a reader, writer, player*: character development, discursive writing on fan sites, FAQ authoring and answering, wiki creation, contribution and monitoring, the writing of an extension pack, live streamed gameplay video with capture cards and editing, synchronous chat, oral presentations, adapting the game for a lower age group and a 'quest ethics' activity that takes in elements of personal, social and moral education. And on to the micro analysis of film language (cinematography, *mise-en-scène*) with *Mean Streets* (1973) and the Cindy Sherman stills, students now making their own, appropriating school *spaces and places*, playing roles, performing. A series of pedagogical 'meta-challenges' (*text events*) arrive at this point, Instagram likes temporarily colonized as a learning experience, informed by Zack Gage's art, and linked to skateboarding, Parkour and next the re-appropriation, through *Be Kind Rewind* (2008)-style sweding, of French New Wave aesthetics (*negotiating authoring and being creative*). Students write video essays using the *Rear Window* (1954) timelapse and Cassette Boy as stimulus for a 'cut and paste pedagogy'. Remixing *Dr Who* presents another 'meta-challenge' – this time competing for numbers of views, and the online media presence of Tom Ska and Zoella are understood as fanzines for the digital age. Students next make a playable game (*Squidverse*) as a synoptic task, with the autotelic dimensions of play (*the look, sound and feel of textual experience*) over-riding any potential recourse to expert/inexpert classroom positions.

Educating Us and *Textual Bake Off* are parallel activities, rationalized in the chapter as Paulo Freire in Cheshire, amounting to a student assemblage of twenty-first century signifiers, on their terms, arising from multiple digital challenges on the theme of 'a cultural explosion made by me' (*associations and affiliations, representing yourself*). The teacher sharing this pedagogic strategy describes this as an 'interpretive bricolage in beta' – a nice summary of our entire project, perhaps. Students are thinking now about performance, *Much Ado about Nothing* is worked together with *Disney Infinity* and the Playstation network in perhaps the closest 'take' in the collection on Nick Peim's teaching of English through *Romeo and Juliet* and *Home and Away*, *Macbeth* with *EastEnders* (*the categories of learning, reading and writing*). The Scary Mary remix of *Mary Poppins* provides a rough template for online parody, informed by Man Bartlett's performance art and Stan Douglas' *Suspiria* installation so students can digitize and exhibit their interpretations of the Shakespeare text in ways that are similar to the immersive experiences around gaming, social networks, live editing and projection (*spaces and places, how textual experience feels, producing and consuming, authoring*).

As well as this rhizomatic text work, the expert/inexpert dynamic is configured by each author, badges awarded to students during live teacher-student blog dialogue in *Edutronic*, whereby form and purpose are inextricable and students are writing to do more than prove they can write. Blogging about English Literature, utilizing the social discourse of the comments field, learning is constructed through the connected text as both the object and subject of study (*the idea of authoring, the categories of reading and writing*). Through constantly publishing themselves, about published writing, students' work enters the same domain as the 'great literary heritage' to which it responds. Our scheme of work concludes with landscapes of food, from the psycho-geography of Will Self to the contradictions of eating – enjoyment and feast, necessity and luxury (*associations, representing yourself*), moving on to food's socio-economic, political and historical contexts; the representation of food, worked through with fieldwork with multiple and divergent paths, as we work with our students on this ultimate 'great leveller' for knowledge, to deconstruct the situatedness of food in the dominant cultural narratives of their communities (spaces and places for consuming textual meaning). Textual landscapes again – menus, photos, adverts – working with our 'funds of knowledge' to re-negotiate food as text through exhibition, fragments, maps, juxtapositional readings, autobiographical writings.

What does our textual experience look like, sound like, feel like and, now, taste like?

Doing text.

Lines, multiplicities, assemblages, a map of text. I'm not sure if we can claim a fully rhizomatic approach on our collective behalf, or that what we offer is entirely non-signifying. But we can start out from any point in the above 'scheme of work' and connect to any other point. As such this teaching strategy could not be 'rooted' in the form of a chronological plan that could be scrutinized by inspectors or 'quality managers', nor are the texts above fixed – they are always modifiable and the connections between them are lines of flight, 'becomings'. Related to this way of thinking, popular culture, for Williams, is not only the 'stuff' of texts but the continuing resistant energy of the people:

> …in the generality of their impulses and in their intransigent attachments to human diversity and recreation, they survive, under any pressures and through whatever forms, while life itself survives, and while so many people – real if not always connected majorities – keep living and working to live beyond the routines that attempt to control and reduce them. (2015: 106)

We are not only teaching about and with popular culture, then, this teaching *is* popular culture. Our teachers writing here are certainly transformative intellectuals, in Giroux's terms; here they are 'making the pedagogical more political and the political more pedagogical' (1988: 127). Some of them write about their writing here as a departure, more or less comfortable, from the 'day job'; others describe how they already work. Nearly a quarter of a century ago, Peim wrote about 'new bearings' for English teaching, towards a 'theoretical self-consciousness about its constitution, attitudes and practices' (1995: 208). In *After the Media*, we offered 'new times, new questions' for Media Studies, attempting an equivalent revaluation. And yet the chapters that follow in *Doing Text*, despite the prominence of networked, digital media across them, seem to exemplify an approach to working with students that is applicable to any time or context, founded not on celebration of new technology but rather, returning to the *Long Revolution*, on the lack of any desire to reduce and control, to exert their own culture as a standard or to mask the power relations at work in the classroom when texts are 'on the table'. These aren't really 'new pedagogies' at all. Rather, they are resources of hope.

WORKS CITED

Bennett, P., Kendall, A. and McDougall, J. (2011) *After The Media*. Abingdon: Routledge.

Berger, R. and McDougall, J. (2011) 'Media Studies 2.0: A Retrospective', *Media Education Research Journal* (2)1: 5–10.

Bourdieu, P. (1984) *Distinction: A Social Critique of the Judgement of Taste*. London: Routledge.

Bowman, P. (2012) 'Rancière and the Disciplines'. Paper presented at *Crossroads in Cultural Studies*, Paris 2012.

Buckingham, D. (2015) 'Oh no! It's an Oh My Vlog blog!' Blog post at http://davidbuckingham.net/blog/ (accessed 28 July 2015).

Burnett, C. and Merchant, G. (2014) 'Points of View: reconceptualising literacies through an exploration of adult and child interactions in a virtual world'. *Journal of Research in Reading* 37(1): 36–50.

Deleuze, G. and Guattari, F. (1987) *A Thousand Plateaus*. London: Bloomsbury.

Fraser, P. and Wardle, J. (eds) (2013) *Current Perspectives in Media Education*. London: Macmillan.

Frau-Meigs, D. (2014) 'No coding without decoding!' Presentation to *Media Education Summit*, Prague, CR: Nov 21 2014. https://www.youtube.com/watch?v=yZpI_iMBqI8 (accessed 28 July 2015).

Gauntlett, D. (2015) *Making media studies: The creativity turn in media and communications studies*. New York: Peter Lang.

Giroux, H. (1988) *Teachers as intellectuals: Towards a critical pedagogy of learning*. New York: Bergin & Harvey.

Gutierrez, K. (2008) 'Developing a sociocritical literacy in the third space'. *Reading Research Quarterly*, 43(2), 148–164.

Hall, S. (2014) Foreword to *The Centre for Contemporary Cultural Studies 50 Years on*. Birmingham: Midland Arts Centre.

Hartley, J., Burgess, J. and Burns, A. (eds) (2015) *A Companion to New Media Dynamics*. Oxford: Wiley Blackwell.

Hills, M. (2005) *How to Do Things with Cultural Theory*. London: Hodder Arnold.

Laughey, D. (2011) 'Media Studies 1.0: Back to Basics'. *The Media Education Research Journal* 2(2): 57–64.

Lopez, A. (2014) *Greening Media Education*. New York: Peter Lang.

Masny, D. (ed.) (2013) *Cartographies of Becoming in Education: A Deleuzian-Guattari Perspective*. Rotterdam: Sense Publishers.

McDougall, J. (2015) 'Open to disruption: education "either / and" media practice'. *Journal of Media Practice* 16(1): 1–7.

Merchant, G., Gillen, J., Marsh, J. and Davies, J. (2013) *Virtual Literacies: Interactive Spaces for Children and Young People*. London: Routledge.

Merrin, W. (2015) 'Fight for the Users! Media education in the 21st century'. *Media Education Research Journal* 5(2): 59–80.

Orr, S. and McDougall, J. (2014) 'Enquiry into Learning and teaching in Arts and Creative Practice' in E. Cleaver, M. Lintern & M. McLinden (eds). *Teaching and Learning in Higher Education: Disciplinary Approaches to Research*. London: Sage.

Papacharissi, Z. and Easton, E. (2015) 'In the Habitus of the New; Structure, Agency and the Social Media Habitus' in Hartley, J., Burgess, J. and Burns, A. (2015) *A Companion to New Media Dynamics*. Oxford: Wiley-Blackwell.

Peim, N. (1993) *Critical Theory and the English Teacher*. London: Routledge.

Pole, C. and Morrison, M. (2003) *Ethnography for Education*. Maidenhead: Open University Press.

Ranciere, J. (2009) *The Emancipated Spectator*. London: Verso.

Readman, M. (2011) *CEMP Conversations*: http://conversations.cemp.ac.uk/ (accessed 28 July 2015).

Unesco (2015) Declaration on Media and Information Literacy: http://www.unesco.org/new/fileadmin/MULTIMEDIA/HQ/CI/CI/pdf/news/paris_mil_declaration.pdf (accessed 25 July 2015).

Williams, R. (1961) *The Long Revolution*. London: Chatto & Windus.

Williams, R. (2015) *A Short Counter-Revolution: Towards 2000 Revisited* (ed. J. McGuigan). London: Sage.

Williamson, J. (1981) 'How does Girl No. 20 Understand Ideology?' *Screen Education* 40: 80–87.

Young, M. (2008) *Bringing Knowledge Back in*. London: Routledge.

2: READING TEXT

Steph Hendry

The age of the consensus audience has passed and the media no longer stands as our cultural centre in the way it once did; we do not share 'cultural moments' via the media in the way we used to. Niche audiences are an important market and they now create small communities around media texts, personalities and media-based activities. These audiences are able to interact with each other and with media institutions and this active nature of audiences is seen to have empowered the user, as:

- Audiences can create their own media products and self-publish online (they are 'prosumers', no longer needing the mainstream media to allow them to have a voice or to speak for them);
- Audiences can access a wider range of media products whenever they please and all modern media is fully portable;
- Audiences are no longer tied to publishing and broadcasting schedules;
- Accessing media products is not only easy but audiences can often do so without paying for products, making audience choice almost infinite but reducing institutional income sources.

Teachers have seen a dramatic change in the way young people engage with the media. Media teachers are no longer teaching 'keen amateurs' but are often dealing with students who have limited knowledge and understanding of traditional forms of media. The institutional changes combined with a different knowledge base in students has added to the challenge teachers face as they not only have to support the development of analytical skills but they now need to introduce students to media forms, genres and institutional information. In particular, sixth form students' use of 'media' tends to focus on the personal and the social and they are accustomed to bringing the private into the public space.

In a valid and logical response to the cultural and institutional changes taking place, Media Studies started to look at the rise of e-media and its impact on the construction and consumption of media products. Always looking to be a contemporary subject, this refocus allowed teachers and students an opportunity to engage with the new institutional structures and audience behaviours. This meant that the focus of the subject had shifted and so some of the basic general knowledge about the media itself and the analytical skills that were the basis of understanding the way meaning is created was reprioritised in favour of issues around audience access to the media and institutional convergence. The subject changed its terminology and no longer focused on 'texts' but on 'media products'. This shift in the discourse identified that the act of 'reading' the media had become a secondary consideration. This move away from what was seen as an 'old fashioned' textual focus has meant that students are often having to deal with complex ideas about how the media works without first developing a confident analytical skills-base.

READING EVERYDAY

The nature of reading is personal. It is something that we do alone. Sitting in a crowded cinema or with the family in the living room may make the act of reading a film or a television programme feel like something we do in public, but the initial act of reading is personal and private. Reading a book is a quiet, solitary pastime, so much so that a love of reading is often assumed to be an indicator of an introverted personality type.[1] Despite this, the act of reading a book still has more cultural capital than the act of reading a film or television programme. Not all acts of reading are seen as equal: film studies calls film audiences 'spectators', making their role clear – they can view and read the film but that is where their activity ends; whereas media studies places 'audiences' in an economic relationship with media producers and they are described as 'accessing' and 'consuming' the media (via technologies).

However, the act of watching and interpreting media texts is still 'reading'. The skills needed to read a book, a theatrical performance, a TV programme, a newspaper, a music video, a game or a person's body language are the same. Certain acts of reading are, however, privileged over others. On 28th October 2014, a story broke regarding the French Culture Minister Fleur Pellerin, who had said that she had not read the work of recent Nobel Literature prizewinner, Patrick Modiano. A discussion on Radio 4[2] differentiated between 'actual' or 'proper reading' (novels) and the wide range of reading undertaken by the French Culture Minister – news, current affairs and briefings, etc.

The latter forms were not considered 'proper reading' and a judgmental tone was taken by the radio station after Pellerin made the statement that she had not had time to read 'literary' novels since becoming a government minister. The Radio 4 presenter seemed astounded as Pellerin 'seems to express no embarrassment about it either'. This hierarchical approach to what constitutes 'proper reading' tends to go unchallenged outside subjects like Media Studies. The maintenance of these hierarchies seems to be of interest to those who are part of the high art discourse as it acts to reinforce established cultural power.

Regardless of the text, the reader:

- observes signs and collections of signs;
- considers what is perceived to be the intended meaning;

- interprets the collected connotations (influenced by cultural and personal experiences and ideas).

Technology allows the act of reading to take place almost anytime and anywhere and does not discriminate between the high art of literary reading or the low art of mainstream mass media. Technology makes high and low art texts accessible to audiences but has the potential to alter the context of reception. The act of reading is impacted on by the reader's relationship with the text and the way it is accessed but, increasingly, the influence of other readers and public interactions are part of the reading process. The act of reading for modern audiences now takes place in a variety of contexts and the challenge for teachers, therefore, is to help students develop reading skills that consider the text itself as well as the audience's relationship with it. Students still need to develop the critical and evaluative skills that allow analysis but the traditional, largely linear approach needs expanding to take in the complexities of the contemporary audience experience.

This is not to argue that personal experiences should replace considered analysis; but by looking at a variety of texts, both conventional media texts and those that are currently seen as 'non-media', the skill of reading can be developed in a way that acknowledges how the different contexts of, for example, live theatre, gaming or contemporary television fiction can be accessed and enjoyed, and different approaches to presenting visual art impact on the meanings generated and received. In all of these contexts the reader creates relationships between the texts that are both personal and public. Encouraging students to recognise the similarities in the act of reading regardless of the text helps reading become a transferable skill.

Reading is, of course, part of everyone's everyday experience. We read people's clothes and hairstyles, we read buildings and their decor and we read people's social status by looking at their cars, shoes and handbags. Of course, the meaning we take from these readings may not always be accurate, but the act of reading remains the same. In this digital age, the act of reading has become a more public activity than experienced in previous generations. As digital technologies have changed the way audiences access the media and as social networking has become more influential, audiences are increasingly involved in a range of activities that draws the act of reading into the public sphere. The notion of the audience engaging in a quiet solitary relationship with the text they are reading is making way for the idea that our interaction with texts is a matter for public record and, more, becomes a communication in itself – a message that is offered for public consumption and interpretation. What we read, how we read and the meanings we create have become public statements that are part of a construction and communication of our own identity and group allegiances. Interaction on social media often becomes an act of public reading and audience commentary becomes part of the textual experience for the audience member who, in turn, becomes part of the experience of the text for others. Therefore, the reader-student needs to engage with their own position as an audience member and the relationship they have with the text and other readers, as well as with the study of reading with teachers.

Students would be able to develop an awareness of the act of reading by engaging in an analysis of their own communications on social media. This would allow a consideration of the way dialogue and conversation act to shape their relationships with others, the world around them and their own idea of identity. In addition, they could be encouraged to consider the way they have actively constructed an identity or even a 'personal brand' and communicated this to others through the careful choice of images, the written word and the selection of links, references and associations.

READING TELEVISION

Much has been made about the democratising effects of new forms of distribution. Online discussion, reviews and social media engagement have become part of the audience experience for many and TV broadcasters are keen to generate something akin to a 'cultural moment' with their products encouraging audiences to watch 'live' (or as near to live as possible) as not only does this reinforce the traditional business model (either encouraging subscription or the generation of advertising revenue), but it also allows broadcasters to tap into free publicity in the form of social media conversations which generate free viral marketing. In 2014 *Game of Thrones* became the most illegally downloaded TV programme.[3] While pirating may not be fully accepted as a valid way for audiences to access TV shows, HBO will have benefited in that pirating the programme allowed non-HBO/Sky Atlantic subscribers to be part of the online community who were active in generating free publicity for the programme. Online debate and discussion reduces the negative impact of the 'loss' of subscription and/or advertising revenue that may (or may not) come from the pirating of the show.[4]

It is to the benefit of media institutions to encourage the desire to read their products publicly and this public reading has, in itself, reinforced its own necessity. Programmes like *Benefits Street* (C4 2014) were criticised for cynically structuring their programme with 'shocking' moments occurring immediately before advertising breaks. '#BenefitsStreet' appeared placed on screen and the traditional ad break activity of 'putting the kettle on' was accompanied by tweeting that expressed strong opinions from all sides of the political spectrum, generating arguments, discussions and, of course, valuable publicity for the programme.[5]

The audience's relationship with texts has changed with the technological and institutional developments of recent times and so the study of reading needs to be considered in a more fluid way than before. Reading as an everyday activity involves a range of interactions between the reader, other readers, the producing institutions and the texts themselves. The traditionally private act of reading has become a more complex act that combines both personal and public engagement and is impacted upon by the context of the way a text is accessed.

Students can look at their own relationships with TV texts and other members of the audience as a starting point for a reframed reading of broadcast media. They could consider how interaction with others informs their interpretation of a text and how multi-screening can enhance (or interrupt) the reading experience.[6] From an engagement with being a modern television audience member, students can begin to use this experience to consider how media institutions are constructing media texts to play into more interactive and communal viewing experiences. Students can consider the impact of audience behaviour on media institutions in the way such institutions respond to criticism, praise and social media trends; and through the analysis of their own everyday acts of reading students would be able to consider the experiences of other audience members and the way modern audiences and institutions interact to create meaning.

READING LITERARY TEXTS: IMMERSIVE/PROMENADE THEATRE

The experience of theatre is both a personal and a public one and for centuries the relationship between the audience and the text has been subject to experimentation. At one extreme, theatres are public spaces that allow the audience to access the text; but, in their traditional context, theatres encourage audiences to approach the reading of the text as a personal activity, remaining still and silent during the production and only engaging with others after the event itself. The level of audience interaction seems to go some way to define a production's cultural capital. Opera and ballet tend to promote a more passive form of audience experience, whereas jukebox musical theatre, for example, encourages audience participation and a more public engagement with the performance itself. Many of the more mainstream successes in theatres recently are adaptations of Hollywood films (e.g. *Ghost, The Lion King,* etc.) or jukebox musicals where pop music is used to stage a narrative (e.g. *We Will Rock You* and *American Idiot,*). Hollywood has returned the favour by turning some of these musicals into films to greater (*Mamma Mia!*, 2008) or lesser (*Rock of Ages*, 2012) success.

Cinema and theatre have been coming together in other ways too. In recent years there has been a move to present more 'high art theatre' in cinemas. Technology allows audiences to experience performances, mostly from London theatres, in local settings. Some productions are transmitted live, others filmed, edited and screened later and the more successful productions are now offered after the theatrical run has finished as 'encore' productions. Two of the most high profile of recent theatrical productions broadcast live at cinemas have been the National Theatre production of *Frankenstein*

(2011), directed by Danny Boyle and starring Benedict Cumberbatch and Johnny Lee Miller, and The Young Vic's *A Streetcar Named Desire* (2014) starring Gillian Anderson. Both productions use literary source material but the star actors have high profiles largely based on their television performances (Cumberbatch in *Sherlock*, Anderson in *The X-Files* and *The Fall* and Johnny Lee Miller in *Elementary*). Unlike the relative informality of television viewing, the merging of theatre and broadcast media here positions the audience as a passive 'receiver' of the text. Audiences experience theatre in the cinema the same way they would experience a film – in the dark and in silence.

There are, however, other forms of contemporary theatre that create new reading experiences and re-position the audience member in a number of roles, both personal and public and as maker and taker of meaning. More experimental theatrical texts have blurred the divide between the audience and the product from the Brechtian destruction of fourth walls to the immersive promenade experience provided by the Punchdrunk theatre company. Punchdrunk create theatrical experiences that are often based around a large site dressed as scenes or locations from within a narrative. The areas contain props that convey information to the audience who are able to walk through the site experiencing the locations for themselves, often finding themselves in the middle of a dramatic scene. Two recent Punchdrunk productions (*It Felt Like a Kiss*, 2009 and *The Drowned Man*, 2014) provided similar experiences for the audience but used different techniques. Both created environments where the audience's experience of reading the theatrical presentation was influenced by the site-specific nature of the production. The audience experience was constructed in such a way that both productions foregrounded the experience of reading the text by challenging the audience's perception of their own role within the production and as an observer of the production.

It Felt Like a Kiss was a collaboration with the documentary film-maker Adam Curtis and it used a warehouse in Manchester to recreate a number of scenes and locations that juxtaposed the idea of The American Dream of the 1950s and '60s with the context of Cold War paranoia. *The Drowned Man* was staged in an old Post Office sorting house in London, using the space to replicate locations within a fictitious film studio. Both productions used the audience's experience of other media – specifically documentary, film and gaming – to help shape the audience experience.

Both productions placed audiences into small groups and sent them to walk thorough the constructed locations with little guidance as to what was expected of them. *It Felt Like a Kiss* largely kept the audience in these groups as they were guided around the location. Being grouped with other theatre-goers created a public space as audience members were able to discuss their experience with their fellow promenaders. The sense of uncertainty in the situation could be shared immediately and so a collective was created from the start of the production. *It Felt Like a Kiss* used audience responses to, and expectations of, documentary and film to create a complex experience that disrupted conventional expectations of the media and theatrical forms. The audience could walk through recreations of US suburban homes, a high school prom-night and a military camp in Asia amongst other locations and they were encouraged to touch and look at the props and to engage with the environments as much as they wanted. Sounds and smells were used to heighten the 'realism' of the environments and the settings were familiar from both documentaries and fictional films/TV programmes set in this period. The military encampment referred to texts like M*A*S*H and the audience was reminded of a host of US sitcom environments when walking through the middle class suburban home complete with manicured lawn and white picket fence. The immersive nature of the experience created the general sense of being both within a fictional setting and a museum. Reading the text became a complex experience that drew on experiences and expectations from representations of both 'real' and fictional.

The audience for It Felt Like a Kiss was split into small groups as they moved through the theatrical space. They were encouraged to communicate with one another in their small groups. The installations of scenes and locations were constructed in such a way that the audience was guided through them in a fairly regulated order. There was little in the way of traditional 'performance' as the audience populated the scenes and tableaus that made up the theatrical space becoming part of the scene being observed by other spectators. Actors were present, though, and at times they encouraged the audience to take part in pre-constructed activities, for example filling out a questionnaire as they were 'admitted' to a medical facility. Actors also infiltrated the audience space and acted to steer audience responses and behaviours. The position of the audience was simultaneously as spectator and participant and the blurring of the line between audience and participant placed the audience more firmly in the public space than is usual within a theatrical experience. Ironically, whilst progressing through the performance space the environment acted to divide and isolate, and what began as a public experience culminated in the separation of individuals as they were steered into increasingly narrow channels that creating an enclosed environment where the audience member was confronted with their own isolation and the implications of this. The controlled movement through the performance space acted to create a narrative where the individual was forced to confront the nature of individualism and the way cultural narratives were part of the construction of ideologies that supported this view of the world and our place within it. The production forced the audience member to make a conscious reading of their personal and public relationship with the production itself.

If it is possible for students to experience participating in an immersive theatre experience, they could draw on this experience to consider the way the theatrical space creates a relationship with the audience that depends on the audience's engagement and interaction with the environment. By engaging with their own actions as both spectators of the production and participants in it, students could consider how the blurring of the distinction between audience and actor positions them as the reader of the text and an active participant in its construction. The student could consider how meaning is made in a number of different ways within an immersive production.

The second Punchdrunk production, *The Drowned Man* allowed audiences more freedom to wander thorough the environment in their own groups than *It Felt Like a Kiss* and all audience members were required to wear a mask rendering them anonymous. Both productions placed the audience amongst the 'action' – this was literal in *The Drowned Man* as audiences moved into a location it would come alive with the performance of a scene from the over-arching narrative. Actors would interact with one another and audience members and performances were punctuated with choreography including song and dance numbers as well as fight set pieces. Like *It Felt Like a Kiss* the space presented a range of different sets and locations. The sets within the space replicated scenes from the film studio's final production (a Western) as well as areas of the studio itself, for example, dressing rooms and actors' caravans. It was not always clear if the scenes being played out were the 'behind the scenes' dramas that came together as a murder mystery story or scenes from the studio production itself. Audiences were so close to the action that actors bumped into them and drew them away from the position of spectator, temporarily positioning them within the drama itself. While being in the midst of the action took the audience member away from the safety of spectatorship it also made the personal experience of the text far more public.

The use of masks anonymised individuals, depersonalising the experience. At the same time, though, being behind a mask intensified the personal nature of the experience as the mask isolated and created the feeling of a singularly individual experience. The experience was close to that of an immersive narrative found in gaming in that the audience/player exists within the fiction of the narrative and has the ability to make choices as to where to walk, where to look and how and what to engage with the environment and those around them. The all-encompassing nature of the environment creates a location that removes the audience from the outside world and its realities, and through the constructed hyper-realities created by the set/gameplay the audience experiences emotions and sensations viscerally. The physicality of surprise within *The Drowned Man* as a group of actors rush into a previously silent and dark set was at least as intense, if not more so, than the adrenaline rush experienced within a game during a violent exchange. In both environments the feeling is created by representations, by fictions, but the feelings experienced by the audience/player are physically and emotionally real.

This was reinforced during one of *It Felt Like a Kiss*'s more dramatic moments of audience involvement. The audience was guided through a number of locations via a maze. At points within the maze the 'lab-rats' found items with instructions attached, all in the negative: 'don't press the button', 'don't touch', etc. If the instruction was ignored klaxons sounded and lights began to flash, prompting the group to get out of the space. The final instruction was not to touch a chainsaw on a table. When 'someone' (an actor?) did indeed touch the chainsaw it started up and someone (an actor again?) shouted 'run!', the audience complied and was pursued by (the sounds of) a chainsaw-wielding maniac. It doesn't matter that the audience recognised the fakery of the situation and the somewhat clichéd situation being created – the fear was real. There was no screen to provide reassurance and the totally immersive nature of the experience caused adrenaline to flow as the 'flight' response was activated. The sound of the chainsaw faded away as the audience found themselves in a darkened room with one TV screen at the far end. As people got their breath back, the TV screen came on and the audience were shown a montage of Hollywood horror images – hardly subtle, perhaps, but a reminder of the safety and security provided by the screen, a reminder of the difference between a fictional representation and an experience based on a fiction. The theatrical experience has been a communal one to this point, but the fear created during the chase acted to create feelings of isolation and it is at this point that *It Felt Like a Kiss* separated the group and forced people to experience the remainder of the production alone.

The masking of the audience in *The Drowned Man* also acted to create feelings of isolation, of being a faceless person in a faceless crowd, replicating the isolation that can be felt being amongst a crowd of strangers. The masks began as a way to identify the audience from the actors but as the experience developed, the positioning of the audience both within the text and outside of it looking in, began to reinforce the constructed nature of the whole experience. Subsequently this created the sense that the signification of the masks could not fully be trusted. Suspicions were raised that perhaps some of the masked and silent viewers were, in fact, participants in the drama and were acting to steer the direction of the audience and instigate dramatic events. The whole experience became one that destabilised the idea of this being a personal or public experience, so much so that it grew increasingly unclear as to who was part of the public performance and who was simply observing.

Students often see themselves as passive receivers of information, both as audience members and in the classroom itself. The idea of immersive theatre could be taken into the classroom in a number of ways:

- **Using Props**. Artefacts could be bought into the classroom and students encouraged to interact with them, enabling the artefacts to act as props or set dressing rather than exhibits. The latter are usually presented for looking at from a distance and an interactive engagement with props would allow creative engagement with the contexts provided, reinforcing the audience's position as the creator rather than receiver of meaning
- **Wearing a Mask**. Students engage with issues in anonymity in their social media interactions and will be familiar with the way being anonymous can offer

a feeling of freedom in the way a persona may choose to speak and act. Those wearing masks may find themselves more able to respond from an individual, independent position due to the feelings of separation from the group caused by being positioned behind a mask. Students could be asked to consider their own emotional responses to texts and, rather than have to declare this publicly, perhaps seeking the 'correct' response authorized by the group, they could wear a mask whilst reading and writing about the text. From this position of relative anonymity it may be easier to communicate personal and independent responses.

- **Role Play**. Some students could replicate scenes from a book or film as a short drama and position the audience of fellow students within the action. The 'actors' could look for ways to engage the audience and encourage interaction with both sides offering their reflection of how the participation added to their understanding, emotional response to or engagement with the source text.

Disrupting the difference between the personal and the public in these theatrical performances creates a constant challenge to the reader of the text. In traditional theatre, the role of actor and audience is clearly defined and delineated. The actor's performance is read by the audience member. Punchdrunk offer new ways of reading a theatrical experience where the reader's private response is as much 'the text' as the narrative, the setting and the performances. The reader's role and the collective experience of the whole audience becomes something that is read alongside the text itself. The public act of attending the theatre has, perhaps ironically, been made more personal through the use of unusual staging and presentation of events and actions. The use of multi-media and audience 'participation' impacts on the reading of these theatrical texts that subvert the idea of the audience as passive receivers of meaning. Punchdrunk audiences are encouraged to read and create their own meaning as they experience the production. Personal identity is simultaneously foregrounded and eroded within the experiences provided by this form of theatre as audiences are both parts of public performance and active in the creation of personalised meaning in this context. These strategies to engage audiences physically in order to enhance the theatrical experience can also enhance student engagement and learning in the classroom.

READING (HIGH) ART ON TV

Punchdrunk brings the 'high art' of theatre and the 'low art' of the media together to create new audience experiences. The presentation of visual art on TV has, however, traditionally followed conventions that positioned the audience as passive viewers being educated by an expert on a 'high art' form. TV art critics such often use a traditional lecturing style as seen in TV programmes such as Robert Hughes' *The Shock of the New*. This approach presented 'authorised' readings to the audience using television, a significantly 'low art' form.

These presenters represented a knowledgeable elite and education and information was prioritised giving audiences an insight into the way fine art should be appreciated.

A convention of the visual art programme is to use a travelogue format that emulates the eighteenth century 'Grand Tour'. Artistic tours of Europe were an upper-class pursuit and so access to Europe's great art works was traditionally reserved for the rich and leisured class. The authoritative expert presenter of the past reflected this elitism whereas modern presenters such as Alaistair Sooke, James Fox and Andrew Graham-Dixon use the travelogue format but have moved away from the formality of the previous generations. Entertainment is a high priority for modern art programmes and the 'grand tour' now reflects the easier access modern audiences have to travel. Graham-Dixon has presented *The Art of… Spain* (2008), *Russia* (2009), *Germany* (2010), *America* (2011), *The Low Countries* (2013), *China* (2014) and *Scandinavia* (2016). His BBC series *Italy Unpacked* (2015), saw him touring Italy with chef Georgio Locatelli. The two traveled together exploring the art and the cuisine of Italy combining two familiar holiday experiences, sightseeing and eating. The informality of their conversations and the fact that each one was shown to be learning from the other subverted the idea of critic as authority and reflected something close to the audience's own experience with travel. These presenters have easy, informal presentation styles and, counter to the cold, objective criticism of the past both are able to communicate emotional responses to the artworks as well as impart their expert knowledge. Fox often pits himself against the received opinion of the formal art world by offering his own subjective readings of art works that challenge the way they are usually seen. This more entertaining style of presentation frames the artwork in a way that encourages the audience to engage (like the presenters) emotionally with what they see. The expertise of the presenter is to provide context to aid understanding of the art works but not to provide the reading itself – this is left to the audience. Fox often uses the phrases 'in my opinion' and 'I think' and in doing so he both offers an expert opinion and also creates a space where personal interpretation is valued. Another presenter of visual arts programming, Sooke recently challenged the traditional reception of an artist in *Constable: A Country Rebel* (2015) and he offers his reading as a challenge to orthodoxy with a youthful and informal style. A more formal style of art programming is still used, though. Jonathan Meades' BBC series *Bunkers, Brutalism, Bloodymindedness: Concrete Poetry* (2014) utilised the language of written criticism as a thesis was put forward and explored. The more academic tone and approach, as well as the (some may say) controversial arguments, made the programme 'difficult' viewing that required that the audience actively engaged with the images and ideas presented. Meades provides an authoritative voice that challenges audience preconceptions. All these expert presenters create programmes that reflect the act of travelling and viewing art in the context of their locations and/or galleries. Audiences are spectators and the works are presented as fetishised high art objects despite the more informal presentational styles and formats often used.

However, recently television has offered another way to access visual art through artists rather than critics. Matthew Collings has made several programmes for BBC4 and retains a lecture style of presentation. Programmes such as *The Rules of Abstraction* (2014) provide the audience with an expert insight that brings together the authority art criticism and the perspective of a creator of art. Collings avoids the gravitas of Hughes and Clark but the programmes are still based on the audience being positioned as those who learn from those with authority. Collings gives his own interpretations on art works based on his experience as an artist. He often interviews other artists to bring in a variety of perspectives from those that create rather than simply 'read' for a living. These programmes are informative and offer an insight into the creative process but the audience experience remains as 'other'. The audience is allowed to observe but is not part of the creative experience itself. Other artists, specifically Rankin and Grayson Perry, offer a much more personal experience that draw the audience in as a participant in art rather than just a spectator.

As an artist, Grayson Perry has created an alternative approach to discussing visual art on television. He draws on the relationships between the creation of art, the reading of art and the construction of personal identity. His TV work has focused on the process of creating art and exploring identity both in terms of a public idea of class (*All in the Best Possible Taste* C4 2012) to more personal ideas of identity (*Who Are You?* C4 2014). *All in the Best Possible Taste* explored the idea of British class identity and demonstrated how class communicates via an aesthetic style and a concept of 'taste'. Perry then used these styles as inspiration for his own artwork exploring the ideas of social class that came through his interactions with people and his relationship with his own class identity. *Who Are You?* explored the idea of the personal and the public nature of identity. He interviewed various subjects about their own personal identities and went on to create portraits of people, families and groups with a range of specific identities from gay fathers and their son, members of a 'fat-positive' group, a woman and her husband who has Alzheimer's, a young transgendered person and a reality TV celebrity, amongst others.

Fig 2.1 Who Are you? Doing Identity

Through each of the episodes and encounters he explored the idea of how we construct our own identities, where they came from, how we use them and what relationship they have with others and the wider public world. In doing so, the audience was engaged in the artist's process of generating ideas and through Perry's own reflections on his subjects and his own notion of self. The audience were able to see the subjective approach of the artist and with this insight a subjective interpretation of the subjects and the object itself is validated. The construction of art and the interpretation of its meaning was moved from the public to the personal.

Rankin's recent exhibition *Alive: In the Face of Death* (2014) worked in a similar way as the photographs were all based on people who were dealing with death in some way – the most personal of human experiences. The construction of the art works was documented and broadcast by BBC2. These portrait photographs brought the personal experiences of the subjects into the public space of both the gallery and a television broadcast – the gallery provided background information on the subjects and their stories whereas the documentary gave the subjects a literal voice. They were shown being interviewed and preparing to be subjects of Rankin's photographic portraits. A relationship was created between the interpretation and reproduction of the sitters' identities by the artist in the photographs, their stories and the audience. Having access to such personal information about the subjects, especially at such a traumatic time in their lives, becomes an act of reading that is largely about the reader his/herself.

Both Perry and Rankin allow the audience an insight into the production process. As a presenter, Rankin offers some objectivity in his approach when he focuses on the practicalities of photography but he also frames the documentary with his own personal experience of death, loss and memory and its relationship to his chosen art form. His film offers his subjects a voice and the artist interacts with them via the production of the pictures. Perry offers the audience his own perspective on the people he is engaging with. Both artists' subjectivity comes through in the way they choose to present their subjects, and the emotional connection made between the producer of the artwork and its subject acts to construct a personal connection to the audience. These personal connections encourage a more personal act of reading from the audience as emotion and feelings are foregrounded as important parts of the production process and are therefore validated as part of the reading process. The portrait is, in itself, the most personal of art forms but the artists draw audiences into the subjects and the art works themselves rather than present them for the act of looking. Critic Laura Cumming's *Ego: The Strange and Wonderful World of Self Portraits* (BBC Four 2010) shows that the traditional presentation of visual art on TV is still the dominant form but artists as presenters offer a personal engagement free from the constraints and the public nature of received opinion.

Students producing creative tasks could consider how audiences construct meaning through the engagement and experience of the artists themselves. In addition to the creative artefacts students could be encouraged to create diaries, blogs, vlogs or similar to demonstrate the personal engagement with both the process of production and the development of the artefact itself. Rather than foreground the formal analysis favoured by traditional assessment processes, students could engage more with the subjectivity of the way meaning is created during creative tasks, allowing audiences an opportunity to engage with the artefact on a personal level but to also engage with the act of creation and the process experienced by the creator.

READING GAMES AND BEYOND: IMMERSION INTO THE OCULUS RIFT

Gaming has long been differentiated from other media forms in the way it offers audiences a more immersive experience than traditional media. The cinema screen creates distance and reinforces the audience's position as a spectator to the action on screen. Audiences have traditionally been placed in a passive position when engaging with fictional narratives and, while the act of reading a film or television programme can create visceral responses to the images, sounds and story-telling, these physical responses are simulacra. The audience can watch events and may have their emotions driven by a manipulative soundtrack and storylines but the audience remains distant to the action. They may laugh whilst watching a comedy, scream when watching a horror or hold their breath during moments of extreme tension but these emotions come from a place of identification and empathy. Being scared whilst watching a well-made horror film is not the same as being scared when walking home alone in the dark (or being chased within an immersive theatre experience).

The reality of the conventional audience's situation is as a passive observer, however emotive, frightening, suspenseful and exhilarating the images presented are. Games, however, draw the audience members in as active participants and so the visceral responses felt by players are one step closer to being 'real' as in immersive theatre. Different types of gameplay offer different types of immersive experiences for players: first person shooters provide excitement and tension; role play games can draw audiences into mysterious situations where tension and suspense are generated; sandbox games create a free space outside of the constraints of the real world where gamers can participate in all sorts of fantasy behaviour that may not be deemed acceptable in a real-life context.

It is, at least in part, the latter aspect of gaming that has promoted it above horror film[7] or rock music[8] as the tabloid media's first port of call when looking for a scapegoat for social problems and concerns. The consequence-free engagement with amoral/immoral situations provided by game worlds is often cited as a cause of real world violence and anti-social behaviour.[9] It is the immersive and (as perceived) personal experience that sets gaming apart from other media. Not necessarily accurate, of course, but the stereotypical notion of a gamer is of a lone player sequestered away from the public sphere in a basement or bedroom. This isolation away from the public sphere is also inherent within the idea that gamers lack communication and social skills and this indicates that, at least in part, the moral panic that surrounds games and gaming stems from the perception of gaming being a private activity generating personal experiences that cannot be shared or accessed publicly.[10]

However, when this perception of gaming is examined it can quickly be countered. Online gaming, multiplayer games and MMORPG environments show that gaming can be and often is a shared public experience. YouTube channels are dedicated to watching gamers play games, games reviewers have become powerful opinion leaders and 'reaction videos' are a popular way to share personal responses to moments within games.[11] The sharing and communication that is inherent within social media is a large part of gaming culture. The level of immersion within a game is also often overplayed. The gamer is distanced from the action by the screen (just like the television audience) and whilst they may have some control over the events within the game and the narrative's development, the gamer is less 'free' than they may appear. Some games are creating narratives that develop in certain ways depending on player choices. *Mass Effect* was one of the first games where the narrative outcome depended on the type of choices (aggressive? cooperative?) made by the player. However, *The Stanley Parable* demonstrates that, however 'free' in-game choices appear to be, the nature of gaming algorithms means that the audience experience will always be predetermined by the game. Finally, gameplay is subject to the same suspension of disbelief as a film or a television fiction. Gamers only need to look away from the screen for a split second to have the fantasy of the world they are 'immersed' in broken.

Oculus Rift is one of a number of headset-based VR technologies. Rift was 'specifically designed', according to its producers, 'for immersive gaming'.[12] Audience members wear a headset and the world represented by the Rift is visually all encompassing and rendered in 3D. It removes any external visual stimulus, creating a virtual reality environment for the wearer. Once headphones are put on, the wearer's immersion is almost complete. Wearable technology is also being developed, from gloves to vests, and work is still ongoing to improve the technology and to find ways that creates movement for the body that matches movements within the technology. These ongoing developments are intended to enhance the reality of the VR experience and to create as immersive an experience as possible.

Even though it is still very new technology the Rift offers a level of immersion that regular games cannot and the exclusion of most external stimuli allows the player to engage with the representational experience more completely. The use of 3D technology and the immersive nature of the headset mean that the audience's experience is immediately a more visceral one. The rational response to the visual messages provided is to recognise them as representations but the fact that the representations are presented to the brain in a way that effectively emulates the 'real world', means the fiction is more easily adopted and adapted to whilst playing. The headset itself acts to physically separate the player from the 'real world' environment and (not unlike the Punchdrunk mask) acts to isolate and reinforce the individual nature of the experience.

VR games that involve the player sitting whilst driving or flying work well as 'walking' in the game whilst actually sitting can create conflicting sensations for the gamer and so, by their nature, they tend to offer more personal experiences. An early VR demo was *Titans of Space*, a space simulator that took the 'pilot' of a spacecraft through the solar system and beyond. Games based on more structured narratives also focus on individual experiences as they can take the player into a virtual reality world and allow them to interact with fictional characters as they 'move' through the environment but multi-player experiences are difficult to accommodate. Currently Rift offers a personal experience that cannot be shared effectively, but the technology is developing quickly and local multiplayer gaming and, therefore, 'in-game' interaction is possible.

The VR experienced can be described but the nature of the technology has meant that making it a public experience is difficult. On YouTube, Rift gameplay is shown as two repeated images (one for each eye's point of view in the headset) on a computer screen. YouTube viewers can see that the player is at the centre of a 360-degree world but they cannot share the immersive or 3D experience. Most YouTube videos communicate the experience of the Rift by showing player reactions to the technology – specifically the visceral reactions created by horror games or by fairground ride simulators.

It is possible to bring this technology into the classroom in a more affordable way in the form of Google Cardboard[13] – a cheap headset that works with smartphones and specially designed apps.[14] Apps are available for Google Cardboard that offer a range of experiences from gaming, in situ poetry readings, gigs, a roller coaster ride and, of course, a whole host of different horror scenarios. Using headsets in the classroom can allow students an opportunity to experience the immersive nature of VR technology and offers a starting point to engage them in discussions about the audience experience in this all encompassing environment. Students could engage in some 'action research' interviewing one another after experiencing the VR 'world' to consider the visceral nature of their experience, the feelings of removal from the class and the isolating effect of the technology. They can also compare the VR experience with more traditional reading experiences. Apps are available that allow the screening of 'home-made' videos through the VR screen and so students can, although currently in a fairly limited way, create their own VR experiences and engage with those created by their classmates.

VR technology is being developed by most major technology firms – Oculus itself was bought by Facebook for $2bn in July 2014 and it is probably safe to assume that the social media company clearly sees a more public future for the software, and predictions for future use will take the technology into the social arena. Facebook founder Mark Zuckerberg thinks that 'immersive virtual and augmented reality will become a part of people's everyday life'[15] and his predictions for the future use of the technology involve creating opportunities for individuals to 'attend' public events such as sports fixtures, theatrical performances, gigs etc. as well as attending virtual classes and visiting a virtual doctor.[16] The business model for VR's development as a platform for 'attending' public events is a simple one – events and performances could be experienced by many more individuals using the technology in the privacy of their own home. Everyone could have a front-row seat and have a virtual experience that emulates being there in a 3D, virtual environment. Of course, this is a long way off but VR is a technology that certainly has the potential to blur the lines between private and public experiences even further. The audience experience will not only influence the way that events are read but also be part of the reading itself. In group experiences, audience members making up 'the crowd' could become part of the VR experience themselves and for others engaging in the experience. The technology could be used to create experiences that cross the high art/low art divide ('attending' ballet performances and cup finals using would work in similar ways). The technology has the potential to democratise access to all forms of text even further. However, as a technology that needs to pay its way, it could also help create an environment where the majority are relegated to reading texts via an atomized, private VR experience leaving the *real* public experience to an elite who can afford to access the performances. The practical reality of 'attending' the event via VR would be an individualised experience taking place in isolation.

Providing different reading experiences for students is the first step to helping them develop an appreciation for the complex art of reading. Encouraging students to engage with their own interactions with technologies, texts and with others can lead to a more engaged understanding of the way texts create relationships with their audience, as well as creating experiences for them and meaning for them to interpret. Sometimes these relationships feel personal whilst at other times these relationships move into the public sphere. The wider the experiences encountered, the more likely students are to recognise both the commonalities of the act of reading that are shared across forms but also the way context shapes the audience experience and, therefore, the meanings taken from texts. The high art/low art divide is removed when reading is seen this way and so the hierarchy between types of texts as well as the privileging of received opinions over personal experiences is removed. Texts do not therefore have an 'inherent' meaning that needs to be learned by the reader, but analysis skills can be taught and developed through practice. In the contemporary media age where audiences are fragmented and the definition of text is in a state of flux, teaching students what to read/think becomes futile when how to read and interpret texts in context has become a daily necessity.

REFERENCES

1. http://www.shiftjournal.com/2011/01/10/the-role-of-reading-for-introverts-and-extroverts/
2. Radio 4: *PM* 28th Oct 2014 5.44pm
3. http://www.bbc.co.uk/newsbeat/30614035
4. Most illegal torrents only become available after an initial broadcast. At the start of Season 5 in April 2015, several episodes of Game of Thrones were leaked and available on torrent sites before the broadcast of the show. (http://www.telegraph.co.uk/culture/tvandradio/game-of-thrones/11530714/game-of-thrones-leak-season-5.html)

5. http://www.independent.co.uk/arts-entertainment/tv/features/benefits-street-twitter-reactions-the-angry-the-idiotic-and-the-defensive-9046806.html

6. http://www.theguardian.com/media-network/media-network-blog/2013/mar/15/multi-screening-behaviours-mobile-study

7. http://www.independent.co.uk/arts-entertainment/films/features/20-notorious-video-nasties-508525.html

8. http://www.dailymail.co.uk/femail/article-566481/Why-child-safe-sinister-cult-emo.html

9. http://www.telegraph.co.uk/news/uknews/1337971/Computer-games-make-children-anti-social.html

10. http://www.video-game-addiction.org/social-consequences.html

11. PewDiePie (https://www.youtube.com/user/PewDiePie) and Yogscast (https://www.youtube.com/user/BlueXephosare) are two of many popular YouTube channels that review games and discuss the experience of gaming. The channels have 36+ million and 7+ million subscribers respectively.

12. https://www.youtube.com/watch?v=KBylGcvRuek

13. https://www.google.com/get/cardboard/

14. https://play.google.com/store/apps/collection/promotion_3001527_cardboard_apps

15. http://www.technologyreview.com/news/525881/what-zuckerberg-sees-in-oculus-rift/

16. https://www.facebook.com/zuck/posts/10101319050523971

WORKS CITED

Adams, R. (2015) 'Media studies survives – but leisure studies doesn't – in final cull of A-levels'. *The Guardian* (online) 26 March: http://www.theguardian.com/education/2015/mar/26/media-studies-survives-but-leisure-studies-doesnt-in-final-cull-of-a-levels (accessed April 2015).

Anon. (n.d.) 'Social Consequences of Gaming Addiction'. *Video Game Addiction* (online): http://www.video-game-addiction.org/social-consequences.html (accessed April 2015).

Anon. (2011) 'The Role of Reading for Introverts and Extroverts'. *Shift* (online) 1 October: http://www.shiftjournal.com/2011/01/10/the-role-of-reading-for-introverts-and-extroverts/_ (accessed April 2015).

Anon. (2015) 'New Game of Thrones episodes leaked online'. *The Telegraph* (online) 12 April: http://www.telegraph.co.uk/culture/tvandradio/game-of-thrones/11530714/game-of-thrones-leak-season-5.html (accessed April 2015).

Byrne, C. (2005) '20 Notorious Video Nasties'. *The Independent* (online) 27 September: http://www.independent.co.uk/arts-entertainment/films/features/20-notorious-video-nasties-508525.html (accessed April 2015).

Chapman, J. (2014) 'Now PM's aides slam Education Secretary for burying Gove's school reforms: Morgan locked in row with 'macho' colleagues who say she should take more aggressive stance'. *The Daily Mail* (online) 26 December: http://www.dailymail.co.uk/news/article-2887192/Now-PM-s-aides-slam-Education-Secretary-burying-Gove-s-school-reforms-Morgan-locked-row-macho-colleagues-say-aggressive-stance.html (accessed April 2015).

Chris Pirillo (n.d.) *Oculus Rift Gameplay This Week / Demo* (video online): https://www.youtube.com/watch?v=KBylGcvRuek (Accessed April 2015)

de Botton, A. (2014) *The News: A User's Manual*. London: Penguin.

Dear, N. (2011) *Frankenstein*. Royal National Theatre, London.

Denham, J. (2014) 'Benefits Street Twitter reactions: The angry, the idiotic and the defensive'. *The Independent* (online) 8 January: http://www.independent.co.uk/arts-entertainment/tv/features/benefits-street-twitter-reactions-the-angry-the-idiotic-and-the-defensive-9046806.html (accessed April 2015).

Donahue, T. (2014) 'The Good Wife's shock twist: the latest in a long line of recent TV bombshells'. *The Guardian* (online) 24 March: http://www.theguardian.com/tv-and-radio/2014/mar/24/shocking-tv-deaths-good-wife-game-thrones (accessed April 2015).

Garner, R. (2014) 'Education Secretary Nicky Morgan tells teenagers: Want to keep your options open? Then do science'. *The Independent* (online) 10 November: http://www.independent.co.uk/news/education/education-news/education-secretary-nicky-morgan-tells-teenagers-if-you-want-a-job-drop-humanities-9852316.html (accessed April 2015).

Green Day, *American Idiot*. 2004. Reprise Records.

Izundu, C. (2014) 'Game of Thrones most pirated TV show of 2014'. *Newsbeat* (online) 28 December: http://www.bbc.co.uk/newsbeat/30614035 (accessed April 2015).

Matthews, A. (2001) 'Computer games make children anti-social'. *The Telegraph* (online) 20 August: http://www.telegraph.co.uk/news/uknews/1337971/Computer-games-make-children-anti-social.html (accessed April 2015).

Medialens (2014) *Newsnight discussion on 'The News' with Alain de Botton, Samira Ahmed and Alastair Campbell* (video online) https://www.youtube.com/watch?v=ZOdL7fPMjCo (accessed April 2015).

Miller, M. (2014) *Creative Industries worth £8million an hour to UK economy*. Dept. for Culture, Media and Sport (online) 14 January: https://www.gov.uk/government/news/creative-industries-worth-8million-an-hour-to-uk-economy (accessed April 2015).

Newsnight (2014) *What's the point of news?* (video online) https://www.youtube.com/watch?v=VQUmcGF73zM (accessed April 2015).

Parkin, S. (2014) 'What Zuckerberg Sees in Oculus Rift'. *MIT Technology Review* (online) 26 March: http://www.technologyreview.com/news/525881/what-zuckerberg-sees-in-oculus-rift/ (accessed April 2015).

PewDiPie, PewDiePie Channel (video online): https://www.youtube.com/user/PewDiePie (accessed April 2015).

Rawstorne, T. (2008) 'Why no child is safe from the sinister cult of emo'. *The Daily Mail* (online) 16 May: http://www.dailymail.co.uk/femail/article-566481/Why-child-safe-sinister-cult-emo.html (accessed April 2015).

Richards, N. (2015) 'The Fifty Shades of Grey Paradox'. *Slate* (online) 13 February: http://www.slate.com/articles/technology/future_tense/2015/02/fifty_shades_of_grey_and_the_paradox_of_e_reader_privacy.html (accessed April 2015).

Williams, T. (1947) *A Streetcar Named Desire*. 2014 production. The Young Vic, London.

Zuckerberg, M. (2014) Facebook Post. Facebook (online) 25 March: https://www.facebook.com/zuck/posts/10101319050523971_(accessed April 2015).

TV, RADIO, FILM & THEATRE

24. 2001–14. Fox.

Alive in the Face of Death. 2013. BBC Two.

All in the Best Possible Taste. 2012. Channel 4.

The Art of… Spain, Russia, Germany, America, China. 2008–2014. BBC Four.

Benefits Street. 2014. Channel 4.

Better Call Saul. 2015–. Netflix.

Breaking Bad. 2008–13. AMC.

Buffy the Vampire Slayer. 1997–2003. WP/UPN.

Bunkers, Brutalism and Bloodymindedness: Concrete Poetry. 2014. BBC Four.

Civilisation. 1962. BBC2.

Community. 2009–015. NBC. Yahoo! Screen.

Constable: A Country Rebel. 2015. BBC Four.

The Drowned Man. 2013. Punchdrunk.

Ego: The Strange and Wonderful World of the Portrait. 2010. BBC Four.

Elementary. 2012–. CBS.

The Fall. 2013–. BBC Two.

Game of Thrones. 2011–. HBO.

Ghost. 1990 (dir. Zucker, Jerry). USA, Paramount Pictures.

House of Cards. 2013–. Netflix.

It Felt Like a Kiss. 2009. Punchdrunk.

Italy Unpacked. 2013–. BBC.

The Lion King. 1994 (dir. Allers, Roger and Minkoff, Rob). USA, Walt Disney Pictures.

M*A*S*H*. 1972–1983. CBS.

Mama Mia! 2008 (dir. Lloyd, Phyllida). USA, Universal Pictures.

Mass Effect. 2007–. Bioware.

Orange is the New Black. 2013–. Netflix.

PM. BBC Radio 4.

Question Time. 1979–. BBC One.

Rock of Ages. 2012 (dir. Shankman, Adam). USA, New Line Cinema.

The Rules of Abstraction. 2014. BBC Four.

Sherlock. 2010–. BBC One.

The Shock of the New. 1980. BBC.

The Stanley Parable. 2011–13. Galactic Café.

Titans of Space. 2014 (last edition). DrashVR.

Transparent. 2014–. Amazon Studios.

The Unbreakable Kimmy Schmidt. 2015–. Netflix.

We Will Rock You (Queen musical). 2002–2013.

Who are You? 2014. Channel 4.

The Wire. 2002–2008. HBO.

The X Files. 1993–2002. Fox.

3: WEARING TEXT

Claire Pollard

CONTEXT

I am a teacher of English and Media Studies in a high achieving, non-selective faith school in Tower Hamlets. Although the majority of students I teach are British, many of them are second or third generation Asian or African. We teach a unit that examines the relationship between the media and collective identity, where students are expected to trace the representation of a particular group over time in at least two media and reflect on the ways that identity is mediated. I allow my students to choose a group to focus on under the broad banner of 'Multicultural Britain' – they may choose to study the representation of, for example, Muslims, young black males, or immigrants. A problem I encounter is getting students to reflect on their own media consumption – they prefer to write about the texts we study in class than whatever they consume at home. This chapter of *Doing Text* seemed to me like an opportunity to try an experimental process with my students with the aim of encouraging them and instilling in them the confidence to bring to class the texts that they consume, in order that the rest of us might analyse the representations within them and the impact this process of mediation might have on identity. As 'wearing' and identity are inextricably linked – the act of dressing in the morning is a process of performance; a construction of an identity that we want to project to the outside world – I decided to use outfits or, for the purposes of this book, 'worn texts', as a way of tracing our identities in each other's textual fields to see how that identity is mediated. Put simply: my students would 'read' an outfit or 'worn text' constructed by me and explore its representation in texts with which they were familiar and vice versa. The outcome would allow us to compare how we see our own identities with how others, as a result of their textual influences, read our identities, and ultimately it would help us to understand the effect the media can have on our identity.

I decided to take a research project approach to the task of exploring worn text and the act of wearing text. One of the things that struck me when reading Bennett, Kendall and McDougall's *After The Media* (2010) was the idea of promoting textual agency among learners in Media Studies. As a teacher of English I experience first hand, and to a certain extent am responsible for, the perpetuation of the idea that there are certain set texts that have primacy within the world of education and in a broader Western culture. As part of my MA I carried out research into the way that specifications in Literature, Media Studies and Film Studies vary in terms of how prescriptive they are about texts studied. In Literature, texts are selected from pre-agreed lists or have certain parameters in terms of period, genre and 'credibility' of the author. Even when units do allow students to select their own texts, they have to be sent to the exam boards for approval. In Film Studies there are also set texts, albeit to a lesser extent; but Media Studies, historically and at the time of writing, has very little prescription, unlike most text-focused subjects interestingly the reformed A levels in Media Studies due for teaching from 2017 include a requirement for 'Close Study Products' specified by exam boards'.

Although this should allow for total freedom (or at least flexibility) when it comes to the selection of texts in reality it's hard to resist the temptation to teach established texts that are well known among Media teachers and academics. Nonetheless I believe it is the responsibility of teachers to ensure that when selecting texts for study, we avoid creating a canon for Media Studies. Texts or areas of study that teachers of a different generation (and possibly social class) perceive to be significant – for example, *The Shining* (1980), the Napster phenomenon in the 1990s – provide an often useful historical context for students but we run the risk of overshadowing contemporary or familiar texts or events rooted in the 'now' of Media Studies by impressing on students the 'importance' of these texts or topics. As teachers, we need to be brave and facilitate students' understanding of the familiar now rather than applying key concepts which we present to them as valid or significant.

However there is a counter-argument that the formulation of a canon of texts and practices in Media Studies would give it a much-needed legitimacy within the broader curriculum. Of course, the premise of this collection of interventions is that these subject hierarchies are at best a distraction from the immediate work of using texts of all kinds as an unfettered resource for 'educating'.

After the Media contends that an established 'Media' no longer exists and therefore this opens up opportunities for studying all sorts of texts. This includes texts that students bring to class – a lovely idea, but hard to achieve in reality. Although I agree with the broader notions that all texts are worthy of study and that we should not impose our tastes onto our students, there are certain factors that prevent this from happening. Firstly, there is the teacher's responsibility to prepare students for further educational study where knowledge of a range of texts might be expected. Several years ago a student of mine was asked to prepare a presentation about the influence of Charlie Chaplin on modern cinema for a university interview. With a limited knowledge of modern cinema and absolutely no knowledge of who or what Charlie Chaplin was, she didn't stand a chance.

Whether or not you believe that it is a job of the mainstream education system to instill in students a level of cultural capital, it is surely agreed that we should be opening students' eyes to texts they would be unlikely to encounter on their own. Secondly, in my experience, students are nervous when it comes to seeing their own textual references as worthy, not so much of study, but of being written about in an externally marked exam by an examiner who may not approve of the application of Gramsci's idea of hegemony to a shoddily made YouTube series.

In the past, when teaching about the relationship between media and collective identity, I have tried to encourage students to reflect on their own media consumption, with varied success. *EastEnders* – a text I haven't consumed since the first departure of Kat and Alfie in 2005 – is often cited, and although popular, can be given legitimacy because the teacher can provide the historical context for representations in that particular show. Similarly, *The Bill*. Both are well established, long running, mainstream shows on terrestrial channels and students feel confident writing and talking about them in relation to their exam question despite their teacher's ignorance of recent storylines. Thus, a popular text becomes 'academic' because the teacher has intelligent-sounding things to say about Sanjay and Gita. In some cases, my students have gone back to find clips and synopses of those events in a bid to seek out the more legitimate Asian characters to write about in their exam because, after all, the examiner, most likely of the same generation as NOT of the teacher, would be more likely to understand and award marks for points about something historical. Even *EastEnders*.

Four years ago, despite having taught a couple of lessons on 'the rise of the web series' and watched several episodes of a range of series that represented ethnic minority communities, a student revealed to me just three days before the exam that he liked something called 'Diary of a Badman'. It turned out to be an amateur comedy web series created by and starring a teenage second generation Muslim in South London. In each episode he comically reflects on his religion, his family and his everyday life. When I expressed confusion that this hadn't been mentioned when we had been looking at other web series the student in question claimed that he didn't think they would be allowed to write about it, that it somehow didn't count. Despite having exceeded 40 million views and one episode having been the 7th most-watched online video in 2011[1] this YouTube series was seen to be somehow 'not a text' because, perhaps, I hadn't presented it to them and therefore the examiner might not accept it as a valid example. Thinking back now, I wonder how many times, within the formal teacher-exposition stage of a lesson, a student has shouted out (yes, my students shout out) things like 'Oh, that's a bit like in…' and then said the name of a text I wasn't familiar with, which then, out of wanting to finish my point (or not seem like an idiot), I steamroll over and carry on giving my own examples.

So for this project I wanted to try and establish a sense of total democracy from the start. I planned for all of us to take a selfie of an outfit that we felt best summed up our identity. This could be something flash or ordinary: the point was that the outfit had to be a representation of who we were. Then using WhatsApp, a technology that the students were comfortable with, we would uploaded and shared our images. Once we were able to see the constructed outfits for each member of the group, we would trace items of clothing worn by that person across the range of text types provided to me by the editors of this book. The items of clothing would act as signifiers of meaning but would the meaning we hoped to project through our constructed identities be read as intended, or, to use Hall's encoding and decoding theory (1973), would the preferred or dominant reading be apparent to the rest of the group?

METHODOLOGY

In order not to dominate this process I decided that it would be better for a student to set up the group. One student had all our numbers so she set up a WhatsApp group which she (imaginatively) called 'Media' and invited each class member. There were 7 members of the group, myself included. The process took place in first half of the spring term and we allocated one lesson a week to our 'identity project'.

There was obviously a question of ethical responsibility carrying out this process in the lead up to their exams. The close focus on clothing is not hugely relevant for the exam question I was preparing them to answer and, at times, it did feel as though this project was an extra burden on a group of already over-worked and stressed students. However, the identity element of the exam topic is often overlooked and historically our students prefer to focus on the question that asks about representation over time to the one that requires them to explain how identity is mediated. By placing a clear focus on identity and briefly covering some aspects of identity theory, I hoped to enable them to answer the more difficult exam question and, as a result, achieve higher marks. This cohort of students happened to be all of middle and higher ability with several of them aiming for As and the elusive A*s. I also made sure to refer regularly to the identity project in our normal lessons to illustrate the connections between representation and identity.

In the first lesson, I began by brainstorming what identity is and what makes up our identity. I explained the project and outlined what we were going to do and what I was planning to achieve. I explained what 'mediated' meant and then shared with the students, via What'sApp, a selfie of me in an outfit which I said I felt most reflected who I was. I explained that this first text, the selfie, constituted one of the text types we would be exploring – an 'aspect of everyday life', this being the act of getting dressed.

Over the next week I invited students via WhatsApp to upload their photos. By the following session, we had three (including mine) to analyse. As with all these sessions, we moved the furniture around so we could sit as a group around a big table. In the spirit of democracy and trying not to influence their responses or text choices in any way, we always worked like this in these sessions and I tried not to deliver from the front of the classroom. Additionally, where possible, PowerPoints were sent via WhatsApp in advance so that during the lessons, I wasn't springing new information on them or giving the impression that I was holding the power or the knowledge.

When the group were reading the worn texts (the outfits we had on in our selfies) the person who had been wearing the text sat apart and was not allowed to correct or add to the discussion being had. The discussions were partly to reach an agreement as a group to what the outfit consisted of ('does hairstyle count?', 'is the jacket black or navy?') and then a discussion of the overall look, and individual items of clothing as signifiers of meaning. As part of this discussion, the students made several references to other media texts and other aspects of life where this outfit or item of clothing had been seen and I made a note of these. While their outfit was being analysed, the wearer had to sit apart and make a list of their own textual references for their outfit although when they were doing my outfit, I transcribed their conversation for the purposes of presenting it in this book.

The theories covered throughout the unit were Butler's Gender Performativity, Foucault's Technologies of the Self and Merton's Self-Fulfilling Prophecy. Theory was introduced idea-first. I put up the following statements on the board and got them to discuss as a group and place them on a continuum from the one they most agreed with to the one they least agreed with. In the allocated time, a full conclusion was not reached but below are the statements in the order most of the class agreed with:

- We adapt our identities to different situations.
- Your identity is not fixed; it constantly changes.
- Society and the media have more control over your identity than you do.
- If you get told repeatedly that you are something, you become it.
- Our identity is just a performance – even our gender identity is learned by looking at how other males and females behave.
- Power does not exist, it is only something you display or not.

Once everyone's selfies were uploaded I posted the list of the different text-types (literary text, art work, online media exchange/social media event, video game, DIY home creativity, 'mass media' text considered 'popular') on the WhatsApp group and waited for them to post examples from their own textual fields. The thinking behind this was that the formal structures of the classroom would be removed and they would hopefully feel more comfortable posting on their phones from the comfort of their own homes creating, what I hoped would be an informal, fluid, constantly evolving space for us to share our ideas. In reality, though, this is not what really happened.

ISSUES WITH METHODOLOGY

Despite the students making lots of textual references in their conversational analysis of the worn texts that were uploaded, the imposing of a list of specific text types killed the flow. The very categorisation of the different types of text was off-putting and confusing as they weren't always sure what fitted into what category. For example, one student uploaded a picture of an actress wearing the same check shirt as one of the boys in the group. This was just something she retrieved from Google images: it wasn't a photo shoot so couldn't be considered 'art' and it wasn't shared via social media so we struggled to categorise it. Another student, when looking at my worn text, started discussing bars and restaurants that he associated with people who dressed a bit like me. In retrospect I could have not shared with them the types they had to cover and either hope that eventually they would fill the gaps or discreetly attempt to steer them towards specific text types. This would be problematic though in contradicting the whole ethos of textual agency among the students. The 'Literary Text' and 'Social Media Exchange' were the most problematic. Literary because clothing is very visual and trying to remember a written description of a specific item of clothing from a book or play or poem was a bit of a stretch, even for me, and very few of their film references could have been classed as literary film (for example, 'Miss, you remind me of the little girl in *Wreck it Ralph*'). The social media exchange was, I think, too far a leap in terms of what they considered to be a media text. As a class, they had never really had experience of analysing this sort of text before. For this process to have been more successful I should have spent more time at the start exploring what constitutes a text and why there are hierarchies in subject media that mean some texts are more worthy of study than others. Bringing them in on the debate about whether there is still an established 'Media' that transmits information or whether the things they create and encounter on social media might count as a media 'text', may have resulted in a richer and more fruitful exploration. Despite my attempt at modeling this by posting on WhatsApp a screenshot of Pinterest board for one of the students' haircuts, no student posted an example of any of the worn texts on social media until I eventually just told someone to do a search in Pinterest.

In order to meet the criteria of the 'DIY Home Creativity' text type, I used a different class of younger students who were preparing for a textual analysis exam in which they needed to analyse how *mise-en-scène* is used to represent a particular group in an unseen clip. Some groups were given the selfie and others were presented with a mood board of the textual references for the same worn texts as represented in the selfie. The students were told that the costume for the characters was fixed but they had complete freedom to choose the storyline. They had to come up with a brief synopsis and 6 frames of a storyboard including one of the characters. This had mixed results – the fact that they were given a male and a female character meant that they resorted to the most obvious gendered storylines and there was too much of a focus on racial stereotypes for the black male student, even from an ethnically diverse class studying representation at that time. And the fact that was carried out as a starter task in school meant it did not meet the 'home' part of the specified text type.

At the start of the project the focus was very clearly on the worn texts but as time went on the students struggled to focus specifically on the clothing. They were unable to separate the person from the outfit and this resulted in a few textual references that were not applicable to the original selfies but did apply to how they saw the identity of that person. Many of their comparisons in the later stages were linked to celebrities and not focused on a specific element of the worn text in the original selfie or any particular moment of representation for the celebrities. For example, in the same lesson where I was compared to the animated child from *Wreck it Ralph* (2012), I was also told I was like the girl from *(500) Days of Summer* (2009). These were not references to my worn text; they were, I assume, comparisons to do with my cutesy, quirky, loquacious and extremely annoying personality.

Another danger was inadvertently imposing my reading of the worn texts on them during the group discussions. Often their communication with each other was patchy and unclear and I had to get them to clarify which, on occasion, resulted in me saying 'do you mean...' and them agreeing or modifying their response (this tended to depend on the personality of the student).

Also there was very little motivation for students to work on this outside of class. Despite my pitching it to them as a fun project, and despite the fact that they were engaged and motivated in the lessons, getting them to participate outside of school was difficult. I tried to post regularly to the WhatsApp group and at times this resulted in 1 or 2 returned posts but more often than not I had to nag them and then eventually give lesson time over to them Googling on their phones and posting up images. I think the use of WhatsApp certainly increased the excitement of the project and in the early days, with the posting of their selfies, was used very well but when it came to uploading the text types it was just one more task to do. It's inevitable that a project lead by their teacher is essentially going to feel like school and as I wasn't actually setting homework and deadlines for this project, it was not a priority and they were not engaged enough to participate fully on their own time (and I don't really blame them).

WEARING CLAIRE (FINDINGS)

Below (Fig 3.1) are the images we started with. This is the outfit that I feel coolest in; the outfit that I feel most comfortable in and the outfit I feel best reflects my identity. This is an image of the PowerPoint I gave to the class for analysis:

Fig. 3.1: My Selfie. A screenshot of the PowerPoint slide shared with my students.

For me this 'worn text' has very specific signifiers that I would expect someone from a similar tribe and of a similar age (mid-late thirties) to be able to 'accurately' read.

I'll start with the shoes: Doc Marten's 10 hole, cherry red boots. My friends and I all started wearing DMs in year 9 when we established ourselves as part of the grunge or grebo subculture. They were readily available on Northampton market and Wollaston village factory shoe shop, just outside my hometown of Wellingborough, where they were, in those days, manufactured. As well as being worn by cooler, older kids who wore baggy heavy-knit jumpers and had army surplus store bags with the names of a hundred bands graffitied all over them, they were something that marked you out as alternative and a little bit aggressive. As A-grade students with tie-dyed dungarees and old granny-coats from charity shops, my friends and I needed something that said, 'Don't fuck with us.'

My first pair were black 8-hole. The 10-hole cherry red – or oxblood as they are sometimes described – became a must-have for me when I bought Blur's *Modern Life Is Rubbish* album. The album has just one picture of the band, a painting by Paul Stephen of the group looking fashionably bored on a District line London Underground train. In the foreground of this image, glinting under the artificial strip lighting, Damon Albarn has the greatest jean and boot combination I ever did see. This marked a shift in my musical identity from grebo to more indie/Mod. It was a look I emulated throughout most of the '90s and it's one I still favour today. (It's also an album I still adore.)

These boots, I should add, are not the original pair – at some point at the end of the nineties I stuck flower pots in them and put them on various windowsills of numerous London shared houses until they eventually went crispy and perished. After *This is England* came out in 2006 I immediately bought a new pair in a bid to reclaim the look before it became 'popular' and to some extent, began to rediscover the slightly tomboy-ish mod fashion that I favoured in the sixth form. Ten years on they're still so shiny because they still really hurt my feet. I guess they used to be manufactured in Northamptonshire for Northamptonshire feet and the Thai manufacturers just don't make them like they used to.

Again, music is presented as key to my identity through the t-shirt. I discovered Teenage Fanclub by reading the army surplus duffle bag of Nat Gordon, a sixth former from Wilby (another village just outside Wellingborough) who was on our school bus. I found the track 'What You Do to Me' on a compilation album (vinyl, of course) and have been a massive fan ever since. This t-shirt was bought in 2010 at the Shepherd's Bush Empire. It's identical to the original navy one I bought at my first gig at the Cambridge Corn Exchange in November 1993, which I still have; but, being a man's XL, it has been reclassified as maternity wear.

The pinstriped velvet jacket I have also had since I was 16. It was bought in a charity shop in Wellingborough, though I can't remember which one. I had a more shapeless black velvet jacket in my earlier grunge days; this marked the shift to a more Mod fashion phase. It was quite unusual in 1995 to wear a blazer. When I went for my first sociology lesson at a cluster 6th form (my school didn't offer the subject so they taxied me to a nearby school 3 times a week) the class assumed I was their new teacher. Socially, I never quite managed to come back from that; the class was dominated by bright, rich, beautiful middle class girls who simply didn't understand *what* I was trying to do fashion-wise. I still wear this now and I can still, just about, button it up.

The last part of the outfit is my hair and headscarf. I've pretty much had short hair for almost 20 years. I started wearing headscarves and handkerchiefs to hide tangled, windswept swim hair on the beaches of the West of Ireland about 11 years ago. I rarely wear any jewellery these days so headscarves are my main accessory. I immediately feel cooler when I wear one.

MY TEXTUAL REFERENCES FOR THIS SELFIE

Worn Text		Textual Reference	What I like to think it says about my identity
Cherry Red DM Boots	Literary	*Clothes Music, Boys* by Viv Albertine: 'I go to Holt's in Camden Town to buy a pair of black Dr Martens. (you can get them in black, brown or maroon, the skinhead boys at school used to buy the brown ones and polish them with Kiwi Oxblood shoe polish ... They also kept them pristinely clean at all times.) I wear my new boots with everything – dresses, tutus – it's a great feeling to be able to run again. No other girls wear DMs with dresses so I get a lot of funny looks.' (p.124)	Similar to Albertine, I bought DMs to be different (to the mainstream, though not my friends). They are practical; I almost never wear heels – not even on my wedding day – just in case I find myself needing to run away. Juxtaposition in fashion is something I have always enjoyed; in the 90s I contrasted DMs with short floral dresses, or, like Courtney Love at the time, feminine slip dresses or nighties: tough and vulnerable in one outfit.
Pinstriped Velvet Jacket + DM boots	Art	Blur's *Modern Life is Rubbish* album artwork.	These guys are effortlessly cool in this image. They're in London and they look so bored by it. As a 14 year old in a shitty corner of the Midlands, I couldn't imagine anything cooler. They have vintage/charity shop look in this picture that immediately appealed to me and soon after this everyone who was anyone in Northamptonshire (about 15 people) started watching *Quadrophenia* (1979) and dressing Mod.
	Mass media text considered popular	*This is England*.	As with *Quadrophenia* this was a story about working class kids with a passion for music and parents who didn't have a clue what was going on inside their hearts and heads. Vicki McClure as 'Lol' in *This is England* is the first portrayal of an attractive girl in boys clothing that I can remember. When this came out in 2006 it made me nostalgic for the way I used to dress between 15 and 19 – polo shirts, vintage shirts, jeans, boots, blazers. It's when I was at my most physically and socially comfortable as well as looking tough, tomboyish and practical.

	Art Work	Aspect of everyday life	Social Media Exchange
Headscarf/Short hair	'We Can Do It!' propaganda poster, 1943.	Travel, seaside.	Strong, tough positive; get off your arse and do something. I have always loved swimming especially outdoors and part of that is loving having swim hair; tangled and matted with salt and sand. It was under these circumstances that I started wearing headscarves. For a lot of women the only thing better than looking good is looking as though you don't care what you look like and still looking good.
Teenage Fanclub T-shirt	*Bandwagonesque* Booties Tweet		I bought some baby booties for some friends of our when they had their first baby with the image from Teenage Fanclub's *Bandwagonesque* (1991) on them. He tweeted them and it got more favourites and retweets than anything I have ever posted. Most of the retweets were from people of the same age, with an interest in same sorts of music and I found this both exciting and heartwarming. It was like connecting with people that I could have known back then, people who were in on the fact that the nineties was the best decade and with whom I felt some deep musical and cultural affiliation.

Although I made a collage of images and descriptions of my textual interpretations of my outfit, I didn't share it with my students at any point over the project. When they got the original images, they were instructed to annotate them alone for a couple of minutes and then they were left to discuss what they felt the worn text signified. I adopted a technique that I have used before when doing Socratic seminars with our classes: I did not partake in the discussion at all, or even start them off. It makes for an awkward first minute or so as they all stare at me and at each other and giggle, but eventually someone who is sure of the task starts the discussion and before you know it they are genuinely discussing together without paying much attention to the teacher.

I transcribed in my school planner while they talked (I felt audio recording would be off-putting for them) and below is the transcription. You'll see that I didn't completely succeed in staying invisible – there were a couple of occasions where it was necessary to interject and they are also recorded below:

TRANSCRIPT OF STUDENT DISCUSSION, ANALYSING MY WORN TEXT

'Genre is Indie.'

'Indie restaurant, smoothies, organic.'

'Casual, smart casual, because of the blazer.'

'Shoes are formal.'

'Headscarf is young. Suggests innocence, childish.'

'Like those 40s or 50s war posters.'

'Indie rock style.'

'What do you mean, Indie restaurant?'

'You know Dalston Road, Brick lane   bares indie restaurant.'

'Bright colour scheme (T-shirt) – *attention seeking?*'

'The t-shirt draws attention in contrast to the rest of the outfit.'

'It's a safe outfit, what everyone else would wear.'

'Blends in with the crowd.'

'Practical.'

'Wear it any time, everyday.'

'It's like in GTA when you chose what [peril?] you have e.g. fug, youngster it's the hipster!'

3: WEARING TEXT

'Cool, elegant. Blazer and tight jeans. Hat.'

'Is hair part of your outfit?'

'Neat practical look.'

'Tomboyish.'

'Like M.J.' (a boy in their year group)

TEACHER: WHAT ABOUT INDIVIDUAL ITEMS OF CLOTHING AS SIGNIFIERS?

'Blazer suggests smartness, acting your age.'

'The shoes are sturdy. Powerful, dominant and chunky.'

'Jacket definitely hipster.'

'Don't know what the shirt means.'

'Is it a band, Miss?'

'Must've enjoyed being a teenager.'

'Symbolic of older times.'

'Still living young.'

'It's an old band. It's a band, right?'

TEACHER: YES

'Still living young…'

'Or trying to?'

'No not trying to…'

'I could see myself doing that. Like a TV show when you were young and you still wear the t-shirt when you're older.'

TEACHER: DO YOU MEAN LIKE COMIC BOOK T-SHIRTS?

'No. Like TMNT (Teenage Mutant Ninja Turtles) I would still wear - you know with just the blue mask - like that, when I'm 30.'

'You can buy old cartoon t-shirts in shops now.'

'What could we say about the jeans?'

'Current style.'

'The cuffed jeans show they're still in touch with trends these days.'

'But the t-shirt- no one would know it, it's in the past.'

All in all I was quite surprised and pleased with their interpretations. The comments about the t-shirt in particular, the 'old band' being both a sign of clinging on to younger days as well as something that only certain people – who were in the know, and in the tribe – would understand. I was surprised that certain fashions, like the cuffed jeans and DMs were considered up-to-date. I should say that I am writing at a time when nineties fashion and grunge chic are back (this week Vogue celebrated the release of the new documentary *Kurt Cobain: Montage of Heck*, the only way they know how: with a grunge fashion special inspired by the dead male icon) and doing this project in 5 years time, with fashion shifting as quickly as it seems to these days, my selfie may have got a completely different response. They were spot on with the 'wear It anytime, any day' which comes back to the idea of carefully crafting an outfit that suggests I haven't made an effort. A few textual references came up, including, impressively, the 'indie restaurant' comment which, although perplexing at first, turned out to be a clever link between the clothing signifiers and a 'smoothies, organic' lifestyle. In fact I spend a lot of time in cafes and restaurants in Dalston, which also suggests that although I think my look is authentically from my past, it obviously reflects where I live and socialise in my thirties

The process of getting the remaining textual references was challenging. Eventually I just got someone to search in Pinterest for the social media exchange and, as a group they came up with nothing for literary text. In the table below I have gathered the references they came up with a few qualifying statements. As this took place over several lessons and through WhatsApp, the comments were not recorded.

3: WEARING TEXT

THE STUDENTS' TEXTUAL REFERENCES FOR THIS SELFIE

Worn Text	Text Type	Textual Reference (specific texts as named by the students are in bold)
Whole outfit as shown above	DIY Home Creativity	Two **storyboards** were submitted by a group of 16 year-old who were given the selfie of myself and of one of my students. In the first one I am described in their notes as *tomboy, geek, studious quite young* (teenage – because of the t-shirt) with *casual jeans and formal shoes*. The disappointing narrative is a female character called 'Alex' who enters the teenage fanclub – presumably some sort of youth club – and watches *Muppets* and plays *Grand Theft Auto* with a boy with whom she swaps numbers and eventually leaves. The second is a parallel edited narrative with a girl and guy getting dressed and taking selfies. They upload them to blogs. The girl likes his post and he sees her t-shirt and falls in love because he also likes Teenage Fanclub. In the final frame they are at the 'teenage fan club', presumably a bar or youth club, where they meet and instantly fall in love. In their annotations of the worn text they make several comments including *sensible, sophisticated, relaxed* – connotes she is *content, committed to idol* (the t-shirt) and in relation to the boots, *motivated, ambitious, sturdy* and *hipster*.
Headscarf	Art	'Those 40s or 50s **war posters**'
Blazer and Jeans	Video Game	**Grand Theft Auto online's 'I'm Not a Hipster Update'** The description on GTA wiki reads: 'Express your incredible individualism and stand out from the herd with the post ironic, artisanal, organic, entirely independent, 100% re-claimed "I'm Not a Hipster' Update now available for *Grand Theft Auto Online*. This new content update features new retro print tees, skinny jeans, hairstyles, tattoos, animal masks and more, as well as additional enhancements to general gameplay to ensure the world is constantly evolving.' Damning stuff.
Headscarf	Mass Media text considered 'popular'	'That lesbian **(Tilly) from Hollyoaks** – It's the hair!' Tilly is a redhead who often wears headscarves and just happens to be a lesbian. Although not massively girly, she doesn't fit the tired and outdated stereotypes of masculine or aggressive looking lesbians. It's a fair comparison.
Whole outfit as shown above	Aspect of every day life	**Indie Restaurant** – the student is referring to hipster café bars around Dalston (where I live) and Brick Lane. This year a café opened up that only sells cereal. You know the kind of thing.
Turned up jeans and DMs	Online Media exchange, social media event	**Pinterest board depicting male and females in turned up jeans and DM boots or shoes**. Including, I'm delighted to add, David Bowie.
Whole outfit as shown above	Literary	No return

51

MY RESPONSE TO STUDENTS' INTERPRETATIONS OF MY IDENTITY

Having shared my worn text with my students and seen the process of having it analysed and then mediated through their selection of texts from their own textual fields, I am not disappointed with the outcome. Some key parts of my identity have been reflected in a way that I find acceptable or in some cases flattering. I don't really mind being compared to a young attractive lesbian character, even if she is from *Hollyoaks*.

Several representations draw on the 'hipster' subculture, which, although annoyingly reductive, is probably reasonably accurate. I live in Dalston, the hipster epicentre of London, and in terms of fashion and lifestyle there are clear similarities. But we were here long before the hipsters invaded and spend much time bemoaning their arrival and laughing at their tiny dogs and ludicrous hats on Broadway Market on a Saturday – while waiting for my decaf flat white to cool.

The students were hesitant when suggesting textual references that were male or homosexual for fear of offending me but it actually makes for a much richer representation and I am proud of the way that they have made clear connections with the outfit and images they have seen in their own media consumption.

Obviously, despite bringing in dudes, lesbians and cafes, the nuances of my identity have been reduced and flattened to a recognisable but heavily mediated one dimensional character type. The storyboards created by the younger students have focused on the fact that I am a girl, they have wrongly deduced from the mood boards that I am young (presumably because of the *Hollyoaks* character) and they have come up with the most common storyline for teenage girls: how to get yourself a man. Both storyboards show a teenage girl without a worry or care in the world, socialising in her 'teenage fan club' and meeting a guy. In these storyboards the hipster element is less prominent than the gender and even reasonably obvious feminist signifiers only result in a slightly less feminine name: Alex.

The process of mediating and diluting one's identity is to be expected and is what I set out to demonstrate to my class, but it was more clear and had more of an effect on my students' understanding of the damaging effects of a mediated identity, when we carried out the same process with one of the students.

WEARING JAIDEN (FURTHER FINDINGS)

Although it was our aim to gather textual references for every class member's worn text, it didn't happen. I put as much pressure on them as I was comfortable with, alongside the pressure of getting coursework evaluations and exam practice answers in. I was also aware that by pushing the tasks, it became my project and not theirs. However, we did get almost full sets of references for a couple of students and here is a brief account of one of them, starting with a screenshot of the selfie image and the textual references:

Fig. 3. 2 Jaiden's Selfie and mood board, L-R from the top: *3 Feet High and Rising*, De La Soul, CJ from *Grand Theft Auto*, Kermit the Frog meme, Karl from *The Simpsons* and a screenshot from Pinterest.

When using this method to get my class to understand how identities could be mediated, I felt it was important to use a student whose 'real' identity they were more familiar with and with whom they might share textual references for the worn text. This also had the result of their being more engaged and indignant when they saw how his identity morphed into something unrecognisable from the person sitting around the table with us.

Getting Jaiden to reflect in front of the class on the construction of his outfit and what it signified about his identity was problematic. He claimed it was just his favourite outfit and he hadn't thought about what it said about his identity, but it's clearly an image of a constructed identity. From the pose and the lighting it is obvious that he has thought about this. The most he would say is that he felt it was smart but not too serious or formal. When confronted with the mood board I asked how he felt about it and he said he was ok with it. He felt it mostly reflected his outfit and that the only reference he was unhappy with was Karl from *The Simpsons* as he felt that made him seem stupid.

At this point we looked at how Jaiden's identity had changed through our assembly of references for his outfit or worn text – they agreed it had changed but was still recognisably Jaiden.

When I showed the group the next step – the storyboards based on the moodboard – we saw a major distortion in Jaiden's identity. The two storyboards created both showed a young black guy dealing drugs out of his car and using guns. Clearly the creators of the text decided to hone in on the textual reference that either appealed to them most or were most familiar with and filtered out all the other information into what was, essentially, a racist interpretation. On all the annotations, both of the moodboard and of the selfie, his race was mentioned.

When I carried out this group discussion with the class it had been a while since the earlier parts of the project and was now very close to their exam. I posed the question, 'What has happened to Jaiden's identity?' and left them free to discuss. They were surprised. They felt that it was nothing like what they thought expected it would be and that the storyline was wildly different from their understanding of Jaiden's identity. They felt that the choice of narrative and situation might be as much a product of the age and immaturity of the producers of that text as it was the source material (moodboard). Another student said they felt that an interpretation based purely on a picture could never be accurate. It was felt that the producers of the DIY creativity text had perhaps misread the De La Soul album artwork and assumed the bright colours and flowers connoted a 'high on drugs' state and that alongside the image of CJ from *Grand Theft Auto* (the image in the top right hand corner of a man on a bike with 2 automatic weapons) they had made one assumption that had overpowered everything else. When asked why this might have happened we discussed the lack of understanding or life experience of the 'readers' of these images, but also how their own personal preferences and practices – in that they would probably be more familiar with the work of CJ in *Grand Theft Auto* than any of the other textual references placed before them – might influence their interpretation.

One student suggested that as producers they probably just went with the most obvious stereotype because it was easiest to replicate and understand. Another student added that the negative stereotypes and negative aspects of identity are often exaggerated because it's the easiest thing to do and they would be mostly likely to attract an audience.

In past lessons we had studied Hall's Reception theory and although the class could probably explain what a preferred or oppositional reading was, they would probably have to use the examples I had given them in class to illustrate their explanations. This process, however, allowed them to actually experience and be personally affected by an oppositional reading over which they had no control. This was a really fantastic and unexpected by-product of this project.

CONCLUSION: EDUCATIONAL OUTCOMES

I set out with two aims for this project the first being to increase my students' textual agency. They did, to some extent, have useful conversations with each other about texts that were common between them that I wasn't familiar with – the Kermit meme, for example, is something they were all familiar with and even when I Googled it, I'm not sure I got it. Despite my ignorance, the girl who put it forward as a text was well able to explain how it was relevant to Jaiden's worn text and was able to read the meme in a way that linked to her understanding of Jaiden's identity – it related to his nonchalance and aloofness which may have been something she read in his worn text but most likely supported by her understanding of him as a person. There were a couple of other moments when the class were talking amongst themselves and discussing texts and I was purely in the role of facilitator because, certainly in the case of video games, I had no idea what were talking about. So in a small way, it did increase their textual agency.

Has this had a lasting impact in our lessons? Not really. There may be a number of reasons for this: for example the culture of the classroom and the school. Although my media department and all the teachers currently teaching media at my school work hard to create a relaxed, mutual working atmosphere in lessons (which I feel is necessary to support the large scale project-based coursework that is required for the qualification we teach) the general 'independent learning' ethos in the school is quite weak. Independent learning is synonymous with using computers and in actual fact we rarely allow students the space to learn and fail independently. Failure is not an option. Also I have to admit that I do like to maintain a clear teacher-student boundary. As a head of department, I have to send nasty letters home, meet with parents, issue threats and targets, and these would not be effective without it. There are clearly established hierarchies that affect the students' agency. Year 13s have had 14 years of schooling and probably very few opportunities in that time to choose any of the texts that appear on their curriculum. Thus the system imposes its own standards and criteria for success through prescribed texts that students either engage with and succeed or reject and fail. And my students, who are determined to succeed, play it safe when choosing texts to write about in their exams.

Another problem with students selecting texts is that they don't always make appropriate choices. Even within this project where the different text types were broad and egalitarian, they were still categories, and students struggled to find things that fit into those. Similar things happen when I ask them to bring in texts for whole class study: the same class have been presenting news articles that represent immigrants in a positive or negative light but reader letters have been confused with the political views of the paper, or they choose things that are too old, or too off-topic. This should, I admit, be surmountable over time but with exams almost always on the horizon it feels irresponsible and amoral to take these risks. They will not thank me for increasing their textual agency if they write something wacky in their exam and get a poor grade.

The second objective was to encourage my students to engage with ideas of identity and mediation and in that respect I feel the experiment was hugely beneficial at bringing to life a concept that in the past they had only been able to engage with in a very simplified way. Through this project they were better able to understand the way the media can have an enormous influence on the representation, and therefore identity, of groups. Firstly it showed how a mediated identity is flattened and one-dimensional and can take one aspect of a character and distort beyond recognition. Secondly, it showed that you have no control over how the readers of a text will respond to it – and that often audiences use texts to amplify already deeply-set beliefs, often based on previous texts they have consumed.

A point made by a student about the media honing in on the obvious and negative when it comes to representing groups opened up a discussion about how the mainstream media targets particular groups that are already negatively represented and reproduces those dominant, negative images in order to play to audience's expectations. The storyboards based on Jaiden's selfie were overtly negative and actually, when considering the ones made for my selfie, they did very obviously hone in on one aspect of female experience – finding a man – that, as a feminist, I might find offensive.

Although it wasn't part of the original plan to outsource the DIY creativity part of the search to a different class, this actually had a much more fruitful outcome. As the students noted, our opinions and knowledge of each other's identities beyond just a captured image of a worn text tempered our interpretations of the outfit. It also had a Chinese-whisper effect – having the storyboards created 'once-removed' allowed for our identities to be completely reinterpreted and reduced to a narrow and often stereotypical focus and helped us to experience how collective groups (such as immigrants, which is our current exam topic) would feel about reductive and negative representations.

REFERENCES

1. Sky News: Talking Dog's top YouTube hit, 2011

WORKS CITED

(500) Days of Summer 2009 (dir. Webb, Marc) Fox Searchlight Pictures, USA.

Albarn, D., Coxon, G., James, A. and Rowntree, D. (1993) *Modern Life Is Rubbish*, Food Records.

Albertine, V. (2015) *Clothes, Clothes, Clothes. Music, Music, Music. Boys, Boys, Boys.* London: Faber and Faber.

Bennett, P., Kendall, A. and McDougall, J. (2011) *After The Media*. Abingdon: Routledge.

Blake, N., Love, G., McGinley, R. and O'Hare, B. (1991) *Bandwagonesque*, Creation Records.

De La Soul (1989) *3 feet High and Rising,* Tommy Boy/Warner Bros. Records.

Diary of a Badman (2010–13) (video): https://www.youtube.com/playlist?list=PLH8ThQDcA78Q3JVmoj0KVTtTojIcUnMA4 (accessed July 2015).

Hall, S. (1973) *Encoding and Decoding in the Television Discourse*. Birmingham: Centre for Cultural Studies, University of Birmingham.

Kurt Cobain: Montage of Heck (dir. Morgan, Brett, 2015) HBO Documentary Films.

Miller, J. Howard (1943) 'We Can Do It!'

Quadrophenia (dir. Roddam, Franc, 1979) The Who Films, London.

The Simpsons, FOX, WFXT, Boston.Sky News (2011) *Talking Dog's top YouTube hit* (video): http://news.sky.com/story/910270/talking-dogs-top-youtube-hit

This is England (dir. Meadows, Shane, 2006) Warp Films. London.

Wreck it Ralph (dir. Moore, Rich, 2012) Walt Disney Animation Studios, CA, USA.

4: WRITING TEXT

Pritpal Singh Sembi

INTRODUCTION

This chapter is intended to be somewhere between a textbook and a purely academic intervention. I want to reflect partly upon my own auto-ethnographic experience to think about how gamers create culture before, during and after gameplay via engagement with wider written discourses. I believe that media literacy needs to be refocused towards an 'ongoing engagement with contemporary culture' (Hall, 2014: 3) and gaming is an expression of popular culture that would benefit from pedagogic engagement.

It has now become impossible to ignore the impact of gaming on everyday culture, wherein time spent on gaming can outweigh time spent in formal education or employment for some. However, since many people use games to *escape* from real-life, how can it be that gaming might actually enhance real-life? Video games offer rewards for those who invest time with them: offering positive and motivating in-game feedback, an ability to pursue virtual world-changing quests, often better virtual relationships than those in real life and the ability to explore and develop alter-egos in a safe environment.

A fundamental suggestion I make is that writing has moved beyond traditional boundaries in terms of *what* is written, *where* you write and *how* you write. Much of the experience of gaming is expressed within discourses that exist outside of the actual gameplay itself which, harnessed appropriately, can have important educational value. I believe that this gamer discourse is rooted partly in what we experience during gameplay but this is just the beginning: it is also rooted in the identity we construct (i.e. how we see ourselves and how we wish to be seen) as well as when we reflect upon the private world of gameplay into, for example, the public domain of new/social media. The *World of Warcraft* Wiki online, for example, is an extraordinary resource that is second only to *Wikipedia* in terms of popularity and visits per day. This is a relatively new form of writing that has emerged alongside the increased interactivity and complexity of next generation video games online; but, more importantly, it is a form of writing that some gamers engage with both voluntarily and regularly. However, we need to question the rather outdated idea of writing as being a 'paper and pen' exercise and embrace, instead, writing as a more creative concept that takes place for the most part within what might be called the 'reflective downtime' between gaming sessions. I believe that we should embrace these existing wider gaming discourses, as well encourage more, but not to the point of intellectualised fetishism – which conflicts with the goal of a more flattened textuality and relationship between teacher and pupil.

It is still rare for a teacher of either English or Media Studies to be as competent a gamer as their pupils. It is also uncommon for such teachers to consider gaming as anything but anathematic to traditional education. Yet the discourse (discussion, debate, Wiki, strategy guides, FAQs) around modern gaming represents a form of writing that is commonplace and familiar to a large community of gamers. As such I believe that we need to develop a pedagogic strategy that takes such writing seriously and explores the role of the inexpert as someone who co-ordinates the expertise of others into a meaningful learning experience for all. We must also consider a pedagogy that values reflection upon the gameplay experience and considers gamer capital to be just as important to education as other forms of cultural capital that students bring to the table.

MY BACKGROUND

Alongside my background in Media & Film Studies I have been a life-long home video gamer from the original 8-bit Sinclair Spectrum 48K to the newest next generation home consoles, amassing thousands of hours of gameplay. Video gaming, for me, is usually an immersive and escapist experience that I have often felt guilty about pursuing since it is too readily considered at odds with educational aims.

To make matters worse, I am a veteran video game player who would probably have been awarded my PhD by now if I hadn't encountered *The Elder Scrolls 5: Skyrim* during my sabbatical. This game, once appropriately described as a 'soul stealer' by an astute student of mine, overtook all of my free time very quickly indeed. Once I was hooked it was absolute: more addictive to me than any video game experience I had ever encountered before, or since, and I am not short of such encounters. Despite moving on to other titles, I still come back to this game very regularly. Part of me craves something to assuage the guilt of my *Skyrim* obsession: something to show for the 'meaningless' pursuit of escapist pleasure that I have succumbed to. A book chapter would be ideal!

THE ELDER SCROLLS V: SKYRIM

Skyrim is the 5th installment of the highly successful *Elder Scrolls* franchise from Bethesda Game Studios. Playing from a first- or third-person perspective, it is set in a wintry Nordic themed mythical land of Tamriel that plays host to the genesis of a civil war between The Stormcloaks and the Imperial Legion, within which the player is asked to formally take sides at some point. However, *Skyrim*'s main story revolves around the player and his quest to defeat a dragon, Alduin, who is prophesied to destroy the world. It transpires early on in the gameplay that the player is the legendary Dragonborn (with the body of a mortal but the soul of a Dragon) and this serendipitous dual heritage becomes vital to pursue the main quest. As the Dragonborn explores *Skyrim* he/she can unlock side-quests and sub-plots by talking to Non-Player Characters (NPCs) and assisting them in some way. Overall, *Skyrim* is an immersive sandbox Role Playing Game (RPG) on a massive scale that, apart from some initial forced linear tutorials, allows the player to negotiate a largely individual path through the game.

Fig 4.1 The Dragonborn confronts one of many dragons on his quest to defeat the main antagonist, Alduin.

Activity: Character Creation & Experience (Beginner skill, within 30 minutes of game time)

a) Ask players to begin the game and choose the name, gender, race and other features of their character.

b) They may choose something broadly similar to themselves (e.g., at least gender) or a projection of their desires (stronger, faster) or something quite unique (e.g., reptile) for novelty or for the abilities of a certain race (e.g., resist magic, powerful physique).

c) Ask students to reflect upon their choices and discuss amongst themselves.

d) What are the reasons for choosing what they did? What difference would it make if they chose another character type?

e) Ask students to play through the game, which is initially quite linear as the dynamics are introduced, and see how it feels to experience the world.

f) How does each player view the world they are discovering? How have they been treated so far? What do they expect might happen next?

g) Ask students to speak to various NPCs to unlock quests and/or side missions.

h) Which quests appeal over others? Why are some quests 'shelved' for now? What is actually going on when quests are prioritised above others (e.g., pursuit of wealth, approval, power, goodness)?

i) Ask students to discuss their particular experiences with others. What is the reason for the difference?

I personally began the game like one might play *Monopoly*: amassing vast wealth & real estate from the rewards and trappings bestowed following commissioned quests and exploration. I then went on to help innocent villagers by protecting them against evil forces and dragons reigning terror upon the land. I made moral choices akin to how I might react in real-life (i.e. still refusing to take on the unsavory and morally ambiguous *Dark Brotherhood* quests) and remained essentially a morally upright character overall. I gained social status by helping others and improved my character to be the most powerful Mage stealth archer I could be: allowing me to take out my enemies using potions, enchanted armour, magical spells and powerful poisoned arrows often unnoticed.

Players who are more trigger-happy can adopt a more aggressive approach to their skills and approach, those who prefer strategy and stealth can remain hidden and only kill when necessary. It makes little difference to the game's progress whether you take the lethal or non-lethal approach. Consider *Dishonored*, by contrast, where the conclusion is completely influenced by how much blood was shed by the player. I realised that I enjoyed having this moral choice, particularly when I was involved in some ethically questionable missions that actually made me uncomfortable as a player (i.e. killing innocent people and torturing others for information). I enjoyed being an honorable and morally upstanding citizen of *Skyrim* and shared my experience with others.

Activity: Character Development (Basic Skill, within 2 hours of game play)

a) Players will have a choice about how their characters develop over time. Some may join the College of Winterhold to be a Mage, others may join the Thieves Guild in Riften to learn about pickpocketing, the Companions in Whiterun to explore mercenary armed combat or the Elders in High Hrothgar to learn about the magical Dragon Shout skills. Each route will have implications.

b) Each of these choices is just a first step. One can step partly into one camp and then refine other skills elsewhere before returning to their original expertise to improve it.

c) The more a technique is practiced (e.g., archery) the better the player gets. A kind of use-reward-use virtuous circle that allows players to hone their skills in the direction they find most appealing or useful (depending upon the motivations).

d) All skills can be used for good and bad reasons (i.e., pickpocketing an evil person may be a good quest, but this skill can also be used to 'rob' innocent people of their gold).

e) Although it is possible to specialise in one skill, it is quite common for players to have a combination of different skills that they favour.

f) Which 'factions' were joined? Why were some avoided? How do students see their characters developing? What skills are important to them or the gameplay? Why?

Activity: Character Status (Basic Skill, within 3 hours of game play)

a) There are quests that improve the status of the player in each of the main strongholds (e.g., Whiterun, Winterhold, Windhelm, Solitude) to the point that you can be considered Thane of the area.

b) Such status allows you extra freedom in the area and the ability to purchase a house. The house provides a secure place to store all 'trappings' of adventure and accumulate vast amounts of wealth if required.

c) It also means that guards will 'turn a blind eye' if you are caught stealing from shops in the area.

d) How important is status within the game? Are you really being altruistic when you perform morally sound quests in order to be given property by one of the Jarls? Have you ever done something knowingly 'wrong'?

PEDAGOGIC PRINCIPLES

As suggested, I believe that we need to harness the informal and largely undervalued pre and post gaming writing activities that are normally undertaken as part of the gamer's world deemed quite separate to education. This moves Media teaching on by re-imagining the concept of writing and by focusing upon a hitherto under-represented cultural form in the classroom. According to Apperley's ideas around gamer capital, once cultural capital around the gaming experience is accumulated it empowers the player to share this wealth of knowledge with others, often via discursive means. Gamers are seldom, if ever, proffered an opportunity to do this in a formal educational setting let alone receive formative and summative feedback as a consequence. As mentioned: this chapter is an attempt to reframe the sharing of gamer capital, as a valuable form of writing, to deem it just as worthy as any other cultural text.

Video games embody pre-written narratives for the gameworld *a priori* before it reaches the point of retail sale. It is this writing that provides the diegesis, marketing, *mise-en-scène*, parameters, etc. that formulate the pre-existing game world that players engage with. *Skyrim*, in particular, has a massive open world with a rich backstory and milieu that can accommodate a wide range of narrative opportunities and in-game options. The active player of the game is unequivocally writing his/her own version of the existing text: each quest initiated represents a new narrative thread that can be explored or ignored. The path taken towards each quest is variable depending upon the player's personal approach, equipment at their disposal and skills they may possess. This provides a wide range of journey permutations for players who are regularly invited to develop their skills by several NPCs in exchange for gold or errands.

There are several avenues when gamers choose to share their experiences and reflect upon their accumulated wisdom such as online chat, multiplayer gaming, FAQs, Wikis, streaming video sites with synchronous chat. Discourses around cultural products can take on a life of their own with fan based websites, avatars to represent players and an app to monitor the availability of their online gamer friends. I suggest that we embrace this lifeworld, or gameworld, and bring it into the classroom to challenge the staid formulations of traditional curricula – allowing students the opportunity to take more ownership over their independent learning. I would stress, however, that although the teaching practitioner may be somewhat undermined as a gaming inexpert, they must still be respected as the main facilitator of learning for all activities. Without careful planning of learning activities the student engagement with gaming texts could become unstructured and informal.

A film text reveals its narrative arc largely through viewing, a book requires more interaction and thought, a game requires increasing skill, rewarding more active repeat play and refinement of player engagement. One is required to interact with a video game in a prolonged and meaningful way before the 'gameworld' is made apparent: it is not evident immediately and effortlessly. Again, this is another part of the multimedia discourse that surrounds the modern gamer, and it is a discourse that expects its participants to familiarise themselves with appropriate gameplay rules, guides and stratagem in order to participate meaningfully. In fact, many players now rely upon engagement with, for example, walkthrough guides and FAQs online to progress past difficult stages in games. So there is an important correlation between the gaming experienced during play and that which we experience *outside* of play. You can't reach the end of a video game without active effort and time commitment: such engagement with *Skyrim* can lead to a uniquely 'written' story of one's own Dragonborn journey, which some players feel compelled to share.

Activity: Strategy Guide (Intermediate Skill, at least 20 hours of game time)

a) Create an online searchable Wiki to consolidate gamer capital to assist players with various aspects of the game. What should be included in this Wiki and what shouldn't?

b) Create an FAQ to guide other gamers who may be 'stuck' at a certain point in the game. How might the discourse of the gameplay and the FAQ feed into each other on an ongoing basis?

c) Ask students to write a formal printed strategy guide for the game. Who should this be aimed at and why?

GAMEPLAY AND CUSTOMISATION

Videogames and video gameplay do not exist in a vacuum. Even if they are played alone, these texts and the experiences of them are located within a set of interpretive practices. Understanding this videogame culture is key as it highlights the myriad ways in which videogames provide a stimulus for social activity and privileges the complex sets of reading and production activity that explicitly decry the designation of videogaming as trivial or asocial. (Newman, 2004: 148)

Skyrim is designed to be played alone, though the discourse around it challenges 'the popular perception of the videogame player as an isolated, withdrawn loner' (Newman, 2004: 148). There is no multiplayer element but the life outside the gameplay has been largely engineered and inspired by an enthusiastic fan base that shares strategy, game modifications, FAQs, advice fora. There is also scope for other written discourse as players synchronously discuss their gameplay with others during interaction in written or spoken 'live chat'. Newman (2004: 157) believes that 'sharing and trading knowledge about games is an important part of the social interactions that take place among videogame fans' and I maintain that this knowledge is *written* when it is compiled, accumulated and shared.

There is also a massive level of customisation, modification and alteration available in *Skyrim* that encourages DIY engagement and creativity around the game. For example: you can mine for ore, smelt it into metal, use this to create weapons, improve these with extra crafting potions and even enchant them with magical abilities – all potentially unique to each player. Each Dragonborn can then have access to countless such artefacts, created with unique powers. The PC version can also be modified via publically shared modifications, or 'mods', shared via the STEAM community (one of several online repositories of PC games, discussion, support and expansion) which can add enhancements to visual detail or gameplay.

Activity: Expansion Pack (Advanced Skill, 30+ hours of game play time)

a) Ask students to design a modification or 'DLC' (very advanced students can make this). This will enlist them to consider deficiencies within the game and/or enhancements they might make. Ask students why their modification is desired and/or necessary.

With such a large number of options, every Dragonborn's journey is inevitably different and evolves as the player progresses. These unique journeys can provide some of the raw material for class based discussion. It is perhaps the social media aspect of *Skyrim* which is the most culturally permeating since 'social spaces exist both within and around videogames' (Newman, 2004: 162) and *Skyrim* is no exception. Fans become new media producers, the discourse from which can feed into the gaming experience too. One major online media exchange for *Skyrim* is Twitch TV, which allows a normally isolated gaming experience to be shared synchronously with the wider community using video-capture hardware, often accompanied with player spoken voice-over and simultaneous text 'chat'. In amongst all this written information exchange I believe that gamer capital is accumulated and the identity of both gamers and their audiences are forged, along with new communities of practice.

HANDING OVER POWER

Hutchison (2007: 35) argues for 'incorporating video games into educational programs in a pedagogically sound way' and wants to 'encourage students to interact with video games as writers, critics, and game developers, not only as players' (2007: 39). I prefer the term pedagogically *appropriate* since I believe that pedagogical approaches should be tailored to specific learning outcomes. However, when people play games as a leisure pursuit, pedagogic possibilities are not necessarily at the forefront of their minds. There are unforeseen opportunities for learning that might also be embraced for pedagogic benefit. So how do we harness the informal, taken for granted experience of the gamer into activities that encourage formal learning?

In the case of video games, the classroom becomes a place where students are also able to offer learning and experience to the teacher rather than readily accepting it from him/her. As such we need to consider approaches that take into account a more 'flipped' or 'flattened' classroom where the expert has become the inexpert and vice versa. The ability to enlighten the teacher has implications for power and ownership of education, whereby expertise flows in the opposite direction to normal activities as the gamer cultural capital of the students becomes increasingly valued. Initial classroom activities should assume that the teacher knows nothing about the game and a process of familiarisation then occurs for him or her. Existing players of the game can be invited to reflect upon their experiences of the game whilst the teacher and other students are invited to ask questions.

Activity: Oral Presentations (Beginner skill, within 15 hours of game time)

a) Ask students to do formal or informal Oral presentations about their experience of playing *Skyrim*.

Once such gamer capital is accumulated students become experts in the field, which they might find empowering when they are given the opportunity to share their gamer capital to others. Players can share information on strategy, observe and learn from the play of others, assist the main player as a 'co-pilot' and much more. Acquisition of gaming capital would normally take place outside of the classroom with home-based tasks based around independent gameplay. The shared space of the classroom is where the isolated experiences of the gameplay come together to inform the learning outcomes of the prescribed activity. It is here that the teacher keeps the students pedagogically focused to make sure that the gameplay is informing the overall educational aims rather than simply the pursuit of gaming as leisure. Differentiation between pupils of varying gaming skills, experience and know-how can be achieved with tasks of varying difficulty: those with advanced experience of *Skyrim* can work upon 'Mods' (e.g., formal software modifications to the game) whilst others can begin more simply by creating their character at the start of the game.

Activity: Race Relations (Beginner skill, within 15 hours of game time)

a) *Skyrim* is beset with racial tension, with a back-story linked to genocide and oppression and easily identifiable racial categories.

b) Ask each pupil to consider how the different races are represented. This may affect whether they join the Stormcloaks or the Empire.

c) Is there a relationship between what they have experienced so far (or expect to experience) and the character they create? (e.g., Argonians and Dark Elves can experience direct racism, and the Thalmor consider themselves a superior race whilst the Stormcloaks can be openly racist as well as being the 'underdogs'.)

d) Is there anything within the game that can be done to improve the plight of the oppressed communities? Is this a major concern of the game?

Activity: Taking Sides (Beginner Skill, within 20 hours of game time)

a) At some point, in order to progress, the player will have to take sides in the emergent Civil War.

b) Having invested time in making moral choices and creating a character journey, players arguably want to continue making good choices throughout the game.

c) Neither side of the civil war is perfect. Choosing one involves compromise and thinking of 'the bigger picture' and invites discussion around political concerns.

d) Since students will find their own *Skyrim* RPG journey they will make choices and go for directions that are their own. Joining sides in the civil war has its own implications: the stormcloaks are the underdogs but also racist, the imperials are elitist and power hungry. Avoiding joining either side is also possible. Teaches about relationships, loyalty, moral and ethical choices, consequences (i.e., some characters turn against you when you have chosen) and dealing with guilt.

As these activities suggest, *Skyrim* has the potential to teach students about politics, power, responsibility, ethics, family, morals, racism, sexism, gender, transgression, wealth, domination, domestic vs wilderness, violence, conspiracy, occult. However this is interactive and experiential research where players can *feel* and *understand* what it is like to experience simulated racism, inflict violence on others, make moral choices (as they 'write' their own story of the Dragonborn) *and* observe the consequences of their actions. It is this personal immersion and moral choice that I believe has the potential to emotively connect students to their learning in a way that library based research cannot hope to achieve. *Skyrim* also allows the player to get married and with an optional DLC expansion, *Hearthfire*, you can build your own home and even adopt children. Even the basic process of creating your own character has implications for how students might see themselves or how they might wish to be portrayed. As a '15' rated game it is ripe for A level teaching since all students would be above the recommended age to play the game.

Activity: Quest Ethics (Beginner skill, within 5 hours of game time)

a) Here is where the ethics and morals of the game get quite interesting. By this time the player should be quite familiar with the gameplay and heading towards their ideal skillset. They will still be some way off but they will be aware of what they would like (e.g., accumulate the best Daedric Armour, become an expert in Smithing to generate wealth, be the envy of sorcerers).

b) Moral choices with *Skyrim* are key. PSHE or General Studies can also be discussed here.

c) There are quests where you can deliver the artefact to the person who asks (and obtain new blessings) or you can keep the artefact for your own benefit (e.g., The Black Star soul gem) thus betraying the sometimes questionable person who set you the quest.

d) Other choices involve returning an unbreakable lockpick to its rightful place or keeping it for your own means (which can also facilitate breaking into bad people's homes to do good things).

e) Hence it is very complicated and there is no right or wrong. What is much more interesting is how students *arrive* at these decisions and how they fit in with their experience so far and their proposed trajectory.

f) There are quests where you need to progress by killing an innocent person (e.g., Grelod the kind) to show that you have a 'dark side' and are worthy of recruiting to the Dark Brotherhood. Other quests involve taking part in a morally ambiguous murder in order to prevent a wider catastrophe that the deceased might have facilitated.

g) Are there any quests that you particularly liked or disliked? Were there any that you wish you had avoided? Do you regret any actions taken during gameplay? Why?

Activity: Age Rating (Intermediate skill, within 10 hours of game time)

a) Consider how the game could be changed to bring the experience towards a '12' rating, which would open the gameplay to a wider audience but may compromise the integrity of the game. Is *Skyrim* still *Skyrim* if it is lowered to a '12' rating rather than a '15'?

EMBRACING AND ENABLING WIDER DISCOURSE

> …videogames are seen by their detractors as not merely responsible for solitary experiences but for isolating ones, too. As a result, they not only *appeal* to loners, but actually *create them*, hence giving rise to the popular conception of videogame fans as reclusive outsiders, distant and disengaged from society, both unwilling and incapable of interacting with others. (Newman, 2004: 146)

This is an idea that I would specifically like to challenge. My suggestion is that far from an isolating experience, pedagogically scaffolded learning activities can encourage a thriving community of engaged and social students that are intent upon meaningful interaction with others. The key here is to allow students the chance to reflect, both intrapersonally and interpersonally, upon their experience of gameplay. Some of this reflection will be done face-to-face and live, whilst some of it will be done asynchronously and online. For example, imagine one student is 'stuck' on a particular level or moral dilemma (i.e. should I kill the innocent Grelod the Kind just because it will give me access to more quests and weapons?). He posts the question on a specific Facebook group and notification of the message reaches his classmates whom offer advice and support. This exchange is now there for all others to see and can go on to form the basis of a WiKi or strategy guide once fully populated. Hence there is an important correlation between offline gameplay and online support, as there would be between times of gameplay and discussion in-class.

Activity: Wider Discourse (Intermediate Skill, various time frames)

[Some activities adapted from http://www.playingtolearn.org/activities.html]

a) Ask students to write a story based upon a week of playing *Skyrim* (English). This would allow students to engage with ideas around narrative and adaptation. However, it also helps them to prioritise narrative kernels so that we discover what is important to each student.

b) Ask students how their collective experience of the game could be novelised. Can we consider multiple perspectives or should we amalgamate all experiences into one? This has implications for democracy in adaptation and re-narrativisation.

c) Ask students to write a screenplay for a movie adaptation of the game. This could also become a storyboard and might be eventually filmed for the most adventurous students.

d) Consider making a trailer for a forthcoming film. *The Elder Scrolls* universe is immense and there is a plethora of material and backstory to cover. Perhaps consider splitting the films into our current crop of film trilogies or even TV serialisation. Reflect upon the reasons why serialisation might be necessary and why it might not.

e) Consider an obituary for a key character from *Skyrim*. Ask students to work on this in small groups to reflect upon what the life of this particular character means to them. Compare this to the experience of other students and how they see a pivotal character.

f) Design a poster aimed at a teacher to convince them that *Skyrim* is a worthy pedagogic tool.

FURTHER ADVICE FOR THOSE UNFAMILIAR WITH *SKYRIM*

In writing this chapter I drawn upon considerable personal gamer capital of *Skyrim*, drawing upon my two disparate worlds of personal gaming and academia. I was not confident it would be possible to weave these two worlds into a meaningful experience and those of you reading this chapter might share this opinion. But I present this chapter since I believe that other teaching staff might benefit from exploring the game as part of their teaching to encourage a more inclusive approach to engaging with popular culture in education. However, I suspect that the majority of teaching practitioners reading this would not have the same gamer capital as I do. How can we ensure that those totally new to *Skyrim* are able to engage with the ideas in this chapter too?

In order to get staff and students to interact with the video game I would suggest it should be provided on PC, preferably via a STEAM account, or installed on PCs onsite at the place of study. This has the greatest potential for permeability within all private and domestic spaces, at the lowest cost, and also allows everyone to access the STEAM fan-based community enhancements. Students and staff would need time to play the game independently to get familiar with the dynamics, mechanics and control system. The potential activities covered in this chapter have been presented, wherever possible, in the order they would be encountered as the game progresses. It is fine for students who are existing players of *Skyrim* to move to later activities as long as they don't volunteer plot spoilers or pre-empt what the other students will experience.

In-keeping with the theme of other chapters in this volume, the 'written' discourse around *Skyrim* permeates all the various text types mentioned by others. The unstructured gaming that students engage with informally is an 'aspect of everyday life'. The DIY and home creativity comes from the application and eventually the creation of one's own DLC, which can be produced outside of study time or within. The literary text would be the potential stories, novelisation and adaption of *Skyrim* from one text to another. The art work might be the poster that students design. Finally the online media exchange would be all forms of media and social media (Twitch TV, Facebook, Wiki, Twitter) where the majority of the 'writing' about *Skyrim* takes place. My suggestion for those teachers entirely new to *Skyrim* is to bring the 'aspect of everyday life' into the classroom in the first instance by asking students what their direct or indirect experience of *Skyrim* might be and discuss this. Then ask the other students to research online (e.g., Wikis and Strategy Guides) and social media to find out more about the game. This would be a quick way to acquire some gamer capital and background information before launching into the gameplay itself: which both teacher and students must partake in for these activities herein to be successful.

WORKS CITED

Apperley, T. and Walsh, C. (2008) 'Researching digital game players: Gameplay and gaming capital' in *IADIS International Conference Gaming 2008: Design for engaging experience and social interaction*, 25–27 July, Amsterdam, The Netherlands.

Bennett, P., Kendall, A. and McDougall, J. (2011) *After The Media*. Abingdon: Routledge.

Crawford, C. (2003) 'Interactive Storytelling' in Wolf, M.J.P. and Perron, B., *The Video Game Theory Reader*. London: Routledge, pp 259–274.

Hutchison, D. (2007) 'Video Games and the Pedagogy of Place'. *The Social Studies*, 98(1), pp35–40.

Hutchison, D. (2009) *Playing to Learn: Videogames in the Classroom* (online): http://www.playingtolearn.org/activities.html (Accessed 14 May 2015).

King, G. and Krzyinska, T. (eds) (2002) *ScreenPlay: cinema/videogames/interfaces*. London: Wallflower Press.

Newman, J. (2004) *Videogames*. London: Routledge.

Wolf, M.J.P. & Perron, B. (2003) *The Video Game Theory Reader*. London: Routledge.

5: PLAYING TEXT

Barney Oram

PLAY?

What is play? How is it relevant to education? How can it fit into the classroom? How can it be used to study text? Play raises a wealth of issues: is it something that as adults you are meant to grow out of? Are we guilty of telling our students and children to stop playing around and by doing so do we relegate play to something that is not serious or worthy?

The erosion of the value of play in society and education has been gradual. In educational terms it made the headlines in 2007 with the building of the Thomas Deacon Academy in Peterborough, a school built without a playground in order to 'maximise learning' as if the process of learning is something that can only take place in the confines of a classroom (Beckford 2007). Play and its role in education is something that is continually in flux. It appears in the Early Years curriculum (Department for Education 2014) and a recommendation was made in the Cambridge report that play based learning be extended to age six (Hofkins & Northen 2009). However, this recommendation has not been implemented.

It would, presently, appear that explicit opportunities for play within the majority of subjects are limited, that the confines of a course specification and the demands of assessment remove the potential for learners to explore and develop ideas through play. This does not need to be the case, indeed it is not something I recognise from the practice of my colleagues and myself, where opportunities to explore ideas and concepts through play are actively encouraged. Arguably with the shifting focus of education toward ever more quantifiable outcomes there is a greater need for learners to have the opportunity to play and to become engaged and curious about the subjects they study and the wider world.

At this point it would be useful to consider what play is and move on to how it can be used in an educational and textual context. Sicart, in his book *Play Matters*, proposes a different way of thinking about play.

> Instead of deriving an understanding of play from a particular object or activity, like war, ritual or games I see play as a portable tool for being. It is not tied to objects but bought by people to the complex interrelations with and between things that form daily life. (Sicart, 2014: 2)

This develops the idea of what constitutes play and sets it within a more varied ecology than most definitions allow. In fact, play is highly resistant to a neat definition, one that does not solely focus on games and one that encompasses the broader edges of what it actually is. Play is a way in which we, as individuals and collectively, engage with the world, something that we have done since we were little children when we did not restrict our capacity to play, to create and explore worlds and ideas. Play can help us express who we are in the world in the same way that film, painting and writing can. In order to help us understand what play is, Sicart (2014: 16) identifies a number of things that he considers play to be:

- Play is contextual. This encompasses the environment in which we play, the technologies with which we play and whosoever the potential companions of play may be. This and the idea of play space will be discussed in more detail when we consider play as an everyday aspect of life.
- Play is appropriative. This refers to play's ability to take over the context in which it exists and the fact that it cannot totally be predetermined by such a context. Skateboarding can be considered an example of play that appropriates space.
- Play is disruptive. Not all play is constructive and indeed pleasure can be gained from disruptive play.
- Play is autotelic. It is an activity that has its own goals and purposes and for its own ends.
- Play is creative. It forces players to think on the fly, to form and reform ideas throughout its duration.
- Play is personal. Though play is often a shared experience the impact and expression of play is primarily individual, it helps one to understand and explore our individual understanding of the world.

Using this framework we will start to examine and discuss how it can be possible to 'play' text, that the concept and experience of playing text should be as valid an approach as reading, writing or performing text.

PLAY AND GAMES

It is hard to write anything about play which does not refer to games. The two things are so closely intertwined that they are often taken as being one and the same thing. This can be illustrated in this definition taken from the Oxford English Dictionary which defines 'Play' as follows:

Play v. I take part in games for enjoyment.

This definition is not alone in considering play and games as being heavily intertwined. Bernard Suits offers the following definition:

Playing a game is the voluntary effort to overcome unnecessary obstacles. (Suits, cited in Kirkpatrick, 2013: 41)

This definition links games and play and the focus is still on the *playing* of a game. It accepts that players willingly accept the unnecessary obstacles (rules) of a game because this helps to make play possible. It is not a definition of a game but rather illustrates the way play and game often interlink. For a more focused definition on what constitutes a game Salen and Zimmermann in the *Rules of Play* (2004) define a game as 'a system in which players engage in an artificial conflict, defined by rules, that results in a quantifiable outcome' (Salen & Zimmermann 2004: 80).

This definition of a game links it with play but also includes the need for a quantifiable outcome, the need for a player or players at the conclusion of a game to have won or lost or to have received some numerical score. This need for a quantifiable outcome is what distinguishes games from other types of play. So is all play a game? Not really; what is evident is that play is a key aspect of games and that the relationship between the two terms is heavily interlinked. Adams neatly summarises the essential elements of a game as play: pretending, a goal and rules (Adams, 2014: 3). All of these elements need to be present to make a game but can also be considered independently of one another. Salen and Zimmermann discuss the relationships that exist between play and games and it would be useful to consider these. The first is that games are a subset of play and the second is that play is an element of games. The first of these takes into account that games fit into a larger ecology of what is considered play whilst the second acknowledges that alongside rules and culture play is an essential part of games. This aligns with Adams who acknowledges the interconnectivity of rules and play within a game. The definition of play that Salen and Zimmermann provide is 'free movement within a more rigid structure' (Salen & Zimmermann, 2004: 304).

This definition is more abstract than the approach suggested by Sicart and covers the three categories of play identified in their book. These are 'Game Play', playing a game with defined rules; 'Ludic Activity', play activity in a less defined structure for example playing catch; and finally, 'Being Playful', where an individual plays with the more rigid structures that often determine behaviour. Sicart discusses playfulness as an attitude as opposed to play, which is an activity (Sickert, 2014). This is an area along with 'play space' that will be considered in a broader educational context.

PLAY IN EDUCATION

As mentioned earlier the idea of play within education is often opaque and rarely foregrounded as a desirable skill. This reluctance to fully embrace the idea of play is not unique to any set of curriculum or subject criteria. Currently the only play-based experiences within formal education in the UK are in the Early Years curriculum and this approach is potentially under threat through the introduction of baseline testing which is likely to lead to the erosion of this progressive approach (BAECE 2015).

There are examples of progressive change toward the idea of play in education. Perhaps the most radical approach is that of The Institute of Play (http://www.instituteofplay.org/), a not-for-profit design studio, which was founded by games designers in 2007 in New York City. The first project was the design of Quest to Learn, a New York City public school. The school covers the 6th to 12th grades and play and games are the key element of lesson delivery.

> Mission critical at Quest is a translation of the underlying form of games into a powerful pedagogical model for its 6–12th graders. Games work as rule-based learning systems, creating worlds in which players actively participate, use strategic thinking to make choices, solve complex problems, seek content knowledge, receive constant feedback, and consider the point of view of others. (http://upperschool.q2l.org/curriculum/overview/)

This school and approach to its curriculum is supported by the Institute of Play and they have actively sought to embed games across all subject areas as the statement above illustrates. They consider games and play to be powerful ways for students to learn a wide range of skills which will assist them in the future. It is a more considered and reflective approach to the power of games than is often found within a more traditional classroom. Rather than viewing this approach as unusual it would be beneficial if game-like elements found their way more readily into broader range of classrooms. As with any new aspect of teaching, the sceptics amongst us will happily say that it all sounds rather progressive but what impact does it have? To this end the Institute of Play and Quest to Learn are open about their practice and there is a wealth of materials available online (Institute of Play 2016).

In contrast to the fully immersive approach taken by Quest to Learn it is likely that learners experience a reduction in the foregrounding of play in education as they progress. This is not to imply that play will completely disappear, it just becomes much harder to explicitly find it within subject areas. However using the framework provided by Sicart, play and the playing of games, can be a powerful learning tool. From my own education I can remember playing a game in a Year 9 Geography class where teams were allocated continents and resources and then had to complete set tasks. The game was a very immersive experience that required a wide range of skills and had a clear rule structure but would generate different outcomes each time it was played based upon the nature of the individuals who were playing it. It was appropriative (the classroom became the play space), it was disruptive (you tried to prevent others from winning through withholding resources), it was creative (as you had to quickly form alliances based on resources that you required) and it was personal. At the conclusion of the game we reflected on what had happened and related this to resource allocation and global trading. It was a much more political exercise than I had realised but it still had an impact upon me as an individual. The impact this game had was not just felt by me but also by other students who still look back in disbelief that one individual, David Tan, was allocated the least resources yet still managed to win the game. This is an event that took place twenty five years ago and was a key element in me taking GCSE Geography.

If you consider a curriculum or subject as a system, it can be viewed as a rigid structure where free movement is challenging and that players, both staff and students must overcome these voluntary, or not so voluntary obstacles to succeed. As with any structure the opportunity exists for play to be incorporated into a variety of subjects and used as a powerful learning tool. As with many games players must follow a set of rules in order to gain quantifiable outcomes in the form of grades and other outcomes. In most cases this idea of education and assessment as play is unlikely to be as pleasurable an experience as a game of basketball, skateboarding at a local spot or building a Lego space station. However, play and play-based activities can provide an alternative way of accessing, engaging with and thinking about material that a more traditional reading would not.

REFLEXIVE EDUCATIONAL OUTCOMES

As previously discussed, play is a participatory form, one in which an individual is active and has the ability to make decisions which can alter events and change outcomes. Individuals engaged with playing (text) have the ability to continually modify it and will often have different experiences each time they participate. This contrasts with the engagement one may have with presentational forms such as a film, TV drama, novel or play where one may be seen as an 'active' participant through the reading of the text but the experiences are not fully interactive as the individual will not be able to modify the text. There will be exceptions to this where experimental works using presentational forms actively encourage participation from the audience where they can create and change the content during the production. Equally, an individual's response to a presentational form will arguably alter and shift over a period of time as their own life experiences allow them to read a familiar text in new ways. Watching *Toy Story 3* (2010) as a father was a very different experience to watching it when I was not. In this instance though my own experience and reading of the text was altered, the set narrative structure and story could not be modified during my viewing. I had no agency over the text in the way I would have had were I playing with a text.

This experience will be one that the majority of learners are familiar with. When presented with a text in a class most learners are guided through it and then asked to express a view on it; this is common when analysing a film or other narrative based text, and may even be the case with a videogame. Often this will move on to a textual analysis where smaller segments are deconstructed, either as a whole class or maybe in small groups. In these instances it is very easy for the teacher to assume the position of expert and deliver the information that is needed before becoming frustrated that this information is not then delivered back to them in the practice essay that follows. At no point does the learner develop agency or have the opportunity to explore a wider context around the text, to play with the text, to alter it, to cut it up and put it back together in a way that means something to them.

There are a number of palpable pressures (masquerading as 'very valid reasons') explaining why this might not be the case: time, access to equipment, need to practise exams, and so on. It is a safe teaching space and a quick and easy way to feel that you are in control. It provides a sense of progression, a linear journey that will end in an exam. While this approach may be beneficial for me as a teacher and provide a sense of 'normal' practice for a student it is not always the best approach for 'learners' and it's interesting to use this ubiquitous tag productively for once to distinguish their 'custom' (as consumers of education) from their 'practice' (even their needs). It is likely that 'learners', living up to their billing, would benefit from 'emergence', a more non-linear approach, one where development can be different and where knowledge and understanding is acquired as opposed to delivered. This mode of 'operation' can be more play based and exploratory, it can allow you to position yourself as 'inexpert' (Bennett, Kendall, McDougall 2011) and encourage learners to make steps on their own. It will not always meet with success and learner resistance at the start is very likely as playing a game is often harder than having a story read to you, reminding us that 'rigour' comes in very different forms.

STARTING POINT IN CURRENT TEACHING

As a teacher I have been very fortunate to work with a range of progressive individuals who have always been willing to develop and reflect upon their own practice as well as create innovative and interesting sessions for learners. Amazingly, this has all been possible in a single institution where the positive outcomes of this approach to teaching has meant that the methods used are not stigmatised, even if they are not whole heartedly adopted by other subjects. In the 14 years I have been teaching I have taught both applied and academic courses and at level 2 and level 3; and though the differing courses and levels have required subtly different approaches, I have not altered my belief that the vast majority of learners are more successful when they are active, be this through making text or playing text.

An example of this is would be the brief series of induction sessions that is used for new AS Film Studies students. The sessions are intended to introduce the following micro elements to the students: cinematography, sound, editing and *mise-en-scène* and run for a period of four weeks. A week involves three sessions of 90 minutes, each week focusing on a single micro element. The aim of the induction period is:

- For students to have an understanding of the four micro elements.
- To learn how to use software and hardware.
- To start to talk about film in a way that moves beyond just liking something or it being 'good' or 'bad'.
- To get to know each other and speak to different people as they are likely to have come from different secondary schools.

Our previous approach to this was for the students to watch a range of selected clips and then have a teacher-led discussion about the finer points of what they have just watched or minor alternatives to this, ultimately the teacher as the 'subject expert'. In contrast, the alternative approach has been to make the sessions active, to establish a range of play-based tasks which students complete. By the end of the first week they have analysed, storyboarded, shot and edited a short Western shootout. A significant number of these are uploaded to social media and shared amongst friends and family. We uploaded the work so that the student has a tangible product at the end of the first week (see https://www.youtube.com/user/longroadfilm and www.vimeo.com/longroadfilm/).

Throughout this teaching staff only demonstrate the basics: how to put up a tripod, how to turn the camera on, how to connect it to the computer and put the files in Premiere Pro. Once this is done we step back and let the students play around with the equipment and task: they can, for example, add effects, turn it sepia and add in music and sound effects. When needed we answer questions about how to do things but otherwise leave them to play with the equipment and create 'footage'. The teacher is deliberately positioned not to appear as the *subject expert* telling them what type of shot to use and why. The emphasis is on the learner to tell the teacher what type of shot it is and why they have used it. The outcome is that a learner will have a greater understanding of what a specific shot type means if they have had to use it.

This approach is also used for the other micro elements, from having students add in all the sound, both diegetic and non-diegetic, to the pool hall sequence in *Mean Streets* (1973) to constructing an edit of the car/train chase sequence from *The French Connection* (1971) having never watched the whole film. They are also set the task of taking stills from an imaginary film dressed as a character that they have invented, in the style of *Untitled Film Stills* (Sherman 2003). This challenges them to participate in the construction of a series of stills, it requires them to appropriate space, to transform a school space into an 'other' space. They dress up and take part in roleplay as they have to become or create a character. On the surface this may seem the most straightforward of all the activities as it requires the least amount of technical expertise, but it is perhaps the one that learners find most challenging as it requires them to play a part, to expose themselves to the scrutiny of their peers and to participate fully in the construction of a text. The previous tasks have been play-based but all used existing texts and have allowed the individual learner to remain hidden behind the work as opposed to taking a starring role.

Overall this set of tasks allow learners to participate in practice based on experiences and activity as opposed to just theory and teacher led sessions. It is an approach that has been built in wherever possible and has had positive impacts both in terms of results and in a sustained growth in student numbers. There has been a commitment for a while now to 'widening participation' in education but a real function of this work, or at least an implication, has been firstly 'realising' this participation and then developing and deepening it. And the 'playing' here is both personal (since we are all, Shakespeare famously claimed, 'players') and professional (since the student 'role' is one aspect of the self-presentation Goffman dubs 'dramaturgical' (Goffman, 1959: xi)). Thus the 'playing' is both playful and dramatic, creative and transactional: the act of being a student is realised by nothing more or less than an 'act'. This is in a subject in which there are more marks for exam-based work than practical coursework yet the benefits of a play-based approach to breaking down and exploring texts has benefits in a learners understanding of how a text works and what it means.

FLATTENED TEXTUALITY

Aspect of everyday life

As individuals it is highly likely that we participate in play of some form or other everyday, transcending race, gender, sexuality or other classification. As we age the actual form and character of how and what we play will alter from a toddler playing with a dump truck and stones to playing *FIFA 16* on a console to a smartphone-based game such as *Threes* on the commute to work or a more traditional crossword with a morning coffee.

> Play is appropriative and play takes place in the context of things, cultures and people, in time and in space. (Sicart, 2014: 50)

My own experiences of play have been altered since becoming a father; my mornings are now filled with two small children being Octonauts, sitting in cardboard boxes as they explore the seabed (the living room) for new adventures. Through doing this they are appropriating existing characters from a popular CBeebies TV programme and using this set of fictional characters to act as a springboard to their own imaginations and adventures. Alongside this they have appropriated the living room from traditionally being a more adult space into their play space. They are appropriating objects, in this case cardboard boxes, that were originally designed for alternative purposes to be used as 'Gups' to explore their imaginary world.

Play modifies and is modified in and by physical and virtual environments. (ibid.)

They are not unique in doing any of this; children everywhere do the same, as adults we become more reluctant to challenge how a space is used. Appropriating the top deck of the number 44 bus as a fashion runway on the commute to work is unlikely to sit well with other commuters but it is likely that a significant number of them will be engaged in their own choice of play, even if this is now using virtual environments as opposed to physical ones. A significant number of games have a sandbox mode which will allow a player to explore the virtual environment. This mode will often allow a player to make a conscious decision as to whether they will interact with the game environment. Will they choose progression over emergence? That is to say, will they try to navigate the environment in an orderly and linear fashion or explore the environment in a more random manner? An example of this would be the approach a player may take with a game such as GTA – do they chose to engage with the linear approach to game play or take an alternative approach and explore the game world as they choose? They may set themselves Meta challenges where they impose their own rule and set their own level of challenge.

What is interesting about the idea of individuals or groups of individuals using Meta challenges is that they can appropriate virtual spaces without other users being aware that a 'game' is being played. An example of this is the use of Instagram, a social media app that is on the surface about sharing a moment with 'friends' but as any regular user of it will know this is not how the majority of users interact with the application. It has become a lifestyle tool, an opportunity for an individual to create and curate a lifestyle that will attract 'likes' and followers. It offers a highly edited and mediated view into an individuals life, one where people are creating a character that is a reflection of themselves, one where the highlights are shared and carefully filtered. It is a similar to the task learners participate in during the Film Studies induction where they create a character and the world in which they live. However, rather than it being an educational game, with all that implies, Instagram is a virtual space waiting to be appropriated. It would be interesting, on reflection, to consider which might best deserve the tag 'learning environment'. One measure is the degree to which each constitute 'experiences' since, as Marshall McLuhan pointed out: 'Everybody experiences far more than he understands. Yet it is experience, rather than understanding, that influences behavior' (McLuhan, 1964: 277). One function of formal education has been to regulate experiences, including grading their value *and* to 'check' learning (critics would say in both senses).

It is all too easy to fall into the false dichotomies of conventional wisdom, which require 'learning' to be 'pre-arranged', bound by intention (trainee teachers are warned that 'failing to prepare is preparing to fail'), asking us to confess when our students were 'off task' as if such a place existed. On a college trip to New York with Media students, a colleague and I, both Instagram users, set ourselves the Meta challenge of getting the most 'likes' for images we posted. We set ourselves rules which we had to follow and then proceeded to post images with alarming regularity adding various filters and hashtags in order to improve the number of 'likes' we could achieve. I would like to say that we managed to rack up a substantial number of 'likes' but the most successful image managed a grand total of 18. Our game was between us, it served no other explicit purpose than to amuse ourselves and pass the time whilst hustling students around the city. No other user of Instagram would have been aware of the battle that my colleague and I were having whilst they were using it, only an unlucky few who have the misfortune to follow us both as they will have had their feeds spammed with heavily filtered images of New York for four days. I had not thought of it as part of my 'work' on this trip as teacher-supervisor, though I clearly had remembered it.

Neither was it a behavior to which our students were oblivious. As we were reminded daily by the students on the trip they managed to rack up well over 20 likes in a matter of minutes without needing to resort to increasingly outlandish hashtagging. Instagram was never designed with this type of activity in mind; it is not a 'game' in any sense, however its users can choose to modify the purpose it serves and play with it in a manner of their choosing. As a learning environment it had been 'produced' and temporarily colonised and we had been hosted. Even if only as an exhibition of our online ineptitude, it had impact, embodying something at least of the discourse of the 'inexpert'. This may be in a similar way to the one described above or it may be through the construction of an 'online self', a character that reflects the best parts of the individual. Other social media applications are also used as a space for play; both Twitter and Facebook allow the users to participate in a range of 'game' like activities. There are a number of example where the appropriation of Twitter invoke what Sicart would describe as playfulness – he cites *horse_ebooks* and 'My Best Day Ever' by the artist Zack Gage as examples of where play and playfulness can be found in an aspect of everyday life (Sicart, 2014: 26). Our learnt suspicion of the playful, of teachers 'entertaining' and others being entertained, is given its most decisive riposte also by McLuhan who wrote tartly: 'Anyone who tries to make a distinction between education and entertainment doesn't know the first thing about either' (McLuhan, 1967: 68).

However it is not only in virtual spaces that notion of Meta challenges can exist; it easily transfers into physical environments. A more conventional physical environment for play in everyday life is the playground. Playgrounds can take many different forms; some are simple and have basic equipment whilst others are all singing and dancing affairs with

5: PLAYING TEXT

rockets, pirate ships and giant towers. If well designed these spaces open themselves up to a variety of play experiences; often the climbing equipment will have a linear route through it from a ladder as a start point through to a slide as an end point but often children will ignore this pathway and seek alternative routes through the equipment, even if this is as straightforward as climbing the slide and jumping off at the ladder. Equally they will also set themselves Meta challenges whilst playing, ranging from not using certain equipment to get from A-B or only using one hand. Children are actively involved in setting themselves their own challenges and whilst young testing out what they can do both physically and cognitively.

What is interesting about play parks is the way in which the space is used. Young children appropriate these spaces during the day, their parents often watching to make sure that they are safe. As darkness descends they become spaces filled with older children, teenagers looking for some reassurance, caught in a difficult phase where they are too young for adult spaces but too big to still be seen to play and enjoy a playground. The equipment will be used but probably not in the manner that the designer imagined. The nature of play may alter; the space will no longer appear as inviting as it did a few hours earlier. A different set of rules will be operating one that has been set by the group. The transitional nature of children can also be seen in the school playground, younger children tearing around chasing one another whilst the older children gather in groups reluctant to play as the younger ones do. The school playground, particularly the primary school one is often dominated by rules. These are their to keep the children safe but a school in New Zealand as part of research removed playground rules and left it to the children to set their own rules and boundaries (http://www.independent.co.uk/news/world/australasia/new-zealand-school-bans-playground-rules-and-sees-less-bullying-and-vandalism-9091186.html). They gained agency over how they negotiated and used the space. This links back to the Sicart quote about how play can modify a space and also how individuals or groups choose to appropriate a space.

The appropriation of space is often how play manifests itself in every day life; urban spaces are now full of disruptive architecture used to prevent skateboarders and traceurs from using the space for play. Skateboarding has a long history of appropriating pubic and private space to use as a key element of play, from draining swimming pools in Southern California to using the Southbank undercroft or Bistro Square as key street skating spots. As skateboarding's popularity, or, more accurately, visibility within the mainstream media has waxed and waned other individuals have begun to use the urban environment in a different way: if skateboarders had the streets then traceurs have taken the roofs. Parkour is now a hugely popular urban sport that has begun to redefine spaces meant for commerce or business as a play space; a city seen through the eyes of a traceur is the equivalent of a play park seen through the eyes of a four year old. It is a space filled with possibility one where objects have multiple possibilities, where routes can be seen and conquered through running, climbing, swinging, vaulting and rolling. As Sicart says play is 'bought by people to the complex interrelations with and between things that form daily life' (Sicart, 2014: 2) So as the tools we use for everyday life morph and change then it is also true that the modes of play that we engage in will alter and shift. In this respect then the majority of people will engage with play in one way or another throughout the course of the day regardless of whether they are fully conscious of doing so. As we come to realise that play is no longer the sole preserve of children and that it is an essential part of daily life then perhaps we will engage with it more fully.

'Mass Media'

A key element of media education has for a long time been the need to decode the messages that are present in 'mass media', to get learners to 'read' texts and then articulate what they may mean. However this approach is becoming problematic in the face of a rapidly changing media ecosystem; as videogames, blogs, apps and other areas become the focus of study it becomes incredibly hard to apply the more traditional methods of analysis to them. It is also failing to fully embrace other ways of looking at text and getting learners to 'play' with a text as opposed to just 'reading' it. There are a number of different ways in which learners can 'play' with text; making short videos can demonstrate conventions of a particular genre or film movement, which can be an opportunity for learners to demonstrate a more sophisticated understanding than may be obvious in an essay. This has worked well for me in the past particularly when studying a film movement with easily identifiable tropes such as the French New Wave.

The example posted at https://www.youtube.com/watch?v=NE_TOYrymuM is a good example of the type of work that can be produced. The task was to produce a short sequence in the style of the French New Wave and was set after the unit had been completed and the learners had watched a variety of New Wave films. To make the task more straightforward they picked a set idea out of a hat, in this case to send a postcard. The task served to reinforce the learners understanding of what they had watched and translate it into something that they understood. It is this process of translating their understanding that is the most important element of the work. If they have failed to understand what it is that they have been studying it will be clearly evident in the finished piece of work. There is no opportunity to hide behind information provided by the teacher as there would be in writing an essay.

This is not an isolated attempt to make the understanding of text more playful. I have also had learners make 'swedes', versions of feature length films inspired by *Be Kind Rewind* (2008) as well as shot-for-shot remakes of opening sequences from films. All of these tasks have elements in them that make play so engaging. They are appropriative, as the learner takes control of the text and can begin to use it as they choose; they are disruptive, as the text that is being played with will no longer be in its original form and the learners have disrupted its original meaning; they are creative, as learners have to think about how to solve problems that they may face, how to adapt to their surroundings and make best use of their resources; and they are also personal, as the individuals participating will each bring their own understanding to the task and then be able to take away an enhanced understanding of the text that they have been playing with.

These activities have been enabled through the use of technology and a willingness to experiment with what can be considered as learning. Recently this has evolved into learners constructing video essays to replace timed essays as a classroom activity. This has been used at both AS and A2 levels sometimes to enable a direct comparison of two linked films or alternatively to explore a focus film or film form in more detail. Throughout this activity learners are fully engaged with the 'texts' that they are analysing and they are able to make direct visual comparisons between films and other forms such as paintings and photographs that they feel have influenced the 'text' they are studying. Video essays are a valid academic approach to the analysis of film and a wide range of examples can be found online: *[in]Transition* is an online academic journal that is focused on video essays as a way of studying film. This approach to playing with film texts is not just for academics; the *Rear Window* timelapse allows us to see the film in a way that Hitchcock never intended us to but to someone who has seen the film it presents a new way of looking at it. That is perhaps what is the most powerful aspect of playing with a text in this way – it forces us, either as the creator or the viewer, to look at something in a different way than we did before. This approach to playing with and altering film texts is also used by current film directors. On his blog Steven Soderbergh wrote about 'staging' in film and to illustrate his point used a manipulated version of *Raiders of the Lost Ark* [http://extension765.com/sdr/18-raiders]. He had removed all colour and sound so it was now in black and white and accompanied by a score he added himself. Soderbergh is arguably playing with a text to enhance and develop his own understanding about an aspect of film, in this case 'staging'. There is a range of other sources for video essays online including Press Play (http://blogs.indiewire.com/pressplay/) and Audiovisualcy (https://vimeo.com/groups/audiovisualcy) , both of which can provide inspiration for a teacher wishing to get learners to create their own.

There are of course other examples of 'mass media' texts being played with. This may take the form of remixing existing texts, disrupting their original meaning and creating something new or allowing an alternative way of thinking about the original text. This type of cut-and-paste approach has existed in music for longer than it has on screen, having roots going back to early hip-hop and beyond, where different elements from records were sampled to create something new. What started out as individuals playing about with records and tapes in bedrooms went on to become a huge social, political and musical movement. What has now occurred is that as digital editing has become more common place and affordable the cut-and-paste artist can now work with images as well as sound. The result of this is work similar to that produced by Cassetteboy who has remixed clips from existing shows to generate new meanings, perhaps the most being *Cassetteboy vs The Bloody Apprentice* (https://www.youtube.com/watch?v=Yxi6QDwQyLU), where the popular BBC show is cut up and remixed. It could be argued that through disruptive playing with this text that Cassetteboy has produced an alternative reading of what the text is actually about, a reading that a significant number of other viewers may agree with. It is due to digital technology being readily accessible by a significant number of people that this type of play is now possible. Yet as with the best hip-hop records the art of playing with text in this way requires both practice and a wider understanding of context.

DIY home creativity

The work of Cassetteboy provides a good stepping off point into learners producing and viewing texts outside of a formal educational setting. It is unlikely that there would be the time or the will to produce something as time consuming as a Cassettboy-style cut-and-paste video within the classroom but that would not prevent a learner from attempting something similar at home. Learners who have acquired new skills within the classroom both technical and theoretical will be able to play with text. This may take a range of different forms from the appropriation of existing characters and TV shows to create their own episodes. This is the case at https://www.youtube.com/watch?v=ZxelW-_QIKk where a pair of students have produced a short *Dr Who* sequence taking on the roles of the Doctor and his assistant while using existing enemies, in this case the Daleks from the original series. The sequence borrows from the original in both style and content and even uses an old BBC ident at the start. It is playful in its approach and the two students who made the video are fans of the TV show who are playing with the text in a creative and personal way.

This is a product that has been created externally from the classroom using equipment that the two learners had access to but it is reliant on the skills that they had developed *in* the classroom. In this respect they had been taught how to use the tools but had also been encouraged to play with them and explore the possibilities. In the piece they demonstrate a sophisticated and nuanced understanding of how *Dr Who* functions yet have made it for their own pleasure as opposed to trying to target a wider audience. The video had received 893 views by 20 July 2015 and the production was primarily motivated for their own satisfaction. It was in many ways another example of a Meta challenge, one based on emergence as opposed to progression. There was no requirement to produce this piece of video, they did so because they wanted to and wished to continue exploring and playing with text outside of the classroom. This has continued even though the students have left college having successfully completed their courses; videos that play with text continue to appear on their YouTube channel.

Dr Who has been joined by *Sherlock* as another text to be played with, again made from the perspective of a fan as opposed to a critic. This type of DIY home creativity is not unusual and is rapidly increasing as the tools for creation and distribution become more accessible. An ex-student of mine now has one of the most popular YouTube accounts in the UK (Tom Ska) and has successfully built up a large following through playing with text outside of the classroom. Though the content of his videos may not appeal to a mainstream audience or have previously been able to find a distribution channel they have found a substantial and global following, something that YouTube has enabled. The same is true of Zoella, whose videos appeal to another niche audience that was not being served by the mainstream media. Both TomSka and Zoella can be thought of as an updated version of a fanzine for the digital age; they are generating content that was overlooked by mainstream media and filling a gap in the market that was not seen by larger outlets. The reach is now far larger than a printed fanzine but the sense of DIY creativity remains the same and obviously is part of the audience appeal. It is unlikely that TomSka or Zoella would find that their YouTube format would translate successfully to the more traditional medium of television, with its need to appeal to as wide an audience as possible because of the costs involved.

Art work

Unlike other forms, Art in the curriculum has a longer tradition of play and playfulness, so rather than try to summarise this when other writers have done so in a much more erudite manner than I could ever manage it would useful to consider it from a different angle. As with the video essay Art can be used to help learners begin to look and think about texts in very different ways. Cindy Sherman's *Untitled Film Stills* have been a useful staring point within my own practice; using a number of images selected at random from the book, learners are required to create the story around the picture.

The activity begins with them in pairs. Students are told that the image is from a film and that they must look at it and decide what is happening and why, who is the person that we see in the image and what is it that are they doing. They can then work in pairs to decide the story and explain what the film is about. They are unaware that they are beginning to construct the background information to a role-play scenario. They will not be asked to act anything out but they are working through a process as this task leads onto them having to create a still for a film of their own creation and having to consider the *mise-en-scène*, framing, and sense of performance. A number of learners will be fairly confident that they know which film the still is from and try to map that film onto it whilst others acknowledge that they have no idea of what the film is but try to establish what type of film it might be from the visual clues found in the image. In some ways the task replicates a guessing game, as learners have to rely on their previous viewing experiences to piece together a credible and realistic scenario for the image. The outcomes are always interesting as learners quickly and accurately produce readings of the images based upon their extensive film viewing experiences. The majority of learners are surprised when they discover that the images are not from any particular film but posed art works and they are often more surprised that the single female in each image is the same person. They find the transformational element to be the most difficult to grasp but it serves to highlight how superficially they may initially look at an image and the need to look harder and be more reflective about what they have seen.

Another approach that is used by the National Film and Television School (NFTS) is the task given to first year students where they have to recreate a 3-D version of a painting; this requires set construction and design, lighting, direction as well as teamwork and communication skills. It also forces the students to study an image for a substantial amount of time and to consider how it has been composed. Having seen a finished example in the NFTS studio it is incredibly impressive and an extremely challenging task for students to complete. It is an advanced version of using the *Untitled Film Stills* but still has an element of learners playing with a text and appropriating it for their own needs.

Videogame

Of all the text types discussed the relationship between play and videogames is, on the surface, the neatest match. You play a videogame; it is what is meant to happen. You do not 'read' a videogame, you play it. In fact, to try and apply the more traditional methods of textual analysis to a videogame is incredibly challenging; they are often multi-faceted texts drawing upon a huge range of references from a variety of media forms; or they are *Tetris* or *Threes*, games that do not lend themselves to textual analysis but to complete player engagement and immersion. Though an increasing number of console-based games now feature detailed and cinematically edited scenes, some of the most immersive games are graphically simple engaging the player with a challenge that gradually increases. Alongside this, as smartphones have become increasingly common more people are playing videogames, even if they would not normally consider themselves to be game players. Companies like Toca Boca who produce games aimed at a young audience that will appeal to both parents and children alike. Apps such as *Toca Nature* are being used as inspiration for music videos and also provide children with a stimulating emergent experience as well. This intertextuality and relationship between texts is an interesting area to explore with learners but it is similar to a more traditional mode of delivering media and film texts.

Perhaps a more adventurous approach to videogames is to get learners to create and attempt to construct one. This requires a more in-depth approach than a traditional A Level allows but it is possible through an applied course. Over the course of an academic year learners have planned, created and produced a playable videogame, *Squidverse*. This is a game developed by two students with no prior programming knowledge but who were willing to embrace the challenge of creating a playable game. It is not perfect but it does illustrate how play can be appropriative. They borrowed the Squid character from the *Dr Who* sequence they had made for fun, and the idea of a platform game is borrowed from *Donkey Kong* and later *Mario*. It is creative in the sense that this character and world had to be formed; there was a huge amount of problem solving in the process of programming the game, they failed and failed again but learned from their mistakes. This reflects a key part of playing videogames, the need to learn from mistakes in order to progress. It was also personal, as it forced them to consider other players experiences, to broaden their idea of what others would gain from playing the game. It also required them to judge the level of challenge needed in order to make players want to try to complete it; make a game too hard and people will not return to play it, make it too easy and it will be played once, so the level of challenge needed is critical in a games success.

THE NEW PEDAGOGY

Having briefly touched upon differing text types and how play can be found in all of them, it is worth highlighting some ways forward with the idea of playing text. It is worth returning to Sicart's points about what play is and altering parts to make them relevant to classroom practice and the type of activities that have been touched upon.

- Play is contextual – this encompasses the environment in which we play, the technologies with which we play and whosoever the potential companions of play may be. Not every task requires technology, lots can be achieved without it, it should not be a crutch that prevents other forms of play taking place.
- Play is appropriative – this refers to play's ability to take over the context in which it exists and the fact that it cannot totally be predetermined by such a context. In some sessions and tasks allowing learners to be the 'expert' or a willingness to take the role of the 'inexpert'.
- Play is disruptive – not all play is constructive and indeed pleasure can be gained from disruptive play. Tasks that allow learners to break down and reconstruct texts can be incredibly powerful in understanding the original context of the text.
- Play is autotelic – it is an activity that has its own goals and purposes and for its own ends. Some tasks do not need to be directly related to assessment

objectives or outcomes, sometimes more powerful learning takes place through emergence.

- Play is creative – it forces players (learners) to think on the fly, to form and reform ideas throughout its duration. Tasks should push learners to make choices, learn from failure and alter original plans.

- Play is personal – though play is often a shared experience the impact and expression of play is primarily individual, it helps one to understand and explore our individual understanding of the world. Not every learner will get the same outcome each time; it may take an alternative task for something to click.

In all of this there should be a sense that playing text can help develop all learners' understanding and that it is a useful way of rethinking how to deliver material that would have otherwise reinforced an expert/inexpert position. The examples provided have been used over a number of years in a range of classes and have had positive outcomes both in terms of learner outcomes but more importantly in learner engagement and enjoyment.

WORKS CITED

Adams, E. (2014) *Fundamentals of Game Design*. London: Pearson.

Bennett, P., Kendall, A. and McDougall, J. (2011) *After The Media*. Abingdon: Routledge.

Borden, I. (2001) *Skateboarding, Space and the City*. Oxford: Berg.

Goffman, E (1959) *The Presentation of Self in Everyday Life*. New York: Doubleday.

Kirkpatrick, G (2013) *Computer Games and the Social Imaginary*. Polity Press: Cambridge.

McLuhan, M. (1964) *Understanding Media*.

McLuhan, M. (1967) 'The New Education'. *The Basilian Teacher*, Vol. 11(2), pp. 66–73.

Sicart, M. (2014) *Play Matters*. MA: MIT Press.

Salen, K. and Zimmerman, E. (2004) *Rules of Play*. MA: MIT Press.

Sherman, C. (2003) *Untitled Film Stills*. NY: MOMA.

ONLINE SOURCES

BAECE. (2015) *Early Years experts unite in the call to block Baseline Assessment*: https://www.early-education.org.uk/press-release/early-years-experts-unite-call-block-baseline-assessment (accessed 16th February 2016).

Beckford, M. (2007) School without play area bans break times: http://www.telegraph.co.uk/news/uknews/1550808/School-without-play-area-bans-break-times.html (accessed 16th February 2016).

Department for Education (2014) Statutory framework for the early years foundation stage (EYFS) (March 2014) (accessed 16th February 2016).

http://www.foundationyears.org.uk/files/2014/07/EYFS_framework_from_1_September_2014__with_clarification_note.pdf (accessed 16th February 2016).

Hofkins, D., Northen, S. (eds) (2009) 'Introducing the Cambridge Primary Review': http://www.readyunlimited.com/wp-content/uploads/2015/09/An-Introduction-to-the-Cambridge-Primary-Review.pdf (accessed 16th February 2016).

Institute of Play (2016): http://www.instituteofplay.org/work/projects/quest-learning-in-action/ (accessed 16th February 2016).

Saul, H. (January 2014) *New Zealand school bans playground rules and sees less bullying and vandalism*: http://www.independent.co.uk/news/world/australasia/new-zealand-school-bans-playground-rules-and-sees-less-bullying-and-vandalism-9091186.html (accessed 16th February 2016).

Soderbergh, S. *'Raiders'* (2014): http://extension765.com/sdr/18-raiders (accessed 16th February 2016).

6: MAKING TEXT

Emma Walters

Pedagogy as Bricolage/ Re-Imagining Textual Practice Through Biographies of Knowledge.

My vantage point for this experiment begins initially with my own biography, accompanied by my associated educational history, career pathway and Continuing Professional Development (CPD) choices as they serve to constitute this piece of writing, my constructed narrative. Critically, I hold a belief that understanding our contribution to both the textual and cultural milieu in which we situate ourselves provides concrete meaning to our existence in the space and time in which we are historically rooted. Of equal importance are questions on the very nature of how our textual and cultural footprint impacts on the wider society we are in the process of creating. I view making texts as a mode of reinforcing this underlying ideology, a strategy of facilitating, locating, constructing and ultimately communicating or for the purposes of this project, 'making' our sense of self and place. I will attempt here to interweave and reconstruct (in a non-chronological order) key story strands that serve to contextualize and valorize this narrativised chapter. It symbolises an assembly of fragments of lived experience, stories and methods. In participating in this experiment, I have to meander and navigate such strands relating to my ideas for making text.

Adapting a term originally coined by Levi-Strauss (1966 cited in 2005: 4), Denzin and Lincoln might describe the assembly of writing this chapter as an act in the making, the work of a (2005: 1084) 'methodological (and epistemological) *bricoleur*', a history shared with other textual comrades who, at the time of writing (July 2016) I have not yet met.

Therefore to initiate this moment and contextualise my framing for this discussion, I will seek to provide a very brief history. I studied Media at GCSE level in 1990, later embarking on a BA in Broadcasting at Falmouth (1993–1996). Post-degree I worked in the media industry for several years before entering Further Education (or FE) 2003-present, where I have predominantly taught Level 3 BTEC Extended Diploma Media Production (TV & Film) and A Level Film Studies, the latter until student enrolment figures were deemed unprofitable. More recently, in 2010, I completed an MA in Creative Media Education at Bournemouth University (BU) when, assuming an autoethnographic approach for the first time, I created a short film entitled, *Death of the Teacher?* (2009). The film adapts the work and methods previously used (however using Play-Doh and other available materials as a more cost effective alternative to Lego) by David Gauntlett (2007), of making by doing identity. Gauntlett justifies his rationale by explaining:

> The notion of 'play' is useful in a process like Lego Serious Play, although perhaps it works best as a fruitful *metaphor* for thinking freely and without constraints… this is not *quite* the same as play, as practiced by children, which usually has no particular goals beyond those contained in the exercise itself. (2007: 134)

Gauntlett uses 'Lego Serious Play' as a means of communicating ones' perceptions of oneself and experience of the world:

> Approaches which invite people to reach down into the 'engine' and pull up a narrative in a different way might, then, reveal different kinds of account and give us a fuller understanding of those subjectivities. (Gauntlett, 2007: 90)

Seven years on, reflecting on *Death of the Teacher?* (2009) as my own attempt at experimenting with making text, enables the identification of the following six limitations of that particular project:

1) Autoethnography was used somewhat superficially; a comprehensive understanding with a clear conceptual framework was not in place.

2) Problematising the visual representational outcomes was not carried out effectively; representations were assumed as truth or snapshots of lived experience. Critical reflections on ideas of constructed and subjective narratives would have further triangulated findings.

3) The project title did not clearly correlate with methodology and supporting literature, giving rise to a sense of incoherency and messy data.

4) Play-Doh proved easily accessible and inexpensive to purchase in large quantities, however neither reason supports the selection of such method.

5) I felt I was simply mirroring Gauntlett (2007). The ability and opportunity for participants to review, reflect and return to the research was something not accounted for.

6) Additional methods of triangulation or 'crystallization' (Richardson, 2000; cited by Hayler, 2011: 40) were needed to validate the findings therefore proving difficult to assert the project produced any new knowledge.

Drawing here on Freire's (2014: 180) 'circle of knowledge' concept then, although flawed, learning extracted from my engagement with that particular process helps to shape the development of my understanding of making autoethnographic practice(s) today.

This pivotal phase in my career marked the foundation of my interest in ideas around 'making text' and to what extent our biographical histories contribute to our selected pedagogic approaches. For the first time I began to view pedagogic practice(s) as research and research as pedagogic practice(s). The classroom became the research field and my students' co-inquirers.

In his book, *Pedagogy of Hope* (2014), Paulo Freire alludes to this duality as a cyclical, mutual and non-hierarchal process. He states:

> All instruction involves research, and all research involves instruction. There is no genuine instruction in whose process no research is performed by way of a question, investigation, curiosity, creativity; just as there is no research in the course of which researchers do not learn - after all, by coming to know, they learn, and after having learned something, they communicate it, they teach. (2014: 180)

My experience(s) of FE, particularly prior to commencing the MA course had been a reticence to accept what Bennett et al in *After The Media* (2011: 231) term 'pedagogy of the inexpert'. However, critically I now embrace the idea of myself as that of the inexpert and openly refer to it as the elephant in the staffroom. Making meaning has become dialogically rooted as I constantly seek connections within and across the multiple silos of textual biographies of knowledge as carried and communicated through my students.

The way I started seeing and thinking about pedagogic practice(s) became transformative and liberating, carrying with it a dislocated and transient identity not to fear but paradoxically accept. Learning to acknowledge and identify the learner within emerges as central. I began to view autoethnographic practice(s) as a route through managing the ever-constraining challenges of FE with liberation and hope counterbalancing a 'pedagogy of the oppressed' (Freire, 1993).

The historical roots of autoethnography and what is broadly recognised as the researcher's biography as present within the study of social science originate in C. Wright Mills who said (1959: 6) that 'no social study that does not come back to the problems of biography, of history and of their intersections within a society has completed its intellectual journey'.

Denzin (2014: 19-20) offers several specific yet varied definitions, which are not especially relevant here, except to reinforce that the prefix of 'auto' makes it almost impossible to establish a singular definition for autoethnography. This destabilises the potential for simplification precisely because each biography carries its own story or more aptly (Sartre, 1963: 143) 'biographical truth', situated, time-bound within a specific period, context, agenda (albeit social, political or other) and set(s) of cultural relations.

Sarah Pink (2013) uses the phrase 'biographies of methods' in relation to selecting appropriate visual ethnographic methods according to the ideological, technical and ethical relevancies of subjects when conducting qualitative research. Reconfiguring her idea within the context of the classroom, I fiercely view learner biographies of knowledge as the starting point to the future possibilities of 'making text' with this chapter aiming to prompt additional discourse on this premise.

Placing emphasis on biographies of knowledge as the starting point for making text position equality and diversity as fundamental to curriculum planning. The public sector has a legal (and therefore pedagogic) responsibility to integrate and promote equality and diversity issues as central not as an additional 'add on'. In the Equality and Human Rights Commission or EHRC, it states that the Equality Act 2010 'will cover all seven equality strands: age, disability, gender, gender identity, race, religion or belief, and sexual orientation'.

The EHRC (2014) specify a new, 'single public sector equality duty will require public authorities to:

> 'Eliminate discrimination, harassment and victimization;
>
> Advance equality of opportunity;
>
> Foster good relations.'

The digital companion and associated activities will make explicit how embedding equality and diversity (E&D) issues can be applied in practice. As part of this experiment with its flattened and socially democratic premise, designed activities ensure that all students are respected, valued and heard with equal weightage. Inclusivity and justice resides within each project design.

Currently I am undertaking a Doctorate of Education (Creative and Media) where I intend to develop on ideas of the kaleidoscopic, somewhat transient nature of our professional identity whilst focusing on transferable skills as raw ingredients for employability across texts; a reliable cupboard staple integrated within the fabric of everyday pedagogic textual practices. Alongside the need to embed equality and diversity in project design, transferable skills are arguably a fundamental feature for the re-imagining of the making text composite structure as we move forward.

The National Children's Bureau concludes their 'Measuring Employability Skills' policy document by identifying actions for future development, actions this project will allude to (transferable skill elements) but does not prescribe. Blades et al (2012) state:

> It seems a sensible next step to agree more widely on a framework of employability skills… which should include some more nuanced analyses examining, for example, which programme components are associated with young people's employability skills… (2012: 35)

In the Learning and Skills Improvement Service or LSIS policy document entitled, 'The further education and skills sector in 2020: a social productivity approach', Buddery et al (2011: 10) state that a key mission for the FE sector is to 'become the 'skills for society' incubators – providing the skills to create the Big Society'. The tone and content of the LSIS findings are mirrored in 'The Wolf Report' (2011) and its notable scepticism (Wolf, 2011: 22) of 'the labour market value' of many vocational courses.

It is important for the reader to note that the ideas and activities suggested in this chapter will not be so prescriptive regarding skills identified in the National Careers

Service (2012) website, nor are they intended to conform wholeheartedly to the LSIS mission statement above. However I will indicate the potential for a range of transferable skills development opportunities in the act of making culture as well as reflecting on the processes inherent in their making.

The 'Eight Learning Events Model' (8LEM), deriving from Belgium and identified in Kearns (2001, cited in Amalathas, CFBT 2010: 14) refers specifically to 'autonomy', 'self-direction' and 'personal mastery' as the nexus upon which all skills hang. The digital companion activities adhere to such concepts as critical whilst position the teacher role as 'an agent in the management of culture' (Bennett el al, 2011: 110). It is not intended as a prescriptive account of integrated skills but rather a collaborative effort towards independence.

In a time of economic cuts, limited opportunities and fierce competition, it would be unethical for me to dismiss and exclude the skills agenda. It is my hope here that I might contribute to the possibilities of how, by making texts, we accrue crucial skills to prepare our students to be work-ready and survive what will continue to be undeniably an extremely challenging social and economic period of contemporary history. As C. Wright Mills aptly observes: 'As images of 'human nature' become more problematic, an increasing need is felt to pay closer yet more imaginative attention to the social routines and catastrophes which reveal (and which shape) man's nature in this time of civil unrest and ideological conflict' (Mills, 1959: 15).

The digital companion will make explicit how the suggested activities position transferable skills as intersecting across and through all making text processes. Therefore, the starting point is, 'Making Text: Pedagogy as Bricolage' and the theme I will use to explore texts is 'Re-Imagining Textual Practice Through Biographies of Knowledge'.

As Church (1995; cited by Short et al, 2013: 5) states, 'the self is therefore understood as a social and relational rather than an autonomous phenomenon' rightfully negating any privileging of the role of teacher over students. This non-hierarchal space for critically interpreting what Fiske (1994; cited by Hayler, 2011: 26) describes as 'culture in practice' facilitates the framing of the stated title within a post structural 'dialogical epistemology and aesthetic' (Denzin, 2014: 73). Such a dialogic-centred conceptual framework is most appropriate to the localised nature or situatedness of textual practice(s). This particular experiment facilitates discourses on the very nature of knowledge and knowledge construction within twenty-first century education. Short et al (2013: 9) refer to this as a 'discursive rather than ontological reality'. The sole objective is not about me the teacher but about we, us, the classroom we share and dialogic exchanges that emerge from those subjective voices unified (albeit temporary) in space and time.

As I write this, I am conscious that the act itself, of re-imagining how we 'make' our day-to-day practice(s) might be perceived by some as a futile, perhaps even fanciful exercise. In response however, as Holman Jones (2005; cited in Denzin & Lincoln, 2005: 765) quotes Tami Spry (2001), 'a self-narrative that critiques the situatedness of self with others in social contexts', as I argue here, is currently under-theorised and insufficiently explored within the FE sector and associated curriculum frameworks. Consequently, it is in my view, that the benefits outweigh the risks of not doing so. This experiment allows the space to action ideas born here providing hope for new ways of working or making.

Although viewing current education from alternate perspectives, Wolf (2011) and Ball (2013) both identify how professionally and emotionally destructive excessive administrative and surveillance systems have progressively come to have detrimental impact on our education system in the UK, particularly during the last decade.

In his blog post entitled, 'Dictator Gove and The Blob', Michael Bassey (2014) succinctly reflects a duty-bound sense of professional purpose:

> Our quest is for classroom wisdom and for ways to utilise that wisdom for the benefit of those who learn. Striving to improve education is built into our DNA. (2014: 1)

As Hayler (2013: 28) points out, 'I realise that you get to know yourself in a new way when you walk with someone else.' More broadly, this project could be viewed as an attempt to re-engage and re-locate what I believe has been lost; moving beyond surveillance systems in the hope of re-establishing meaningful value-free human relations by focussing on the processes of knowledge construction and the roles we assume in the formation of it.

Sartre (1963) and later Derrida (1976) point their readers towards the omnipresence of 'the self' as a shadow that never leaves and therefore dismiss notions of absolute or concrete objectification.

In his paper on Nietzsche, Derrida (1976; cited in Peeters 2013: 1) purports:

> We no longer consider the biography of a 'philosopher' as a corpus of empirical accidents that leaves both a name and a signature outside a system which would itself be offered up to an immanent philosophical reading – the only kind of reading held to be philosophically legitimate.

Over a decade earlier, in his explanation of 'The Progressive-Regressive Method', Sartre implicates biography as fundamental within the 'regressive moment' by stating 'the heuristic method must consider the "differential" (if the study of a person is concerned) within the perspective of biography' (1963: 139).

More recently, Denzin (2014: 26) acknowledges the fusion of roles between the researcher and researched as fundamental to auto-ethnographic practice-led inquiry by succinctly emphasising that, 'the ethnographer's writing self **cannot not** be present, there is **no** objective space outside the text'. Consequently, I suggest that issues of presence and absence, the other and self, reflexivity and verisimilitude emerge as central to pedagogic approaches to making text. Manifestations of this thinking and suggested practical application of them will be evident in resources associated with the *Doing Text* digital companion.

Pink (2013: 51) discusses how the choices of visual modes of recording lead onto the 'notion of biographies of methods'. She elaborates, stating that 'methods have their own trajectories, biographies and transformations' (ibid.). This corporal and sensory element to the students' uses of selected methods is integrated into designed activities. Pink additionally positions the ethical issue of control and ownership under the spotlight, visual ethnographic elements I hope to incorporate in activity design for the digital companion. She asserts 'joint control of the uses that can be made of visual materials, ongoing consultations and re-negotiation of consent, along with input into the question of what images might be used and produced and how' (2013: 63).

Elements of our discourse can be located in our uses of media, contributing to the complexity of deciphering and comprehending what constitutes knowledge itself. Such conversations are inherent in activities designed. However, Foucault talks about consequences due to the absence of language. He states, 'we are not everything… even the philosopher does not inhabit the whole of his language like a secret and perfectly fluent god' (1980: 41).

In this sense, I agree, that the camera, the physical eye, and perception itself can only constitute temporal representational artefacts. However they do remain splinters of fragmented memories and thoughts waiting to be seen and heard. Student reflexivity in making their biographical text will formulate the basis for designed activities enabling an embedded approach to equality and diversity issues so closely entwined with student biographies. Additionally, I intend to identify transferable skills (as I understand them) associated with each activity to reinforce the personal, learning and thinking skills (PLTS) for purposes of contributing to the employability agenda in twenty-first century education.

It is not an intention that you, the reader, be expected to agree to or necessarily replicate suggested ways of making discussed here, although the accompanying session plans will facilitate this should you wish to test the ideas out in your own setting. It is more a prompt that you might consider readdressing the relationship of the teacher-learner dynamic as one of collaborative textual learning and making. To restate the point, this chapter is about developing a conversation about the reconstructed ideas of artefacts produced (not necessarily realities of lived experience) extending to questions about what constitutes knowledge, expertise and mastery when it comes to deconstructing meaning(s) extracted from any given textual artifact.

Although in her imagined game of chess, by design Alice's mission is to become 'Queen Alice' (Carroll, 2011), the motive here is not to win, as there is no game to be played, but rather the proposition of this chapter is founded on a simplistic duty of care being that 'learners everywhere of all ages deserve nothing less' (Swaffield, 2009: 14). The designed activities are intended as a pragmatic solution to creatively engage across political educational policy, equality and diversity obligations (Communication Act 2010) and student biographies of knowledge.

In the final two 'waking' chapters of *Through the Looking Glass and What Alice Found There*, Alice's encounters remain in her imagination for her to interpret, reflect upon and re-tell at some point in the future. In this respect it could be claimed that this *Doing Text* experiment bears traits of what Bakhtin identifies as a 'polyphonic' text:

> …a plurality of independent and unmerged voices and consciousness… with equal rights and each with its own world, combine but are not merged in the unity of the event. (1984: 6)

Alice's adventures signify conversations about conversations. I suggest the 'Looking-Glass House' with its unconventional rules into which Alice is projected serve to dislocate or at the very least destabilise her voice as central. Alice's journey is littered with counter-arguments and perspectives challenging her somewhat limited and narrow worldview, as she perceives it. I view *Doing Text* as an extension of this. It is an emancipatory calling to action for all teachers to destabilise their role, voice and ways of making pedagogy in order to rethink traditional boundaries of practice, cultural assumptions and institutional policy. It is about using a social platform to engender social support and reform for those at the coalface. By holding up the mirror to ourselves at this particular epoch and by reimagining how we might do things differently, we reflexively seek restoration of the soul and spirit in what we do.

Sartre refers to 'crystalized meaning' (1963: 154) as a result of exploring the 'hodological space' of the field. The 'Progressive-Regressive Method' facilitates the exploration of memory pathways; whilst vast, the teacher's role in this case, is to identify how interconnecting ideas merge, intersect or splinter off, where patterns emerge on a collaborative journey of discovery. It repositions the teacher role as subject to ongoing student reflection and therefore making all perceptions and understanding (regardless of position) objects of critique. Therefore in addition to 'presence' and 'absence,' this experiment is, by its very nature, dialogic and our discourses here about inquiry into issues of ideological conflict.

The classroom as a context and in daily practice is in effect a zone of multiple methodological perspectives. Almost four decades on, Richardson adopts Sartre's idea of the crystal as a more apt metaphor than the triangle for establishing rigor and depth whilst exploring pedagogic inquiry of this kind, observing that, 'crystals grow, change, alter… Crystals are prisms that reflect externalities and refract within themselves creating different colours, patterns, arrays' (Richardson, 2000; cited in Denzin and Lincoln, 2005: 6).

Assuming the crystals are our students then, it is the role of the teacher to manage emergent dialogue on the processes of making text including student perceptions, interpretation, prior knowledge and experience, ideology, representation, semiotics, history, reactions to peer review etc. across texts produced. Actively seeking to solidify and clarify meaning(s) alongside students' making text as well as what other students make of the texts produced, pertinently through a shared language no longer reliant on one subjective judgment in isolation.

In her contribution to a 'Manifesto for Media Education' (2011), Natalie Fenton alludes to this notion in her re-imagined statement by placing emphasis on cultural, political, indeed textual critique. She states that the bottom line, 'is to critique power and the power of meaning making including contesting the meaning making of others; to understand and then to play an active part in how our social world is framed, organized, monitored and regulated.'

The 'semiotic guerrilla warfare' (Eco, 1994; cited in Ball, 1995: 268) between Humpty Dumpty and Alice (Carroll, 2011: 222) exemplifies the fundamental role that language has to play in our relations both with ourselves and with others. In her chapter entitled, 'Creatures of Difference', Belsey makes direct reference to this exchange to convey her belief that 'ideas are the effect of meanings we learn and reproduce' (Belsey, 2002: 7). Meaning(s) are to be viewed as textual constructions rather than containing an origin, therefore aligning this experiment within a post-structuralist framework.

The polysemic structure (liberating multifarious voices) and tone of this particular project can be closely aligned to the spirit and work initiated by the Centre for Contemporary Cultural Studies (or CCCS) back in 1964. It signifies a collective enterprise of academic and practitioner voices, yet no one chapter elevated or centralised as the dominant discourse. The unification lies in a celebration of our different responses to what the various strands of doing text might mean to us. This represents a stitching together of our equally disparate narrative strands and associated professional contexts and identities constituting a unified whole. In the same way the Birmingham University student sit-in protest demanded the right 'to participate in the decision-making process of the university' (Dworkin 1997: 168), similarly this project enables us as educators to actively participate through language and action and in doing so we hope to revive our community of practice. Our subjective experience, imagination and companion tools produced and made available (as part of this re-imagined ideal) serve to unite those in the field today. The themes selected for the devised digital companion seek to incorporate popular cultural references and focus on student biography. In part the digital tool activities serve to give voice to the multiplicity of biographies we encounter each academic year. It could be viewed as an act of pluralism that will liberate all involved by positioning hope as integral to the development of our conversations.

Half a century on from the work of the CCS, I would contest that it is only through problematising our biographical histories and positioning everyday cultural experiences as central to pedagogic practice(s) that much-needed discussion and reflexivity on why and how we make texts are simultaneously yet paradoxically ever more prevalent and confusing. The time to deconstruct textual meaning making needs to be built into the curriculum as our biographic footprints and diasporic identities become increasingly more important in the textual economy. In my view it is only through autoethnographic practice(s) combined with textual deconstruction of the artefacts we make that education itself will stand a chance of surviving the textual transformations of our time.

This chapter is about celebrating people in education. It is an acknowledgement of solidarity amongst textual comrades as it attempts to critically analyse reconstructed self-reflexive narrative accounts with the goal of more meaningful re-engagement and restoring a belief in what we make.

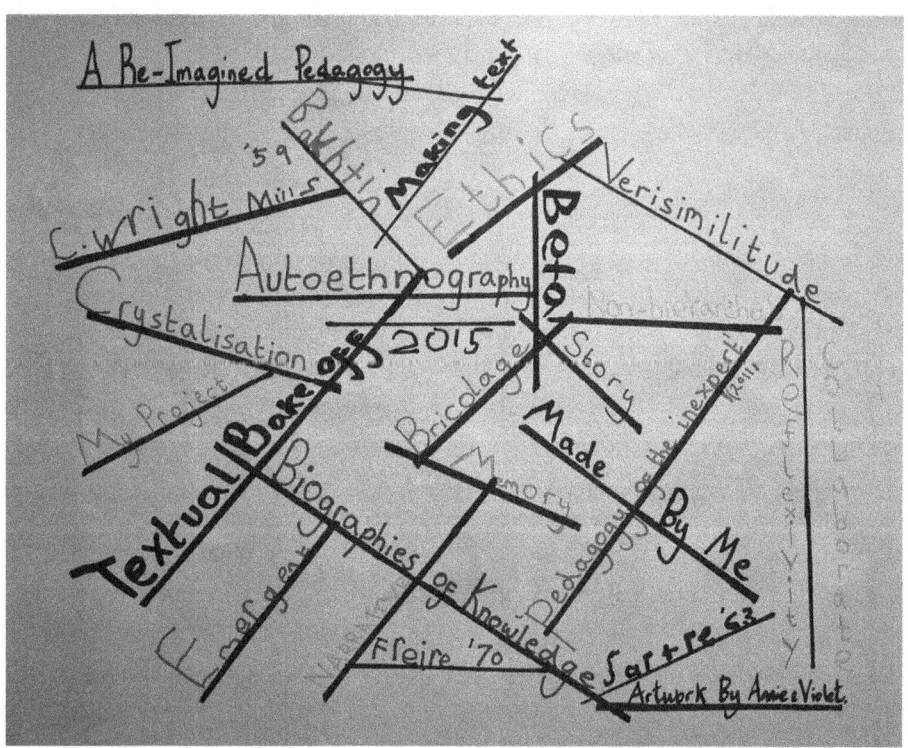

Fig. 6.1 A (Re-Imagined) Pedagogy – Artwork by Annie and Violet 2015 (personal collection)

Pedagogy of The Oppressed (Paulo Freire, 1993): Revisited in Cheshire, 2015

The current barriers to me working this way with texts in my teaching are the BTEC specification itself (it is out of date and fails to reflect contemporary textual activities) and associated criterion (19 units over 2 years, on average 4 criterion per unit equating to 76 different criterion in total). Also, the revised assessment guidelines (beginning 2014) and its 'teaching to the test' ethos only serve to compound and hinder the possibilities of textual exploration and experimentation, as sustained periods of 'no guidance' must now be evidenced.

The out of sync internal focus on assessment data has exploded; each individual criterion per student needs to be uploaded onto three different systems (electronic brief, ProMonitor, CoLin). And currently all student work must be internally verified, as opposed to the previously required four samples by the External Verifier, eroding further possibilities of learning and trust in teacher ability to assess work. The course approval process relies heavily on courses operating in silos, engendering a culture of competition (adversely affecting budget distribution, success rates and morale).

Furthermore, the revised rules adhere to Assessment *of* Learning rather than Assessment *for* Learning, therefore contradicting the original premise of vocational education. This only results in a reduction of creative opportunities to explore the potential for biographies of knowledge as a route through reimagining textual practice(s) by creating a more tailored and personalised programme of study. Learning has become consumption, arguably more akin to what George Ritzer (1983) terms the 'McDonaldization' of FE; a system where our subjects now have shelf lives and our students viewed as customers.

By placing student biographies of knowledge and ideas of inclusivity and differentiation as central to designed activities the potential for authentic self-directed learning becomes possible, rather than formulating boxes to tick, a process often forged and contrived for observational and audit purposes.

Pedagogy of Hope (Paulo Freire, 2014), Revisited in Cheshire: 2015

If the barriers discussed above were removed, I would design textual scenarios or projects centred on the application of making biographies of knowledge, giving equal weight to the teacher and student. To explain, teacher participation would mirror (as well as document – time and resources permitting) student participation. The teacher becomes object of critique also. Rather than regurgitating project briefs on a yearly basis, the teacher would revisit the work made (including work generated by the teacher) the previous year. Thus, transforming the role into one of constant revision and reflection and one that would reflect cultural and textual evolutionary factors affecting practice(s), as determined by each new cohort.

Perhaps, at this point it is worth us returning to C. Wright Mills and *The Sociological Imagination*:

> Continually work out and revise your views of the problems of history, the problems of biography, and the problems of social structure in which biography and history intersect. Keep your eyes open to the varieties of individuality, and to the modes of epochal change. (Mills, 1959: 225)

At the beginning of each academic year the new intake of students would contribute to the content and design as part of the induction process. Through deliberated discussion and democratic decision-making, all students would contribute to reconfiguring the shape of learning for the year to come. The cohort's biographical footprint would differ year on year as each new group would constitute a unique collaborative voice reflecting its textual culture. Assessment would largely be collaborative and involve peer assessment, placing autonomy and responsibility for assessment as a founding design premise. I would also reduce the number of project briefs to three or four per year to avoid duplication and repetition of criterion and more pertinently to reflect real-life freelance time frames whilst facilitating adequate time for ideas development and experimentation, peer review, feedback and reflections on process.

Projects would be interdisciplinary and exhibitions would involve cross-college events to celebrate collaborative efforts and texts produced. Interim college wide events would serve to promote learner research and celebrate institution, cohort as well as individual identity.

Designed activities will provide pedagogic strategies for weaving together the following textual practices into two distinct experimental projects. It is worth highlighting that the popular culture references, as made explicit in the suggested project title(s), serve as a relational anchor only. Any signification extracted can only be drawn out through our own practice, understanding and biographical knowledge, therefore it is expected that outcomes will differentiate across cohorts, for no two cohorts look the same. However, it is pertinent to note that both Project 1, titled 'Educating Us' and Project 2, titled 'Textual Bake Off – Made by Me' will comprise of the following four key narrative components that underpin rationale and design:

- Celebration of Biographical Knowledge
- Reflection, Reflection, Reflection
- Transferable Skills
- Equality and Diversity.

PROJECT 1: 'EDUCATING US'

Alluding to the codes and convention of Channel 4's *Educating Essex* (2011) series, Project 1 involves English, Media and Drama students working collaboratively (to be integrated and then regrouped into 3 distinct groups) on reconstructing their own version of college life through their own eyes and based on their experiences. Students would need to explore generic conventions, language (scripted and unscripted), performance (rehearsed and unrehearsed), and representation of character and story through editorial decisions. During the planning stages they would need to conduct production meetings and contribute to how they think it should look, reflect on their own biographies and how they might represent themselves. By making 'Educating Us' students will come to understand constructed reality programming as literary. The project relates to their understanding of 'everyday life' whilst simultaneously connects to the processes inherent within writing, listening, film making, speaking and visualisation as making. The project repositions the students as both carriers and re-producers of biographical knowledge, as contributors to 'popular' culture opposed to consumers.

Recent American case study examples accessed, Beeman-Cadwalladera et al (2014), Koster & Van Den Berg (2014) and Taylor et al (2014), not only purport but valorise the local as opposed to the global as a site for change. Here, I represent to you my classroom as my local and textual field of practice(s); your classroom belongs to you. As Denzin affirms, 'a cultural studies that makes a difference… seeking instead a radical, nonviolent pluralism that represses no one and liberates all' (2014: 23).

This project is about seeking connections and meaning within practice as opposed to the disruption of it, in the hope of filling the deep onto-epistemological void that I argue exists between what I believe to be my current everyday practice contrasted against what I wish it should or could be. It is about problematising representation in contrast to valorising representations, lived experience or truth for that matter. 'Educating Us' is about initiating this process.

Denzin (2014: 70) reminds us that 'memory is fallible', however dialogue can be used as a tool to prise out meaning, revisit, reify, nullify as a process towards a 'totalising movement' (Sartre, 1963: 155) and not to be viewed as an end.

By asking the students to initially regress and draw on their ideas of how they would represent themselves, this signifies and activates what Sartre would consider a 'progressive' moment for both students and the 'Educating Us' project. Sartre (1963: 153) explains this as 'knowing is simply the dialectical movement which explains the act by its terminal significance in terms of its starting conditions. It is originally progressive.'

Rather than claiming to capture snapshots of reality, 'Educating Us' seeks only to open pathways of knowledge and meaning through representations of the student experience as they see it. As Denzin reiterates:

> Language and speech do not mirror experience; rather, they create representations of experience. Meanings are always in motion, inclusive, conflicting, contradictory. The task is to understand what textually constructed presence means because there is only text. (2014: 36-37)

The origin of his position can be traced back five decades earlier to Sartre (1963) who rejects and destabilises the notion of complete truths. Each biography carries its own story or more aptly 'biographical truth' (1963: 143) situated, time-bound within a specific period, context, agenda (albeit social, political or other) and set(s) of cultural relations.

'Educating Us' is not to be viewed as a route to accessing student truth, for as Foucault warns us, we can never claim, 'universal truth' for 'general right are illusions and traps' (2000: 62). However, I am interested in how the tools used to express products created by students constitute textually constructed forms of expression as well serving to facilitate discourses on deconstruction, conflicts of interpretation and analysis that those choices bring to bear. However, 'Educating Us' is not about seeking universal outcomes but rather it is designed to open up discursive opportunities on the very problematic notion of 'truth.' Instead, emphasis resides here on transforming ideas of identity through reconstruction, or making the self. By design, it is for the benefit of those involved in terms of self-perception over and above the search for truth.

PROJECT 2: 'TEXTUAL BAKE OFF – MADE BY ME'

Project 2 follows similar themes to Project 1, but it differs in that it represents an opportunity to explore and utilise diverse materials and techniques available to students in order to 'make' their perceptions of their culture. The artefact(s) produced alongside materials and techniques used will differ depending upon whether the institution decides to collaborate with for example the art, games, horticulture, or fashion departments, etc. However, the critical point is that the themes will remain the same regardless of participating departments. This commonality will facilitate debate on the processes of constructing culture as perceived and made by students, encourage self-expression whilst placing the learner biography of knowledge as central. A documentary made by film students would serve to trace processes encountered and culminate in a 'making of' documentary on the project.

Ideally this together with all the artefacts produced would be showcased at an organised event or public venue (marketing and management of the event would also to be student-led) with invited guest critics (one member from each area of specialism) to critique learner work.

Post-exhibition, a question and answer session would allow the makers to justify their approach and product in addition to responding to public opinion and feedback. Ticket sales for the event could generate additional capital to be fed back into the courses engaged in the project. Participating students will be given the autonomy to decide on how the money should be spent. The event would constitute a celebration of aspects of everyday life as cultural signifiers of meaning through making.

As discussed earlier in the chapter, Pink (2013: 49-69) warns about the perils of pre-determined method selection primarily relating to issues of context, appropriateness and ethics. If the twenty-first century classroom is viewed as a zone of inquiry then her guidance is relevant within this experiment. This is factored into the designed activities here where participants will have time to explore and self-select a method and indeed textual artefact of choice. Facilitating individual learning styles by encouraging the use of various tools and materials that best fit each individual is integrated into differentiation planning and worksheet activities.

It would be deemed unethical to assume that all students are comfortable working with one prescribed text. I know from diagnostic data calculated on entry that 80% of my 2014 cohort, for example, are multimodal, therefore constructing activities to facilitate diversity and range seems the most appropriate and ethically considerate approach to take. To enforce students to work with one text in isolation for instance would be to engineer a specific mode of response and detract from richness of character and ways people might learn best.

Pertinent to the design and rationale for this experiment is to create a space to play and assess the suitability of working with various self-selected methods by testing and discussing their strengths and limitations with students. Utilizing one text in isolation would not permit this opportunity.

Pink (2013) recognises that context should shift methodological choices; responsive to each new project or culture encountered. Pink asserts, 'methods themselves have biographies with them, inviting and inspiring new methodologies through their practice and findings' (2013: 11). She extends this idea further by elaborating '...the important differences do not necessarily always lie in the medium one is using, but the context in which they are being developed, and the theoretical ideas that inform their use' (ibid.).

Neither project idea is prescribed or claims perfection. Conversely, in the spirit of this chapter, it attempts to facilitate diverse contexts.

The two projects outlined below in Figure 6.2 merely signify a premise on which you, the reader, might wish to adapt to suit your own professional and cohort biographies of knowledge and/ or geographical setting (taking into account variable resources available).

WK	Project 1: 'Educating Us'	Project 2: 'Textual Bake Off'
1	SCREEN *Educating Essex* (2011). Deconstruct key sections. Discussion-based analyses (jigsaw method)/ workshops on genre, language and performance. KEY ISSUE: The Constructed Reality Paradox - A Textual War: Reality Versus/ With Fiction.	ANALYSIS: Semiotics? Students to explore textual meaning creation through a series of semiological-based activities (mixed-media) and the creation of multiple digital collages of perceived key signifiers of 21st century culture. KEY ISSUE: The Author of the Mash-Up. So What's New? Paradox – An Ideological War in the Making. Reconstruction Versus/ With Originality.
2	Create individual character biographies - based on own history, personality and cultural influences. Discussion-based workshops on the ethical implications of representation. Create three production crews 'Team Reality', 'Team Fiction' and 'Team Making Of'. The 'Making Of Team' can be used to triangulate outcomes and prompt discussion on process. Devise in-house contracts and consent forms.	Fashion, Games and Art students to collaborate (self-manage) throughout. All students to explore and gather various materials (they should not be restricted to their subject specialism, e.g. a fashion student does not have to make an outfit) to begin the process of creating an artefact on the theme of 'A Cultural Explosion: Made by Me.' Students can decide to either work in pairs, small groups or individually. Teacher to facilitate logistics.
3	NARRATIVE STRUCTURE: Discuss on-based workshops on 'What makes a good story?' Identify key protagonists, dominant and secondary story strands. Conduct a recce of the building and identify appropriate locations. Plan and manage auditions. Allocate production roles. Students to devise scripts/ storyboard if identified as a requirement.	FRAGMENTS: Students will spend the week continuing to gather materials (various) needed. Whilst doing so, they are required to examine individual materials selected in terms of personal signification (students to use personal blogs to reflect on this process). In weeks 4 and 5 (to follow) students will assemble fragments identified above and again use personal blogs to rationalise their presence. In doing so, reflect on those items or materials that remain absent.
4	PRODUCTION (Schedule to be student-led).	MAKE ARTEFACT (Schedule to be student-led).
5	PRODUCTION	MAKE ARTEFACT
6	POST-PRODUCTION (Schedule to be student-led)	Students MANAGE logistics of creating an exhibition space (Enterprise-in-the-Making) for visiting critics and members of the public (who will be invited to leave comments). Students to contribute to peer assessment activities focused on the construction of meaning, identity and our conflicting ideological cultural assumptions.

7	POST-PRODUCTION	SHOW/ EXTERNAL CRITIQUE: Students engage in a Question and Answer session (Fashion Designer, Games Designer and Artist) on work produced, discussing relevant themes.
8	PLENARY: On screening all three films, students to complete comparison workshop activities. Teacher to chair student discussions on: Problems of representation (scripted sections and the presence of camera). Editing techniques/ selected cuts used help shape viewer reading(s) of character/ context. What is real about reality TV? Watching the everyday. Making Learning. Identify and discuss transferable skills used. Students to self and peer assess each film according to criteria they set in the final week.	PLENARY: Review photographic images of all artefacts created via teacher (triangulating) blog. Teacher to chair student discussions on: The multiplicity of interpretation. Method as biography. Identity and the signification of the whole. Problems of absence. What makes an artefact original? Making learning. Identify and discuss transferable skills used. Students will discuss feedback received from the 'professionals' and contrast that with peer assessment outcomes as well as public comments received from the show.

REFLECTION: Each day, all participating students and teachers will write a reflexive 'tumblr' blog entitled, 'Text in the Making'. The teacher can utilise this resource as a focal point to instigate discussion and appraisal of progress encountered throughout, ensuring every voice is listened to and documented.
COMMUNICATION: All students will also be required to chair and minute their own production team meetings (daily) to ensure individual challenges and merits are clearly communicated.
LOGISTICS: The above projects are based on a block of 8 full 5-day weeks.
NOTE: For Equality and Diversity (E&D) and Transferable Skills (TS) see digital companion.

Fig. 6.2 Overview: Weekly Breakdown for Projects 1 and 2 (personal collection)

Although the tasks involve interdisciplinary planning, ideally the projects would run parallel alongside at least one or two other local colleges. Exhibition events could then host textual work made, serving to: 1) promote student public exhibition opportunities and experience; 2) disseminate good practice across college; 3) open networking opportunities for students; 4) celebrate biographies of knowledge whilst develop student confidence and self-esteem.

The realisation of one's value and purpose is critical to professional identity, believing that what we do can and does make a difference, it is about reclaiming those beliefs. As Denzin states, 'if we want to change how things are, we must change how they are seen, written about, and heard' (qtd. in Ellis & Flaherty, 1992: 21). This project signals an opportunity to reappraise what we do and re-imagine how we do them.

To return to the starting point, at the end of each project, I will reconsider my own biographical lens and practice(s) and reflect on what students can teach me about making textual constructions in what I can only refer to as the 'teacher-maker-learner-maker' dynamic.

By implementing strategies to enhance more authentic modes of personalised textual encounters and engagement, a more flattened, non-hierarchal pedagogic structure emerges. Therefore constituting textual practices that could be classified as interpretative bricolage; decoding texts in the making whilst identifying and extracting key learning moments as part of this 'Doing Text' beta experimental project.

WORKS CITED

Bakhtin, M. (1984; twelfth printing 2011) *Problems of Dostoevsky's Poetics*. Introduction by Wayne C. Booth. Translated by Caryl Emerson (ed.). Minneapolis: University of Minnesota Press.

Belsey, C. (2002) *Poststructuralism A Very Short Introduction*. Oxford, New York: Oxford University Press.

Bennett, P., Kendall, A. and McDougall, J. (2011) *After The Media*. Abingdon: Routledge.

Carroll, L. (2011; originally published 1865). *Alice's Adventures In Wonderland and Through the Looking-Glass*. London: CRW Publishing Limited.

Denzin, K. N. (2014) *Interpretative Autoethnography*. Thousand Oaks, CA: SAGE.

Denzin. K. N. and Lincoln. S. Y. (eds) (2005) *The Sage Handbook of Qualitative Research* (3rd edition). London: SAGE.

Denzin, K. N. (1992) 'The Many Faces of Emotionality,' in: Ellis, C. and Flaherty, M.G. (eds) *Investigating Subjectivity Research on Lived Experience*. Newbury Park, CA: SAGE. pp. 17–30.

Dworkin, D. (1997) *Cultural Marxism in Postwar Britain*. Durham and London: Duke University Press.

Foucault, M. (1980; originally published in 1977) *Language, Counter-Memory, Practice*. Introduction by Donald. F. Bouchard (ed.). New York: Cornell University Press.

Foucault, M. (2000; originally published in 1994) *Michel Foucault Ethics Essential Works of Foucault 1954–1984 Volume 1*. Paul Rabinow (ed.). London: The New Press/ Penguin Books.

Freire, P. (1993; originally published in 1970) *Pedagogy of The Oppressed*. Translated by Myra Bergman Ramos. London: Penguin Group.

Freire, P. (2014; originally published in 1992) *Pedagogy of Hope*. Translated by Robert R. Bar. London, New York: Bloomsbury Academic.

Gauntlett, D. (2007) *Creative Explorations – New Approaches to Identities and Audiences*. Abingdon and New York: Routledge.

Hayler, M. (2011) *Autoethnography, Self-Narrative and Teacher Education*. Rotterdam: Sense Publishers.

Holman Jones, S. (2005) 'Autoethnography: Making the Personal Political', in Denzin. K. N. and Lincoln. S. Y. (eds) *The Sage Handbook of Qualitative Research* (3rd ed.). London: SAGE. pp. 763–791.

Peeters, B. (2013) *Derrida A Biography*. Cambridge: Polity Press.

Pink, S. (2013) *Doing Visual Ethnography* (3rd ed.). London: SAGE.

Sartre, Jean-Paul. (1963) *The Problem of Method*. London: Methuen & Co. Ltd.

Short, N. P., Turner, L., and Grant, A. (eds) (2013) *Contemporary British Autoethnography*. Rotterdam: Sense Publishers.

Wright Mills, C. (1959) *The Sociological Imagination*. Oxford, New York: Oxford University Press.

ONLINE SOURCES

Amalathsa, E. (2010) 'Learning to Learn in Further Education: A literature review of effective practice in England and Abroad', *Centre for British Teachers or CfBT*: http://www.campaign-for-learning.org.uk/cfl/assets/documents/Research/LearningToLearn_v5FINAL.pdf (accessed 10 February 2016).

Ball, J. Stephen (2013) 'Education, justice and democracy: The struggle over Ignorance and Opportunity.' *Centre for Labour and Social Studies (classonline.org)*: http://classonline.org.uk/docs/2013_Policy_Paper_-_Education,_justice_and_democracy_(Stephen_Ball).pdf (accessed 10 February 2016).

Ball, S. (1995) 'Intellectuals or Technicians? The Urgent Role of Theory in Educational Studies.' King's College London. *British Journal of Educational Studies* (1995): http://www.jstor.org/discover/10.2307/3121983?uid=3738032&uid=2134&uid=2&uid=70&uid=4&sid=21104645864663 (accessed 10 February 2016).

Bassey, M. (2014) 'Dictator Gove and The Blob.' *Free School From Government Control.Com* (2014): http://www.free-school-from-government-control.com/Challenge-of-the-Blob.html (accessed 10 February 2016).

Beeman-Cadwalladera, N., Bucka, G. and Trauth-Nareb, A. (2014) 'Tipping the Balance from Expert to Facilitator: Examining Myths about Being a Teacher Educator'. *Taylor & Francis Online*: http://www.tandfonline.com/doi/pdf/10.1080/17425964.2013.864967 (accessed 10 February 2016).

Blades et al. (2012) 'Measuring Employability Skills.' *National Children's Bureau*: http://www.ncb.org.uk/media/579980/measuring_employability_skills_final_report_march2012.pdf (accessed 10 February 2016).

Buddery et al. (2011) 'The further education and skills sector in 2020: a social productivity approach.' *Learning and Skills Improvement Service*: http://www.rsa2020publicservices.org.uk/wp-content/uploads/2011/05/The-Further-Education-and-Skills-Sector-in-2020.pdf (accessed 10 February 2016).

Equality and Human Rights Commission (2014): http://www.equalityhumanrights.com/public-sector-equality-duties (accessed 10 February 2016).

Fenton, N. *Manifesto for Media Education* (2011): http://www.manifestoformediaeducation.co.uk/2011/01/media-education-should-be-5/ (accessed 10 February 2016).

Koster, K. and Van Den Berg, B. (2014) 'Increasing Professional Self-Understanding: Self-Study Research by Teachers with the Help of Biography, Core Reflection and Dialogue.' *Taylor & Francis Online*: http://www.tandfonline.com/doi/pdf/10.1080/17425964.2013.866083 (accessed 10 February 2016).

Ritzer, G (1983) 'The McDonaldization of Society.': http://sociology.morrisville.edu/readings/SOCI101/Mcdonaldization-excerpt.pdf (accessed 20 February 2016).

Swaffield, S. (2009) 'The misrepresentation of Assessment for Learning and the woeful waste of a wonderful opportunity.' *AAIA National Conference (Association for Achievement and Improvement through Assessment) Bournemouth, 16 – 18 September.* http://www.aaia.org.uk/content/uploads/2010/07/The-Misrepresentation-of-Assessment-for-Learning.pdf (accessed 10 February 2016).

Taylor, M., Klein. E. J. & Abrams, L. (2014) 'Tensions of Reimagining Our Roles as Teacher Educators in a Third Space: Revisiting a Co/autoethnography Through a Faculty Lens.' *Taylor & Francis Online*: http://www.tandfonline.com/doi/pdf/10.1080/17425964.2013.866549 (accessed 22 February 2016).

'Transferable Skills' *National Careers Service* (2012): https://nationalcareersservice.direct.gov.uk/advice/planning/Pages/transferableskills.aspx (accessed 18 February 2016).

7: PERFORMING TEXT

Pedagogical approaches to understanding performance in the digitally literate classroom

Mark Parsons

> All the world's a stage, And all the men and women merely players. They have their exits and their entrances, And one man in his time plays many parts, His acts being seven ages. (Shakespeare, 1623: *As You Like It*, Act II Scene VII)

TEACHING WITHOUT SUBJECTS

The concept of Performance is a core element of a number of different subjects including Media Studies, Drama and English Literature. For this chapter I am going to take aspects of these varying but intrinsically linked subjects into this hypothetical post-Media Studies learning environment and explain how I would teach this concept as a contemporary understanding, utilising approaches from each subject. This will be pedagogically similar to the recently introduced Teaching by Phenomena method in Finland where instead of focusing on particular subjects, learning is developed through certain topics and concepts, with Geography, History, Economics and Foreign Languages being covered in the study of the European Union: 'It is not only Helsinki but the whole of Finland who will be embracing change. We really need a rethinking of education and a redesigning of our system, so it prepares our children for the future with the skills that are needed for today and tomorrow' (Kyllonen, 2015). From experience, Media Studies is regarded as a populist subject as the students tend to find it accessible due to having some familiarity of the texts they study; this is an opportunity to develop a course of learning for the students rather than the teachers.

Beecher suggested that our current system of teaching by subject was detrimental to the progress of the students: 'For children, however, subjects of any kind, however conceived, hold no inherent interest, meaning or use. For them the world has simply not yet so fragmented itself. It will do so eventually, as the children gain experience and as they mature, but not for a presently known number of years' (Beecher, 1972: 420). Beecher's thesis is something that has been considered and discussed in Western education since it was published over thirty years ago and now seems to becoming a reality at a national level in the Finnish education system. It is my idea that [applying] a combination of Beecher's thesis, the recent developments in Finland and an understanding of the media saturated environments that the modern student engages with, that teaching a concept as broad as Performance should be a multi-subject and multi-media experience. If we are destined for this format of curriculum, then Media is a subject that is more adaptable than most. If we consider topics such as the European Union or global warming, the relevance of teaching through media is unavoidable. Media is one of the most accessible, adaptable and appropriate subjects if this approach to the curriculum is to be implemented. For example a media teacher could approach the phenomena of global warming through *An Inconvenient Truth* (2006), *The Guardian* newspaper's extensive climate change coverage, *The Truth about Climate Change* (BBC, 2013) and the online *Oxford Climate Forum* and this would allow students to explore different mediums as well enhance their understanding of one of their generation's greatest challenges. The focus of this chapter, however, is on Performance and how we utilise the teaching by phenomena approach whilst replacing the phenomena itself (such as global warming or the European Union) with performance as the central media concept.

This approach to curriculum development would go against current trends in the UK as many are suggesting that the more traditional subject based teaching needs to be maintained and advanced. 'Subject-centred education is sometimes denounced by educationalists as Victorian, outdated and elitist. This is a new development. In the past, distinguished educational thinkers writing from radical, conservative or liberal standpoints all supported versions of subject-centred education. With few exceptions, they thought it appropriate for all pupils. The content of the subject-centred curriculum may have changed over time to include the sciences and modern foreign languages, but all these curricula were broad and included some practical subjects' (Hayes, 2010: 8). It is important that if we do begin to exist in a post-Media Studies world that we strive to identify and highlight its relevance and importance for young people and challenge ideas. This is not an argument against subject teaching – the current subject of Media Studies is academic, rigorous, challenging and teaches a strong balance of knowledge and skills – but rather it is preparation for a time when Media Studies is not on the subject list.

PERFORMANCE AS A CONCEPT

Arguably one of the most important aspects of teaching Performance through a contemporary position is that there are significant moral implications of how young people are engaging and performing through digital media platforms. A key part of this chapter will look at the potential moral and legal issues about the differences in how we want to perform in an online society and the issues regarding the audience's position and response to this performance: 'And to the degree that the individual maintains a show before others that he himself does not believe, he can come to experience a special kind of alienation from self and a special kind of wariness of others' (Goffman, 1959: 229). If we look at recent examples of young people who have chosen to perform through online media such as the trend of NekNominate we can see the impact that these performances can have on the health and social aspects of young people's lives. 'The game has seen people drink blood from the severed artery of a deer; alcohol mixed with dog food, olives and soy sauce; a live goldfish; and large mixes of spirits. Facebook said it was reviewing videos linked to the craze but said that the posting of such material is not a breach of its rules or community standards. Its in-house rules define harmful content as organising world violence, theft, property destruction or something that directly inflicts emotional distress' (Fishwick, 2014).

With the international exhibitors of these performances offering accessible platforms and then distancing themselves from its potential harmful effects it is surely essential that students and all young people are educated on the impact their performance can have on themselves and others.

When asking someone about what performance means to them it is usually followed by a discussion of the theatrical aspects of performance, performance in a theatre, you in the real, physical world performing in front of a real, physical audience. Removing the intended audience and theatrical setting of performance is far from a radical idea. Goffman's idea of *The Presentation of Self in Everyday Life* (1959) is not only relevant to this pedagogical approach but is highly appropriate for applying to aspects of Media. The idea that we adapt who we are and therefore our performance, depending on who we are with is more difficult when our digital performance is to an audience of unknown quantity and origin. Even with further application of Goffman – 'The individual may attempt to induce the audience to judge them and the situation in a particular way' – if we consider that there is no true self, we are just a series of performances and characters, how is this exacerbated by digital media and our performance within it as we to an extent mediate ourselves? This theoretical approach will not be studied in a factual sense: 'So I ask that these papers be taken for what they merely are: exercises, trials, tryouts, a means of displaying possibilities, not establishing fact.' (Goffman, 1981: 1). Applying Goffman to an introduction to Performance in the age of digital media will provide students with an opportunity to discuss and debate their roles and responsibilities within their performances.

TEACHING PERFORMANCE AS MEDIA

Beyond an introduction to this new understanding of performance is a need to explore how Performance can now be analysed, produced and interpreted in a modern media landscape. As a concept that is more associated with Theatre Studies, Drama, English Literature and Film Studies my intention has been to incorporate aspects of all of these subjects of study in the teaching of Performance through Media.

New 'Learning Objectives' are required in order to develop suitable tasks, forms of assessment and consistency across the different approaches and texts. The following learning objectives are an amalgamation of learning objectives found in various specifications for subjects where Performance is integral to the course of study. They are by no means the only way that the concept of Performance can be assessed but offer a point to begin this discussion.

LO1: Apply practical and digital skills to communicate in Performance.

LO2: Relate performances to their social, cultural and historical contexts; explain how performances have been influential and significant to self, and other audiences in different contexts and at different times.

LO3: Demonstrate knowledge and understanding of how performances communicate meanings, evoke personal responses and engage audiences.

In this pedagogic approach one of my key objectives is to ensure that 'the Media' is still taught and we do not turn this opportunity into just a hybrid of already existing subjects which would be easily done with a concept as apparently traditional and rigid as Performance. This should be done in two key ways; the first the analysis of Performance through an understanding of Media Language and the second the application of key media theories to the texts and performances that are being studied. Developing a way you can incorporate theoretical approaches of key media concepts such as Genre, Representation, Narrative and Audience will create paradigms where core elements of the teaching of media as we know it can remain. Applying the concept of Media Language to Performance is something media teachers will be familiar with, whether it is the analysis of *mise-en-scène* from a still frame of a film, or a more complex analysis of the performance of a character throughout an entire TV drama. It is the application of theory that may at first appear slightly more difficult to crowbar into the study of Performance but if we see performance as an element of text then they can still be applied as rigorously. Below are a number of critical approaches I will be discussing or making reference to throughout this chapter and questions arising:

Audience

How can a certain performance appeal to an audience?

To what extent do the audience contribute to the performance?

How does one perform when the audience is not identifiable?

Genre

How can a performance be deemed conventional?

Is a user's online performance influenced by the genre?

Narrative

How can characterisation be analysed?

How does a performance impact the events and outcomes of a text?

Representation

How can someone use performance to construct a certain representation?

How can representations be decoded differently depending on how they are mediated?

FLATTENED HIERARCHY

As text-based study is the approach of the subjects I have previously mentioned, I will try to present a coherent way of delivering this topic through text. Each of these texts can be linked to at least one other text being studied through aspects of their contained performances, a transperformance approach will allow for a more holistic understanding and lessen the opportunity to fall back into segregated traditional subjects. For this to truly be an example of performance analysis through different texts, then a flattened hierarchy must be referred to. No aspect of this course can value the original Shakespeare text of *Much Ado about Nothing* over its contemporary film interpretations and nor can either of them be viewed as more academic or applicable than a videogame. Each text, medium and the form of performance that is associated with them must be given equal recognition and measured against the same criteria.

Performance in a Literary Text – *Much Ado About Nothing*

If we begin our text-based study with something that is contemporary and yet offers a sense of familiarity when we concern ourselves with the analysis of performance, we can take the Joss Whedon film adaptation of *Much Ado About Nothing* (2013). The film offers a modern setting that replaces Messina with an upper-middle-class Californian suburb. Analysing this film interpretation would offer insight into how the use of camera, sound and editing can change how a performance is interpreted and convey certain meanings to its intended audience. Analysing media language opens up a whole different approach when analysing a performance as compared to analysing a physical performance in a theatre for example. How a brutal editing cut could cut a character's speech short, how a change to the frame rate might influence an audience's interpretation of the performer's movement, how the use of sound, both diegetic and non-diegetic, can reinforce or challenge certain meanings encoded in a performance or how the positioning of a camera can reconstruct a certain representation are just some the of ideas that students would have to consider when analysing a performance through a moving image media text. As media practitioners we will all be familiar with the impact that media language can have on a performance but it is ensuring that the students understand the power of the medium in this instance and that arguably a director of a film or TV drama has a wider choice of creative opportunities to influence how an audience interpret a particular performance.

This aspect of studying performance would be accessible as it is hoped that students' understanding gained from this analysis would enable them to produce any independent presentations or investigations to a higher standard. How to analyse a performance within any medium is something that can prove difficult, even in a more traditional scenario: 'Most analyses of cinematic performance focus on three areas of an actor's performance style: his or her gestures, facial expressions and vocal qualities' (Marcello, 2006: 59), elements that are very familiar to Media practitioners and students as they fall within the *mise-en-scène*, but a performance-specific course would require a much more rigorous look at the performance of actors and actresses something that could prove more challenging than initially expected. 'The task of performance analysis [in Theatre, Dance and Film] is enormously demanding, so much so that it is perhaps beyond the skills of any one person. Effectively it requires one to take into account the complexity and range of types of performance, using series of available methods or even inventing other methodologies better suited to one's particular project and objectives' (Pavis, 2006: 1). Developing this new methodology to work across different forms of performance and types of text within different subject areas, and equally across a flattened hierarchy, would enhance a sense of continuity across the course of study and strengthen students' understanding and confidence through the repeated application of the same methodology.

Studying *Much Ado About Nothing* as a transmedia text would allow students to challenge the dominant misconceptions that some forms of media are worth more than any other. Giving the film interpretations the same amount of time for discussion and justification to add further insight and to reinforce the concept of a flattened hierarchy would be a method for enabling their validity. One could also deliver teaching on the BBC series ShakespeaRE-Told (BBC One, 2005) that had its first episode, in a similar way to Whedon's interpretation, contained in a contemporary setting.

One of the notable differences in the performances within this interpretation as opposed to the original text is the visual motif of drinking. 'Among the numerous clever touches is the constant drinking, both at the parties and in between, with hangovers confronted by hairs of the dog and Claudio and Don Pedro sharing a hip flask. Why do these people behave so oddly and believe anything they're told? Because much of the time they're half-sloshed' (French, 2013). These subtle differences in how the performances are constructed between this and a more predictable interpretation of the text such as

Kenneth Branagh's film adaptation from 1993 (which offers a period setting in Messina as opposed to modern California). Historical context could be approached from different angles, such as an exploration on the impact of sociocultural context on performance such as when it was originally produced (sixteenth century England) compared with contemporary versions. This text would allow for an investigation into the performance within genre and how an actor/actress may perform within a particular genre such as romantic comedy, for which *Much Ado About Nothing* is credited as being a huge influence: '*Much Ado About Nothing* has been the most influential. Almost the entire history of Hollywood romantic comedy, beginning with the first screwball comedy, Frank Capra's *It Happened One Night*, in 1934, flows from its font' (Vineberg, 2013). The film theory of the genre cycle would allow for different analytical approaches depending on the phase the text was in; can a performance be innovative, classical, parodist or revisionist? I believe it would be best that if we are teaching Media through revisited concepts such as Performance, then where possible we need to ensure the application of Media theories and approaches is maintained.

Much Ado About Nothing – Forms of Assessment

LO2 and LO3:

Evidence for Assessment

- An Analysis of Performance
- An Artefact.

For assessment of LO2 and LO3 for this text, the Literary Text, a written analysis and an artefact could be produced. A comparative analysis lends itself to the written form and allows students to articulate their interpretations clearly and in detail. This analysis would enable them to compare the social, cultural and historical aspects of each text as well as explain how the performances of certain characters have been influential and the impact they have had on different audiences at different times. For example a comparison between Michael Keaton's (1993) and Nathan Fillion's (2013) Dogberry would offer an insight in how historical context and setting of a media text can influence a performance. Keaton approached his performance as a clown whereas Filion's was reimagined as a police officer: 'There are a million ways to play Shakespearean clowns – back in '93, Keaton went in a big, totally insane direction, and audiences loved it. Fillion played it as this really dumb but officious cop who's quietly insane, and audiences are loving that, too' (Russel, 2013). Whedon's attempt was not to make the performance more serious but if anything to encode a more humorous meaning for the intended audience. 'Here, Dogberry (Nathan Fillion) and Verges (Tom Lenk) are turned into a highly amusing pair of dumb flatfoots from a B-movie, a good cop and bad cop team, who keep confusing their roles and wear dark glasses to look sinister. But they're the ones who, for all their bungling, catch the White House plumbers in Messina's own Watergate scandal. For once they're really funny' (French, 2013).

This comparison could also be extended beyond the characters and their development and could consider the location, setting and the medium in which the performances are contained. A comparative analysis between modern interpretations of the text in a contemporary setting such as Whedon's or David Nicholls' adaptation (2005), with a film where characterisation and setting are much closer to Shakespeare's original productions would provide examples for in depth discussion. Branagh's 1993 version was well received for its understanding of the original text, and in 2014 theatre critic Michael Billington listed it in his top two adaptations: 'But I'd finally plump for two other versions. In 1993, Kenneth Branagh made a first-rate film that began, unforgettably, with the sight of the returning soldiery galloping apace over an Italian plain: Branagh and his then wife, Emma Thompson, invested the raillery with real wit' (Billington, 2014). As the requirements for a group of students to see a live performance of the text may prove too demanding and to also consider that some may perceive theatre performances as not being mediated in a way that a Media Studies course would conclude, it would still be beneficial to compare the adaptations that are accessible and it is useful to be open to this opportunity should it arise: 'Communication as a social tool includes a wide range of functions such as instruction, persuasion, education, entertainment, development and so on. Over the ages, all the communication mediums have evolved themselves to accommodate the various functions of communication and this is true of the theatre as well' (Bhattacharyya, 2013: 2).

Performance in Videogame and Online Media Exchange – *Disney Infinity*

With a grounding in the traditional and a modern interpretation of Performance, students could then be in a position to apply this to an existing text for a case study. The obvious candidate for this would be an online, multi-player videogame. This would challenge students to employ their understanding of Performance and apply it to a more familiar text. One of the more successful forms of videogames are currently those that offer a sandbox mode. This format of game reached mainstream success with *Minecraft* (2009) which allows users to create their own world within the game and is not limited to a particular narrative structure, hence the term sandbox. *Disney Infinity* (Avalanche Software) offers a sandbox mode with the added element of real world physical elements that are required to play the game. This is something that was explored with *Skylanders* (Activision, 2011) but *Disney Infinity* combined the physical elements with both a sandbox mode, referred to as ToyBox mode within the game itself, and the online multi-player aspects. Therefore, for a user to make significant progress within the game world they are required to both perform in their own physical world and within their online world using various Disney Characters to visually and physically represent their online avatar identities.

As a case study *Disney Infinity* would allow students to explore their own understanding of Performance in contemporary media context and apply what they have gained from any previous more traditional analysis of a text such as *Much Ado About Nothing*. The often-used theories of Uses and Gratifications (Blumler and Katz) and to some extent a number of narrative theories, explored in real depth. could be an effective approach at this point. The narrative being entirely driven by the users' real world and online/digital performance brings a challenge to the majority of theories that would be explored on a typical A level Media Studies course.

How a student could apply Goffman's theory of self-perception to a game where a user selects a fictional Disney character to represent their identity could offer interesting results that would allow the students to reinforce their knowledge of Goffman's ideas as well as further their understanding of the moral and social implications of performing to an invisible audience. With aspects of the game not necessarily requiring online multi-players but with users finding the game more cohesive and in-depth as a result of collaborating with other users online, the game is designed to encourage online performance and participation. 'Speaking of multiplayer: I've played these levels cooperatively on the couch so far (the screen splits to give each player their own view of the action), but it seems to me that this is the ideal way to play it; having a friend to team up and tackle challenges with is probably the most efficient way of getting things done.' (Kohler, 2013). To form a consistent analysis through the entire scheme it would be useful to utilise some of the more familiar techniques that are used in studying Drama, the analysis of characterisation. The three areas that are the foundation for this form of the analysis body language, vocal qualities and their reaction to events within the drama can be applied to a text such as *Disney Infinity*.

Analysis of body language could be carried out on the user's interaction with the physical toys of the game and the responses that their real world performance has on the gameplay. Vocal qualities are the second aspect of characterisation analysis and could be used to investigate the vocal commands and the use of communication employed by the users. This would allow for an exploration in the relationship between users as well as how the vocal commands influence the performance driven narrative of the game. However, it is the third aspect of this method of analysis I feel would reveal the most interesting analysis, the way in which performers react to events in the drama/videogame. Analysing the characters/users reactions could also allow us to measure the reactions to other gamers depending on their actions and online identities opening an opportunity to apply Goffman's theory once again.

Disney Infinity – Forms of Assessment

LO1 and LO3:

Evidence for Assessment

- A written investigation on their own experiences
- A demonstration
- An evaluation.

As *Disney Infinity* offers the students the most unique example of performance, the method in which they are assessed must reflect this. Over this course of study students would be expected to investigate and take part in the videogame keeping a record through the use of an evaluative commentary. They would be considering how they felt the physicality of the game potentially made it more engaging and how they responded to constructing their online identities. Blumler and Katz's Uses and Gratifications theory, Goffman's presentation of self and Henry Jenkins' thoughts on the impact of our online identities would be key media theories that could be applied to this section of work. 'The last several decades of observation of the digital world teaches us that the digital world is never totally disconnected from the real world. Even when we go onto the digital world to "escape" reality, we end up engaging with symbolic representations that we read in relation to reality. We learn things about our first lives by stepping into a second or parallel life which allows us to suspend certain rules, breakout of certain roles, and see the world from a fresh perspective' (Jenkins, 2007). Applying these three models would require the students to regularly ask themselves three important questions: Why would I play this videogame? (Uses and Gratifications); In what ways do I alter my online performance and what are the reasons behind this? (Goffman); and How does my online performance impact on myself in the real world and vice versa (Jenkins)?

After students have demonstrated an understanding of these theoretical approaches and applied them to their engagement with the text, they would be in a position to formalise their findings into a written investigation. Like many current Media Studies courses, investigation into this combination of primary research and relevant theories could be reinforced with the results of secondary research, focus groups, interviews and class discussions. One aspect of this investigation would be to analyse the performance of others within the game, so it may be beneficial to have them complete some of their work in groups, asking questions about other users of the game before analysing their performance within it. As a method for further assessment of the performance aspect students could summarise their findings in a performance. This performance could comprise of a presentation that summarises their key findings as well as a demonstration of the game and a discussion of how they interact with the physical and digital worlds to drive the narrative forward. An evaluation on how the process has affected them, to what extent they think the theoretical models apply and how they view engaging with the videogame as a performance could be the final form of assessment on this case study, ensuring that they reflect on any assessment criteria such as how playing the videogame evoked certain responses from them and how the physicality and the performance aspects of the game may make the text more engaging for an audience.

Performance in Mass Media – *The PlayStation Network*

The users who are familiar with playing *Disney Infinity* on a PlayStation will also be familiar with the PlayStation Network (PSN) and despite its controversial history (a security intrusion occurred in April 2010 affecting 77 million users) it has gained in popularity. There are currently over 150 million users registered on the PlayStation Network (Gamesindustry.biz, 2013), such popularity is perhaps down to the fact that registration is, to a point, forced; in order to access the online capabilities of a game such as *Disney Infinity* you must become a registered user. It appears that one of the objectives for the PSN is to allow the audience to engage (perform) with one another on a series of different in game and out of game interfaces. The motivation for this is to increase the audience engagement in the videogames and give them a clearer sense of identity online as we as a social platform: 'First and foremost we just want to help people discover content. It'll certainly help get the word out... but the intention is really to give gamers a place to show off their accomplishments, show people what they're doing, what they like, and get them talking' (Lempel, 2013). The use of the terms 'show off'' and 'to show people' is clearly linked to this idea of online performance; rather than showing off our sport skills on a pitch in front of friends we are now showing off our gaming skills to a potential audience of millions. From our everyday performance to our online performance we have seen an exponential increase in the audience size. Online our performances are more accessible, editable and to an extent out of our hands. This study into the PSN expands on what was explored in the introductory section on the implications of applying Goffman's theories on the online age and the moral and dangerous implications of anybody's online performance. To make this performance available across multiple platforms, allowing your online identity to be altered more frequently, Sony has developed an app that is available on Android and iPhones. This app allows you to 'See what your friends are playing, compare trophies and view your profile or recent activity. Chat with your friends, receive notifications, game alerts and invitations' (Sony, 2015). Allowing the users to utilise the PSN from almost anywhere through a mobile device gives them the opportunity to maintain a consistent performance. The appeal of see *what your friends are playing* is an invitation to witness their performance and compare it with your own. The other side to this is the possibility that not being able to visibly see your audience would reduce your ability to communicate as a result of the lack of social cues. The idea is that as are performances are being communicated and mediated through an online interface we are less concerned by the implications of them compared to when they take place in reality.

The PlayStation Network – Forms of Assessment

LO1 and LO3:

Evidence for Assessment

- Video Blog
- Written Report.

Similarly to and possibly even as an extension of the *Disney Infinity* case study this element of the course could be assessed through a video blog with an accompanying written report that documents the students' own experiences, thoughts and findings. It would be useful for them to refer to key theorists on the gratifications gained from being an audience to other peoples' online performances as well as the way they construct performance themselves. The video blog would allow them to deepen their understanding of post-performance analysis and using the SHAREfactory tool on the PlayStation network that would allow student record and share their in-game performances. The students would also be able to record the additional audio commentary provided by all the gaming participants via their headphone sets, allowing for a recording of both the visual and oral performances of each individual. An analysis of these performances within this type of interface also lends itself to the production of video artefacts; the PSN allows you to exhibit highlight reels of your latest online gaming performances to specific audiences and via social networks. It would be expected that a discussion of how those performances relate to the real world performances, the online personality and the more conventional profile that the performer utilizes would take place. This would be an opportunity for students to refer to key media and social theories and explore the meaning of performance in this context.

Referring to Goffman once again students could explore to what extent the lack of a true self and a life-long performance are extended by the use of an online gaming environment and what factors cause users to perform differently within different genres of games, depending on capacity of other users. An exploration into the differences between the performance of everyday life and the online gaming performance would also be a tool to encourage students to explore the definition of performance.

Remixing Performance with DIY Home Creativity

> DIY media in this sense are very much characterised by people being able to produce their own media – whether they be radio-like podcasts, original remixed music, animated video shorts, music videos – by making use of software, hardware and 'insider' skills, techniques and knowledge that were previously the domain of highly-trained experts who had access to specialised and typically very expensive media production know-how, resources and spaces. (Lankshear and Knobel 2010: 10)

Without getting tied down to the idea that a lot of the technical and production based skills that would be traditionally taught in a media lesson, it is important to accept that the production of professional standard media is now more accessible and consistent amongst young media students. Producing a performance in this mode would allow students to explore their ideas and apply a reflexive approach to their production. An existing understanding of modern media practices would be a key aspect for this and would ideally exist based upon prior learning. Having this would also allow students to develop and apply critical and digital skills to construct a performance within its new definition. This performance could be presented in a variety of different interpretations influenced by one or all of the case studies that have been explored. Students should be challenged to take control of the DIY media tools available to them and given freedom to produce a performance within a media product.

They could make a short film or music video considering the use of film language in constructing a performance, building on what they learned through their analysis of *Much Ado About Nothing* or a similar text. As a big part of DIY Media is the 'remaking' or 'remixing' of existing products, they could take an existing performance from a moving image media source and remix it. Enabling them to change the meaning of a performance by altering the pace of the editing, changing the music or cropping a frame would be an extension of learning earlier in the course applied through new technical tools. This practice would not only allow students to hone their DIY Media skills but extensively explore their understanding of how performances in the moving image media are constructs of the producer's intentions. Initially, DIY Media was seen more for an opportunity to voice political ideas that challenged the dominant classes and the perceivably biased mass media. 'Today a small number of large companies own, control and produce most of our popular culture. The remix video (as an example of DIY Media) process provides a powerful way of taking back to this mass media machine. It is a way to communicate using that audio –visual language in poetic, humorous, poignant and entertaining ways' (Jenkins, 2010).

Ultimately, the majority of DIY media that is now constructed by the 'audience' is intended to change the meaning of something that already exists, and the performance of characters within these texts is a large part of this. This would be an investigation that truly explored the influence that aspects of media language can have on how performances can be interpreted and the meanings that they communicate. A classic example of the success of DIY Media, and one that I believe many students would find accessible and entertaining, is the *Scary Mary* (2006) remix of the *Mary Poppins* (1964) trailer by Christopher Rule. The trailer is a complete change of tone from the original text and the performance of Julie Andrews as Mary Poppins is switched from the authoritative and caring nanny to an almost supernatural, intimidating and frightening character. For this remix no additional visual footage has been added – it is just an altering to the soundtrack and the editing structure. Sound and editing are key aspects into how this performance has been constructed. Leading with this example would demonstrate to students the impact that media language can have on a performance and allow them to expand on the points that were raised when discussing the idea of theatrical performances being less mediated than their audio-visual medium-based counterparts. It also raises significant questions about the impact that existing media concepts can have on performance, the visual style of a film switching from the bright coloured London to a low key, shadowy and almost gothic aesthetic challenging the audience's understanding of the character.

DIY Media – Forms of Assessment

> LO1 and LO3:
>
> Evidence for Assessment

- A remixed media product.

To truly reflect the DIY emphasis on this part of the course students could be expected to complete elements of this task outside of lessons. There would also be pedagogical opportunities for innovative use of differentiation through selecting trailers or clips for the students, asking them to manipulate how audiences read the performance of characters. A presentation by the students of the video with an explanation of how it was constructed and a comparison of the intended readings of the original and the remixed version would allow the students to demonstrate their skills and knowledge clearly.

PERFORMANCE ART

> Performance art is where an artist uses their own body as an art medium and the artwork takes the form of actions performed by the artist. (Tate Gallery definition, 2015)

Utilising Performance art to retain the more traditional and typically known aspects of performance whilst combing those ideas with a broader understanding of the term would allow students to demonstrate a wider spectrum of what they have learned. Performance art is interdisciplinary. The interdisciplinary aspect of this is what reinforces the course of study that performances and subject are limited by boundaries but are dynamic paradigms that audience and producers can manipulate, engage with and construct. All of these possibilities could be reflected in a final assessment in the form of a Performance art piece. 'At the heart of performance art is a strong social critique. It asks important questions about how we perceive the world around us and our place within it' (Skinner). There are some strong moral and critical questions that are raised within this course of study and encouraging the students to critique and challenge these ideas would lead to more independent and thoughtful work. The interdisciplinary aspects of this would allow students to demonstrate their understanding of performance in all of its interpretations and provide a transmedia performance that remixed the physical world with the digital. Blurring the lines of our online and real world performances is not a new concept and is something that has been explored by contemporary performance artists as they respond to the world around them. Brooklyn artist Man Bartlett uses his physical performance and online performance to try and engage people with rethinking how they use social media: 'Bartlett has turned New York's Port Authority bus station into a platform for an interactive online experience with #24hPort and translated tweets into sculpture with "Kith and Kin"' (Chen 2012).

An example of a transmedia approach to Performance art would be the *Suspiria* installation by Stan Douglas (2003). This was an example of digitally enhanced performance that embraced different technologies and was an extension of an existing media text. The installation involved a live cast, projectors and live editing and image manipulation at various places in the German town of Kassel. The actors were acting out some of the classic Grimm fairy tales to a soundtrack and visual style that reflected the Italian horror film *Suspiria* (Dario Argento, 1977). The majority of the audience would never actually 'see' the performances but instead a manipulated live projection at various places in the town, predominantly places that reflected the tone and atmosphere that Douglas and Argento were trying to convey in their works. As Nell McClister explains this is an imaginative exploration of the concept of performance. 'In Kassel, live surveillance footage of the empty, dungeon like labyrinth beneath the Herkules monument (one of many follies in the area) was projected in the Fridericianum across town. Scenes from the Grimms' fairy tales, acted out by a contemporary-looking cast in the grotesque, translucent palette of a color television with bad reception, were superimposed at intervals on the black-and-white surveillance video; sporadic voice-over and fragments of music accompanied the actors' dialogue' (McClister, 2003).

The relevance of this example of performance art is the aspect of multi-media and transmedia storytelling, which would be an effective way of assessing any students who would be required to produce an artefact in this form. Performance art is potentially the most fluid and interpretative form of performance and would allow a great opportunity for a final summative form of assessment. In a similar fashion to the way that current Media students are expected to reflect on and evaluate on their practical controlled assessment in their external exams as well as apply a number of key media theories to their own work, this would allow for a cross-media task. As an example a student who may have studied some of the texts that have been mentioned earlier in this chapter could incorporate their interpretations of *Much Ado About Nothing* and engineer methods that this could be digitised and exhibited in ways that would be identifiable as similar to videogames or social networks. This task would also require the students to provide their first example of their own performance in the traditional sense, although it should be expected that this performance is still mediated to some extent, such as the use of live editing and projectors from Douglas' *Suspiria* installation.

As I write this the future of this integral subject becomes more unclear, an unfair and troglodytic approach to Media Studies consistently undermines the subject, its teachers and its students. Therefore if we are thrust into a position where we are asked to meet certain criteria rather than shown a space to walk into, we need to ensure that whatever the outcomes are that the version of the subject that remains finally gains the respect and the legitimacy that other subjects gain without exertion.

WORKS CITED

Billington, M. (2014) 'Best Shakespeare productions: Much Ado About Nothing', *The Guardian*.

Bhattacharyya, K.K. (2013) *Interpreting Theatre as a Communication Medium*, Centre for Journalism and Mass Communication, Bengal.

Brightman, J. (2013) 'PlayStation Plus has seen 'significant growth' says Sony', *gamesindustry.biz*.

Fishwick, C. (2014) 'NekNominate: should Facebook ban the controversial drinking game?', *The Guardian*.

French, P. (2013) 'Much Ado About Nothing – review', *The Guardian*.

Garner, R. (2015) 'Finland schools: Subjects scrapped and replaced with 'topics' as country reforms its education system', *The Independent*.

Goffman, E. (1990) *The Presentation of Self in Everyday Life*. London: Penguin.

Harris, B. (1972) *Schools without Subjects?*, The Association for Supervision and Curriculum Development.

Hayes, D. (2010) *Education in an 'information age', A defense of subject based education*, IOI Education.

Jenkins, H. (2011) 'Announcing Transmedia, Hollywood 2: Visual Culture and Design', *Confessions of an Acca Fan*.

Kohler, C. (2014) 'Disney Infinity is massive, a little broken and a lot of fun', *Wired Magazine*.

Knobel, M. and Lankshear, C. (2010) *DIY Media: Creating, Sharing and Learning with New Technologies*. London: Peter Lang Publishing.

MacDonald, K. and Cousins, M. (1998) *Imagining Reality: The Faber Book of Documentary*. London: Faber.

Marcello, S. (2006) 'Performance Design: An Analysis of Film Acting and Sound Design', *Journal of Film and Video*. Illinois.

McClister, N. (2003) *Suspiria*. Stan Douglas, The Art Forum.

Pavis, P. (2003) *Analysing Performance: Theatre, Dance and Film*. Michigan: University of Michigan Press.

Russell, M. (2013) 'Interview with Nathan Fillion', *The Oregonain*.

Shakespeare, W. (2015) *As You Like It*. London: Penguin.

Vineberg, S. (2013) 'Much Ado About Nothing and Romantic Comedy, Critics at Large'.

8: CONNECTING TEXT

Christopher Waugh

AGENCY

Students in my secondary English classes no longer write in books. They exist and work in an open online community. We shifted our work online in pursuit of a set of key goals.

As an English department it was our desire to increase their agency as learners. We wanted to make their learning experience a more authentic reflection of how they engage with the world and we aimed to raise their autonomy in the process. To do this we created a personal blog, open to the outside world and unique to its owner, for every teacher and student in the school. We built class blogs and blogs for clubs and groups and we brought them all together under the umbrella we call *The Edutronic*.

Some might imagine our primary motive was to attract students with the lure of modern technology and methods, but this was not the case. The clear imperative, if we were to solve the challenges we faced in motivating and inspiring our cohort of inner London boys to engage with their English learning, was that we had to shift the locus of control, and responsibility, in the classroom from the teacher, to the space between us and the students. It's in this space to which we have shifted the heart of the learning experience, and it's in this space that we position the core artefact of our collaboration – the students' work, our primary text.

Schools and classrooms have maintained a degree of isolation from the outside world that is making what we do in them increasingly rarefied. If the product of the classroom has no referent or context outside the classroom, the value of it will also be steadily diminished.

The connected text, posted onto an online blog, is a fluid, interactive entity. It is the central pivot around which all other learning balances. Teachers, students, collaborators, family, peers, audience and critics all engage with the text produced by the student and each leaves their unique mark. The text enters the flow of the great literary heritage about which we often learn in the classroom, and in doing so, the student-author builds a sense of their own agency in the world and the impact they may have on it. To explore how this might affect the study of a Shakespearian play in English, throughout this chapter I will introduce a range of characters from my classes, the play *Romeo and Juliet* and *The Edutronic*.

Even in the early stages of the study, students avidly use their blogs to record their learning experience, whether it be summaries of scenes and captured quotations, or initial exploration of language and themes. So far, so familiar. Quickly, new players enter the fray, adding a frisson to the plot, as can be seen here in the comments made by the students' family under an entry exploring language in *Romeo and Juliet*:

Armend:

Very well described, through your understanding of the play and excellent use of vocabulary....Well done!!!

Myrvete:

I am very pleased with you and your positive attitude towards writing. Great piece of work and I am always looking forward to reading your work. Keep it up :-))

Myrvete

From the journal of Lis Fejzullahu, age 13.

http://lis.community.edutronic.net/analyse-language-english-project-part-2-act-1-scene-4-act-4-scene-2/

And thus, the family are engaged in the learning experience.

Authenticity – the now

We dispute the notion that the classroom is primarily a venue for the preparation of students for the 'real world'. To us, and our students, the classroom is very much the real world. In the classroom, our experience is rich, complex, unpredictable and frequently demands everything of us. We don't come to the classroom in order to be ready for some imperceptible future, we come to luxuriate in the now. This being the case, it becomes inevitable that the product of our time in the classroom, often a text, should also be invested with a status and integrity that befits the setting from which it arose. In this way, students create text that has purpose beyond the instruments and culture of the education system.

> Hi there people, this is Samy welcoming you to Edutronic. Edutronic is a site where you can be able to talk to the world from your very own computer. You can tell the world about how you're feeling or just what your homework is by publishing your work like I am doing now. When you send your work you can either choose if you want your work to be seen by the world or you can just send it to your teacher by using the private button. Edutronic is a new exciting way to produce your work. So have Fun.

Samy Salim, age 12: First entry to his online journal.

http://samysalim.student.edutronic.net/2012/10/05/welcome-to-edutronic/

8: CONNECTING TEXT

In our department the notion of writing text in order to achieve a grade is an anathema. Our students create texts to communicate ideas, feelings, fragments of their real and imagined lives. They write to record experiences and sometimes to help themselves to think through a complicated idea. We work to help them to create texts that achieve these objectives, and as part of this, we will employ the tools we have created to measure and acknowledge thresholds through which the students may pass in their development as writers.

These thresholds are not the objective of the writing. It does not follow that while a teacher must define and record students' attainment and progress in order to identify opportunities for further learning – or simply to feed the state school bureaucracy – that this measure should be treated as the primary outcome of the students' efforts.

This fluidity of the students' connected texts has led to a complete redevelopment of our means of assessment. Our new schemes of summative validation and feedback are set up as fixed standards. These are published online too, supported by detailed exemplars and represented by badges. Students can put their work forward for consideration and, if successful, are able to unlock multiple achievements with one piece of work. If they are unsuccessful they will go back to the work and further refine it.

Like everything else in the learning experience the assessment processes orbit around the primary text, validating aspects and skills demonstrated, but never over-shadowing it or exerting so much of a gravitational force as to distort its central purpose, as defined by the author.

Here Jamie is exploring the use of personification in *Macbeth*.

> Shakespeare uses a wide variety of dramatic devices in the play Macbeth. A dramatic device Macbeth uses is personification in this extract from Act 2 Scene 1. Macbeth sees a dagger before him which is an illusion and potentially a sign of madness. He says
>
> 'Thou marshall'st me the way I was going; and such a instrument I was to use.'
>
> Macbeth uses personification by using the object - in this case a knife - as if it were a living being. In this quote Macbeth uses the words 'marshall'st me' which means it is guiding him. He says this to the knife which he is imagining to see in front of his eyes. He says to the knife to guide him as a metaphor to control the way he is going. The quote chosen shows hints of remorse even if he continues with the plan to kill King Duncan. In the play Macbeth sees a dagger because he is uncertain whether to kill Duncan or not. He feel weakness if he doesn't continue with the plan but will feel remorse if he continues so he needs guidance on what he is going to do. He uses the dagger to justify his actions.

Comment:

Chris Waugh: Jamie, your work is always impressive and this analysis is no exception.

I'd like to address some aspects of the mechanics of your writing. In particular the sentence structure. Could you have a look at the sentence:

'A complex device is personification in this extract from Act 2 Scene 1.'

and let me know if you can't think of a way of making it more clear. If you can't, I'll help you out.

This piece clearly meets the criteria for the Discovery badge – so well done. It has now been awarded to you!

Fig. 8.1 The Discovery Badge

If you'd like to develop it further and try for the Stage 3 'Figure it out' badge, then you'll want to add more exploration of why Shakespeare is using this personification with Macbeth at this stage of the play – what's it telling the audience about Macbeth's state of mind and what motivates him?

Righto!

CW

Jamie Souffrin-Watts, age 12. http://jsouffrin-watts.community.edutronic.net/personification/

After receiving the comment, Jamie has clearly gone back to his analysis and developed it further to explore the wider implications of the invisible dagger. Further to this he then made a prop of the dagger from this scene, which was rendered with a transparent blade, indicating that it is in fact a 'dagger of the mind'. Another student produced a wireframe outline of a dagger to represent the same effect. They all uploaded images of these made objects to their blogs to sit alongside their written analysis.

The student's connected text has its own integrity, its own purpose and it is as much judged by its audience and author as it might be by the teacher. In this way we do not assume we are always the founts of all knowledge, and I will often cede my role as arbiter of all value. Instead the teacher becomes an ally in the process; sometimes we are a guide, sometimes an editor, sometimes a reader and at other times an active and avid contributor to the conversation the text has stimulated. Connecting a classroom text allows for it to reach an audience, be archived for future reference, be modified, replicated, contested. A connected text can fulfil its human purpose, whatever that may be.

Students' learning should not be devised in such a way as it divorces the form and its purpose. I have seen students being given a pen and paper to 'write an email' to an imagined employer to ask for a job. This 'email' is then taken in by a teacher and marked for written accuracy and stylistic fidelity. No-one would argue with the value of being able to perform this kind of writing task, but there must be a strong argument against this kind of activity in terms of the confusion of purpose. Few people write to prove they can write. They write to think, to record and to communicate. With this impetus denied them, is there any surprise that students lose interest in writing?

Surely students could simply be asked to do a similar task: write an email. The email should be written on a computer and should address a real query to an actual person who exists in the world of the student. This is real. The students will care more about their spelling and form in this scenario than any kind of high-stakes system assessment could ever enforce. The holy grail of students' concern over the accuracy of their own writing is achieved with shocking ease, it is as natural as the actual process of making the corrections needed.

AUTONOMY

The benefit of a connected text is not as simple as merely 'having an audience'. The act of choice in sending something out into the world, under your own name, and of your own creation is a singularly autonomous act. This assertion of self is not uncommon for students in a school classroom, in fact it is an important part of what makes the school such a real and authentic place for students and teachers alike, but the formalisation of this in text is unique. The affordances of this self-assertion are often immediately clear. The text, which frequently represents the most tangible product of the classroom experience for students, extends their voice. The value they place on it is reinforced by the fact that they have the power to publish the text to the world. It has to pass through no gatekeeper and no filtering system, it simply comes into existence as a result of their will. Once again, they are not rehearsing for the real world, they are entering it.

Yet, blogs provide a number of mechanisms for moderation and mediation. Students can act autonomously and, at the same time, adults can observe and subtly moderate the whole process. Young people need this mediation in the online world, and the leap of faith that adults make when engaging with students in the online domain is one that instantly engages them as moderators and guides. Working with students and the text they create online also allows another conversation to progress, the one about the online identity and the far-reaching, often indelible, impact of putting anything online under your own name. A conversation about the future web-search performed by a prospective employer will often help bring to sharp focus the substance of any online utterance.

Students already use connected texts via a wide range of social media platforms to engage with the world and define and discover who they are - to us it's imperative that the work we do with them, exploring the world's great texts and developing language and self-expression, happens in this setting too, so that they may continue to incorporate what they learn in the classroom into their own fabric of experience.

THE ESTABLISHED WRITTEN TEXT

We believe it is again time to rewrite the rules about learning in English that are being continuously refined over the centuries of what some might call the great English Literary Heritage. As teachers have always done, we simply, and humbly, hope to introduce more students more effectively to the world of the text and ensure they have access to it for their entire lives.

In our classrooms the established, canonical literary text is still an object of great importance. We work hard to develop lines of inquiry that originate from ideas and features in the literary texts selected from the canon. In finding transformative value in connecting these texts to our students' own experience, we haven't abandoned our belief in the great value of the printed plays, novels and poetry in our curriculum - nor their existing modes of transmission. It is also not our view that the connected text has usurped these other forms in literature. Instead we see the connected text as a venue for the exploration of these texts - and potentially a catalyst for the creation of great literature of the future.

Students can use their online blog to record quotes and data about a literary text they are studying. They can record themselves reading or performing excerpts or store images of related objects. They can even readily assimilate third-party information into their own responses, further augmenting the role a single teacher can play in developing the range and sophistication of their responses to a primary text. We will often engage in a conversation with the student as part of their online text that allows them to support and refine the use for this extraneous information. In this way the online text enables the development of the skills of selection and deduction of information, as well as assimilation from external sources - as opposed to the typical 'online research' procedure which largely consists of the reproduction of existing, authorised, facts and information.

> **Henry:** (27 December 2012) Hey Sir, I was just wondering if you had read my piece yet, as you're normally very speedy at replying to things. Hope your breaks going well.
>
> **Chris Waugh:** ...The observation and thinking inherent in this answer is outstanding, Henry. Genuinely outstanding. I'd now like to work with you to craft your writing so its sophistication matches that of the ideas you're expressing. Let's discuss it on Tuesday. In the meantime I'd like to show you a couple of examples of other pieces of writing

that you might like to use as a guide for your own development. I'll upload them here to your journal.

Dr Ovenden: Henry, I agree with Mr Waugh's comments on your insightful analysis. I look forward to reading the redrafted version. Good luck!

Milo: Well, Henry I used some of your work for my English essay

Henry: I am continuing with my essay on fate, but have a look at this article I found online: [URL removed] I'm not sure what you will think of it, but I was looking at the script, then was wondering why they blame everything on fate. This is a testament to that.

Henry Howeld, age 12. Excerpts from the comment stream on drafts for an essay on fate in *Romeo and Juliet*.

http://henryashoweld.student.edutronic.net/author/henry/page/10/

These online texts allow our students to engage in their writing or analysis as a crafted process. Henry has taken complete ownership of the process of drafting his essay, and instead of concentrating on what answer the teacher seeks, or what will get him the best grades, he's acting in pursuit of the best answer to the question of fate in the play. The level of autonomy shown by students working online is difficult to achieve in on paper, and their writing demonstrates in content and form a real sense of audience and purpose.

The problem with current methods of teaching is that these core elements are often expressed only as theoretical. Even those text concepts, audience and purpose, have been made abstract in the education system. Whereas an adult writer would consider the purpose of a text or its audience as an integral part of determining its form and content, school student writers have to learn formulae to make the same judgements. They have to determine who the audience 'would be' and what the purpose of the text 'would be' as yet another abstraction of motive. They are then taught forms that match particular purposes (rhetorical questions and the 'rule of three' for persuasive writing, metaphor for descriptive writing).

The crime in this is that as social beings, students already have enormous reserves of knowledge about relevant language registers for various situations and purposes. The abstraction of the context for the texts they create in English at school alienates them from their own experience. They are left having to be taught things they already know, or could determine for themselves based on experience. This in turn devalues their own sense for how language might work in a text. The rigidity of the formulae stifles the infinite variety and nuance in language. The genius that is shown to them in the seminal texts they study is denied in their own writing in the rush to ensure their text fits the prescribed formulae.

THE EDITABLE TEXT

Secondary teachers play a valuable role in the classroom, and the time students spend with them is an extraordinary investment. Placing the students' writing online and thereby shifting the locus of control towards them as authors doesn't imply the devaluation of the expertise of the teacher. If anything, it removes many of the usual social impediments in order to facilitate proper academic engagement.

In connecting the students' writing to the online domain, new options for its use as a cognitive tool are enabled. The primary texts in the classroom have largely been those from the canon that are determined by the syllabus - and this is as it should be. A great deal of metacognitive benefit can be derived from any text where reasoning patterns inherent in the study of literature such as understanding the writer's intention relating to technique, narrative structure, figurative language, symbolism, genre, are explored in pure and comparative terms.

Students' connected texts add a capacity to perform these higher order procedures in relation to their own writing by virtue of one of the key features of an online text: its editability. The students are able to respond to feedback on minute details. Currently in English secondary schools, there is a fad for the requirement that students write a response to the written feedback from their teacher. While this 'green pen rule' is largely a reaction to the desire to make all teacher actions visible to an avid inspectorate, it could not be further from the natural process of editing work. It is designed primarily to provide evidence of assimilation of the feedback by the student, as opposed to being a means of improving their writing. This 'performance of learning' further alienates the writer from the inherent value of engaging in creating text as an artefact, as they are now writing, usually in a green pen, a separate text to validate their understanding of the criticism of the initial draft. Nothing could be less satisfying, or less purposeful.

By contrast, as the connected text remains permanently editable, when feedback is offered, the writer can experiment with that input. They can, should they wish to, engage in a conversation about the recommended change and even seek more - or wider - input. The ease of this process, and the fact that revisions are always stored which allow for the resurrection of older versions, leads to extensive new possibilities for learning about language in writing.

> The silence is deafening and the still air blocks your way like a brick wall. From a distance classroom you can hear the muffled noise of a teacher's music. You will never guess what they listen to, it is torture to your ears.
>
> COMMENT:
>
> **Chris Waugh**
>
> As we discussed, the main job for you to do now is to concentrate on strengthening the imagery in your piece – the notion of 'showing, not telling' will help a lot here.

I like the use of the second-person pronoun 'you' as it offers a real sense of 'being there' to me as a reader.

We also discussed the idea that you may be able to generate an extended military metaphor throughout the piece. If you can do that successfully, you'll lift this work into a new level.

Nice going!

CW

The silence is deafening and the still air blocks your way like a brick wall. **You take every step with precision trying not to get spotted by the enemy. Capture at this point would be the end of the world.** From a distance classroom you can hear the muffled noise of a teacher's music. You will never guess what they listen to, it is torture to your ears.

George Flannagan, age 15.

http://george.student.edutronic.net/2015/02/01/school-from-8-30-to-6-30/

One area of great potential here is the exploration of the literary dimensions of grammar and punctuation. Students are able to explore and implement a range of grammatical formulations in a single piece of writing to experiment with their effect. In doing so they're operating at a highly sophisticated cognitive level. This enables discussion of questions like: 'What effect does combining those two sentences using a relative clause have on the reader's appreciation of the relationship between the two otherwise-unrelated characteristics of the setting?' This can be done online without the student being stifled by the high-stakes effect of making a change that would cause the piece have to be re-written in its entirety for the alteration to be integrated into the work. What's more, the current version is always available to all.

In overcoming the terror of the blank page, the text becomes fluid and responsive, something that is always available for further development. The fear of error is reduced and replaced with a designer's approach to creating texts. The text becomes a made thing, an artefact.

Many of the affordances of visual texts are also present in the connected text. The process of creation is frequently non-linear. Information can be sequenced in many different ways and can incorporate material from many different sources. It can be laid out and re-ordered, re-purposed and placed into new contexts alongside other texts, written or - just as readily - drawn, photographed, filmed or spoken.

Frequently students will leave a piece of work to lie fallow, only to return to it with vigour and energy at a later stage, thereby bringing new knowledge and skill to bear.

THE SOCIAL DISCOURSE

Every text entry on a student's online blog carries with it a comment field. This invites a discussion around intended effects and a reader response that has previously been impossible to achieve. A writer's close relatives and friends will subscribe to their blog and receive any new entries by email the instant they're posted. Students thus already know there's an interested audience there for their work. Comments from teachers enter into a stream where comments also appear from the entire literary world, which both delineates the value and purpose of the teacher's comment. This provides the student with a whole array of other feedback, centred, as always, on the text they create.

Texts are constructed socially through comment-based conversation, discussion in class when the work is displayed on the board, through the gathering of responses from a wide array of people, and ultimately from anonymous readers.

Chris Waugh: Tyrese,

You have created a thing of beauty here. There are many things I love about this poem, but the feature that stands out the most to me is the choices you've made about the line breaks.

I keep going back to read this:

'As fresh as the air,

Like a blade slicing through the wind,

We glide as one you and I,

Even as one lives and one dies.'

…because it really evokes such a strong feeling of exaltation and sadness. What would be a good title, do you think?

Please read this to the class tomorrow.

Colin Tovey (Tyrese's Father)

What he said.

As I told you earlier, Son, you've learned more about the English language in the past year than I've learned in the last 42.

You're a very gifted young man and if this is how you start out then who knows what you can go on to achieve.

We're all very proud of you.

Penny (Internet reader)

Wow! What a great poem, really evocative. It reminds me of the ospreys I've been watching on the web in Wales (they have their own webcam…). That first verse is really powerful – controlled and carefully crafted. Good work.

Kerry Pulley

Hi Tyrese,

I am an English teacher in another school. I hope you don't mind if I comment on your poem. One of the things that I thought was most beautiful, particularly in the first stanza, was the way the number of 'beats' in the lines links so closely with the meaning of the words you have used…

Kaiyum (Peer)

I like the first stanza when you wrote:

We glide as one you and I

Even one live and one dies

This was like a bird eye view as a friend I like it

I would never give you a criticism because it just too good

John Potter (University Lecturer)

Tyrese, I hope that you don't mind that I shared your poem at a talk I did for teachers and other educators at the United Kingdom Literacy Association at the weekend. Also, Mr Waugh, your comments! And all the others. This was after a great talk from the writer Aiden Chambers about the power of writing in our lives. I hadn't planned to do it I just suddenly remembered the last great example I'd seen and shared it and it was your work! There's more to come from you I know! Keep going with it and good luck!

John

Tyrese (Author)

Thanks I would love it.

Tyrese Peters-Tovey, age 11. Selected comments from the Poem "Bird's Eye View" http://tyrese.community.edutronic.net/poem/

In this case the comment stream built over a period of just a few days, clearly demonstrating the power of the social discourse around a connected text. Tyrese was simply performing a classroom task, in this case writing a poem, but the range of responses, from the emotional affirmation from his father to the detailed technical evaluation from the teacher online, lead to him experiencing the empowerment of having his creative work appreciated by others. Again, in this sequence, the teacher played a role, but was not the gatekeeper. Tyrese could access an audience and a response independently of the teacher, which subtly authenticates the creative work of the classroom. Again, the work they do in school becomes the most pressing reality for the student.

Students also engage with the work of others, including students from other classes and other years, as part of their daily work. They look into the texts that others are creating in the same task as they may be performing. The connected text enables a much higher degree of mutual collaboration and peer-teaching than do most clumsy classroom strategies aimed at stimulating this. They inform each other's work, and they show appreciation for each other's success. Their work shows signs of their peer audience and often has encoded within it subtle irony and in-jokes designed only for their specific peer audience. All this is rich and alive, and neither can nor should be described by a curriculum or assessment rubric. While the text is functioning as an expression of the author on the instrumental level - as it fulfils the requirements of the task provided - it also operates on a social level, where it engages in an interplay with selected peers.

This form of multi-level textuality also heralds a new form of 'privacy'. While the online world increasingly moves in the direction where all information is available to everyone all the time, the youth in our classrooms are devising ever more subtle ways of encoding their social messages underneath the surface via idiom. This rich vein of nuanced language is enabled in the connected text by virtue of its existing in the public domain.

TEXT COMMUNITY

Knowledge is important, but what's even more important is knowing what to do with it. In the past, students would closely guard their written answers for fear that one of their peers might gain advantage by accessing their best material. These days they are becoming increasingly aware that the real capacity that is going to be of value, once they have acquired the requisite knowledge to be able to effectively evaluate and analyse their current problem, is their ability to express their ideas with clarity and effect.

Some of our students' journal entries that provide effective and detailed analysis of core English texts already gain first page rankings on popular search engines for even the most generic of search phrases. They have accessed the academic world for themselves, and they have added something that is of value to others.

8: CONNECTING TEXT

The endurance of an online text allows a narrative to build as years pass. Old work is not discarded; rather, it passes into the history of the students' wider body of work. Ultimately, through this publishing format their work enters exactly the great literary heritage from which it first arose. The students' work enters a temporal stream, accessible to all, and retrievable at any moment by any person. Our classrooms, far from being a cul-de-sac, have a direct connection to the main line of the world and its texts.

9: EATING TEXT

Gill Burbridge

The cultural landscapes of food

Tell me what you eat, and I will tell you who you are.

Jean Anthelme Brillat-Savarin

INTRODUCTION

As someone who has no inclination for cooking, ostensibly sees the consumption of food as merely functional and, left to her own devices would live off a diet of toast and avocado, I can claim no personal vantage point from which to invite and challenge others to experiment with how food makes meaning, and can be experienced, interpreted and understood within a pedagogical framework. However, there are three significantly intersecting contexts that have encouraged me to both reflect on the educational value of reading the diverse cultural landscapes of food specifically and, more widely, to re-examine my understanding of texts and what it is 'to do' in relation to academic enquiry.

My involvement in this project is primarily a product of having been fortunate enough to have spent a decade teaching A Level Communication and Culture, a genuinely multi-disciplinary course to which reading the meanings and practices of everyday life (such as food/meals/eating/cooking) is integral. I have, like many teachers of this subject, metamorphosed from an earlier incarnation, in my case as an English and Drama teacher and, in doing so, found myself simultaneously liberated by the absence of 'set' texts and, at times, overwhelmed by the abundance of meanings that culture creates, to the point that *everything* is text. It is entirely plausible that an entire scheme of learning could be woven around the ways we encounter and understand food on a literal, analogical and metaphorical level. In envisaging the text as the curriculum in this way we are getting close to the 'projects' described by Ron Berger, in *An Ethic of Excellence*:

> We have a thematic curriculum: teachers use multidisciplinary themes (architecture, amphibians, Ancient Greece, and so on) for weeks or months at a time, and within these themes students complete projects. These projects are the primary framework through which skills and understandings are learned. They are not extensions of the curriculum or extras when the required work is done. They are themselves at the core of the curriculum. (2003: 65)

The second context, borne out of the first, is that as Principal Moderator for the AS coursework unit, I have offered 'Food' as a topic for the Investigation; an 'active reading' which invites students to understand the relationship between food and personal identity. The placing of food as text within a formal specification raises interesting issues, not least how we read that which has a material reality as opposed to that which exists purely within language. As Joe Moran suggests, 'The everyday cannot simply be read like a literary text, because it is lived out in spaces and practices as much as in language and discourse' (2005: 22). The 'living out' of food is intimately captured by Luce Giard when she describes the process of 'doing cooking':

> I discovered bit by bit the pleasure.... of manipulating raw material, of organizing, combining, modifying, and inventing. I learned the tranquil joy of anticipated hospitality, when one prepares a meal to share with friends in the same way in which one composes a party tune or draws: with moving hands, careful fingers, the whole body inhabited with the rhythm of working, and the mind awakening, freed from its own ponderousness, flitting from idea to memory, finally seizing on a certain chain of thought, and then modulating this tattered writing once again. (2005: 320)

The reading of any text, whether it has a tangible, three dimensional existence, or is constructed and experienced primarily through language, is as much an act of reading ourselves as it the subject of our enquiry. To acknowledge this is to invite students to engage with important epistemological issues and the ways learning is influenced by, and in turn contributes to, our understanding of what comprises the world and how we come to know it. Hans Lenk (2009) highlights the interpretative social construction of knowledge when he argues that:

> We have no last, ultimate foundation which cannot be doubted at all, which would render a conceptual or linguistic formative basis to build a safe intellectual construction on it. We however do not operate like a rope artist without net, but we ourselves - on the basis of biological fixed dispositions and formal - operational necessities ... would knit or construct our nets in which we try to catch or capture elements and parts of the world. Thus we elaborate our own net including the rope on which we try to balance ourselves. These nets and ropes may be extended and modified ... Any 'graspability' whatsoever is interpretation-laden. The world is real, but 'grasping' the world is always interpretative. (2009: 20)

A final challenge of reading the everyday is that, as the extract from Giard suggests, we both experience and create it. Our relationship to food exemplifies this since we plant, grow, harvest, produce, market, buy, prepare, present and consume, just as we depict it - in terms of both literal and symbolic representation - in photographs, paintings, illustrations, songs, literature and moving image. Food cannot be isolated from its myriad contexts, for as with all texts, its signification is dependent on the structures that help to organise it, along with the many places and spaces where it is read and understood, as well as produced and consumed. Reading food as text, then, is to explore the methods, skills and contexts through which we create, interpret and understand meaning in a multitude of ways. It is this intersection of lived experience, sensation and cognition that Giard describes and that Lenk conceptualises as 'grasping':

> The concept of grasping implies that the active dimension of acquiring knowledge is a genuinely constructive activity and not primarily a representational task of trying to represent external structures. 'Grasping' should not only be interpreted in the literal sense of gripping something, it should be understood in the figurative senses of 'understanding', 'knowing' and 'getting inside'. (ibid.)

The third context that has produced a fundamental interest in, and commitment to, the importance of text and its 'doing' is that, as a Vice Principal of a large sixth form college in London, I spend much of my time thinking, reading and talking about how, as well as what, students learn and what it means to educate and be educated in the current socio-economic and political climate. An experiment in learning beyond the boundaries of a formal curriculum is particularly pertinent at a time when curriculum and qualification reform is bringing into view a range of ideological and pedagogical values, publicly tested and contested. Emerging out of this discourse, which has taken the form of both substantial, informed debates and point-scoring rhetorical skirmishes, is a not unfamiliar tension between 'accountability measures' that equate educational 'success' with assessment outcomes, and a widely held belief, on the part of educators, that learning is often constrained rather than substantiated by assessment methodologies. A commentary produced by the Assessment Reform group highlights the extensive research available which catalogues the impact of an educational structure preoccupied with performance indicators:

> These include the often excessive and inequitable focus of many schools on pupils whose results may be key to a school hitting particular achievement targets; the repetition involved in months of focusing on what is tested and on test practice, which also serves to narrow the curriculum; and the consequent undermining of professional autonomy and morale among teachers. (2009: 25)

Similarly, in their exploration of the potential of new technologies to extend and refigure pedagogy,

Fullan and Langworthy (2014) have argued that:

> More than at any time in history, an individual's educational attainment is vital to her or his future success in life. Yet our mainstream education institutions are increasingly portrayed as obsolete, designed for the purposes of an earlier, mass-production, industrial era. Study after study and TEDtalk after TEDtalk highlights how the high-pressure focus on surface content knowledge measured through traditional exams pushes students and teachers out of school. (2014:1)

The concept of 'doing' education is central to the discourse that surrounds academic or vocational study. Students frequently refer to what they are doing at college, by which they mean the subjects they are taking. There is clearly a semantic difference between 'doing', 'taking', 'studying' and 'reading' a subject, but is this distinction experienced in practice? What does it mean to 'do' English Literature (or History, Geography, French or Physics) and is this qualitatively different from 'studying' or 'reading' English Literature?

At a basic level, whatever academic discipline we pursue, we access only a version, mediated by a whole host of filters, from the ideological whims of government ministers and shifting ideas about the nature of educational 'standards', to the contents of the stock cupboard, or the interests of individual teachers. In this sense it could be argued that rather than 'doing' subjects they, to a large extent, 'do' us. Despite significant shifts in pedagogy over the last fifty years and successive educational policies designed to increase inclusion and promote equitable access, it remains difficult to create spaces of learning that resist the transmission and reproduction of dominant culture, constructed through a selective process of emphases and exclusions. Ritchhart offers the following summary: 'Rather than working to change who students are as thinkers and learners, schools for the most part work merely to fill them up with knowledge. Although some may see intelligence as a natural by-product of schooling, in reality the curriculum, instruction, and structure of schools do little to promote intelligence and may even impede it in some cases' (2002: 7).

The model of education in which we operate is still, essentially, what the Brazilian educationalist Paulo Freire refers to as 'banking education'. According to this concept, the act of teaching students risks actually obstructing their intellectual growth by turning them into passive 'receivers' of information that has no real connection to their lives. Freire states:

> Implicit in the banking concept is the assumption of a dichotomy between human beings and the world: a person is merely in the world, not with the world or with others; the individual is a spectator, not re-creator. In this view the person is not a conscious being (corpo consciente); he or she is rather the possessor of a consciousness: an empty 'mind' passively open to the reception of deposits of reality from the world outside. (2008: 247)

Classrooms around the country display taxonomies of learning which foreground the importance of creativity, evaluation and critical thinking, and yet the very structures that underpin the education system negate their development. The current emphasis on league tables, performance indicators and impact measures impose not just practical limitations upon the freedoms available to individual teachers within individual lessons but psychological constraints as well. In his application of Freire's work to African education, Nyirenda (1996) argues that:

Knowledge becomes a donation from those who know to those who don't know...It denies the learner and the educator the possibility of dialogue. Banking education fails to stimulate intellectual discipline. Instead it kills curiosity, creativity and any investigative spirit in the learners and encourages ... passive behaviour. (1996: 13)

CURRICULUM BOUNDARIES

Curriculum content and assessment methodology lie at the heart of our education system and impose significant constraints on the degree of flexibility and innovation possible. John Hattie's meta-analysis concludes that the 'biggest effects on student learning occur when teachers become learners of their own teaching, and when students become their own teachers' (Hattie, 2011: 14). From this perspective, feedback, as a form of visible learning, is critical in enhancing the quality of the teaching and learning experience. Winne and Butler (1994) provide a useful definition of feedback as, 'information with which a learner can confirm, add to, overwrite, tune, or restructure information in memory, whether that information is domain knowledge, meta-cognitive knowledge, beliefs about self and tasks, or cognitive tactics and strategies.' (Winnie and Butler, 1994: 48) A model of learning which puts student feedback at its core would enable students themselves to direct, shape and refine the structure, content and process of their learning. However, the reliance on content driven curriculum and the privileging of formal testing as the dominant mechanism of assessment means there is little space to allow students to 'be creative curriculum makers who are critical thinkers willing to take appropriate professional risks' (Key, 2013: 181).

Creative and experimental approaches to the imparting and acquisition of knowledge and the capacity to develop a deep understanding of the intersections between academic disciplines require students and teachers to question and contest fundamental assumptions about the purpose and process of education. These issues have a heightened resonance at a time when the most significant reforms to the structure and assessment requirements of academic qualifications since Curriculum 2000 are about to be implemented in schools and colleges across the country. One consequence (and indeed the purported rationale) of the narrowing of the curriculum both at GCSE and A Level has been the discontinuation of subjects which involve significant overlap. It is with a dark irony therefore that qualifications predicated on a fundamentally interdisciplinary approach and which require students to grapple with complex and substantial relationships between socio-economic, historical and cultural contexts (the very skills that are integral to higher education) may no longer be available. This seemingly regressive preoccupation with rigidly differentiated subjects is also at odds with recent innovations in Finland, the highest ranking European country in the Programme for International Student Assessment (PISA) rankings. Here, subject-specific lessons are being replaced by 'phenomenon' teaching (i.e. teaching by topic) involving a more collaborative approach.

The educational benefits of interdisciplinary learning have been well documented. Allen F. Repko's research, for example, argues that:

> Interdisciplinary studies is a process of answering a question, solving a problem or addressing a topic that is too broad or complex to be dealt with adequately by a single discipline and draws on disciplinary perspectives and integrates their insights to produce a more comprehensive understanding or cognitive advancement. (2008: 12)

Such a claim is pertinent to the issues of pedagogy explored throughout this chapter and to the practical approaches and responses described later. In particular, the ability to see intersections between different disciplinary perspectives, to 'integrate their insights' and to explore these practically and creatively are, it will be argued, essential to the 'cognitive advancement' of students. The suspicion that the ideological impetus of curriculum changes positions A Levels as the preserve of those already imbued with sufficient cultural capital to meet the 'intellectually demanding' (Gove, 2013:) rigour they require, is lent weight by the funding cuts within the post-16 sector, which have resulted in an erosion of enrichment and extension provision, and the breadth of the curriculum offer.[1]

The approach to learning and enquiry explored here is, in part, an act of resistance and re-appropriation, genuinely committed to challenging and contesting imposed assumptions about the relationship between curriculum content, academic rigour and the development of critical thinking and deep learning. Such a challenge to accepted orthodoxies invites a dialogue between those who see 'more facts' as the route to 'good conceptual understanding' (Christodoulou, 2014: 20) and those who question the very distinction between factual knowledge as a schema for understanding the world and the process of interpretation:

> Reality is not easily legible. Ideas and theories are not a reflection of reality; they are translations and sometimes mistranslations…We should be realistic in a complex way, understanding the uncertainty of reality, knowing that the real holds invisible potential. (2001: 70)

Morin's argument is echoed by Gillie Bolton's work on the potency of substantive reflection in which she suggests the extent to which learning journals, as a form of reflection and evaluation, can problematise notions of reality: 'Unpredictable horizontal reflective dialogues are potentially a subversive discourse with their exploratory and conflicting realities' (Bolton, 2005: 178). The unstructured nature of the journal accords with the playful and experimental approach to learning which underpins this project. Prefaced with Rilke's maxim, 'Live the questions', Bolton's research highlights the need to position the student and their lived experiences at the heart of the learning process. It is possible, perhaps, to see a parallel here between the value of quotidian experience as a subject of academic enquiry and ordinary language philosophy. Paul Ricoeur (1977) suggests that, 'the variability of semantic values, their sensitivity to contexts, the irreducibly polysemic character of lexical terms in ordinary language', meaning that the discourse of the everyday, and the texts that result from it, can be understood as 'a kind of conservatory for expressions which have preserved the highest descriptive power as regards human experience, particularly in the realms of action and feelings' (1977: 380).[2]

In the following section I will consider how, as educators, we might negotiate with our students these realms of 'action and feelings' and encourage them to see the organic power that language has not just to depict but also to create. In doing so we are inviting them to engage with food as an act of communication, 'a body of images, a protocol of usages, situations, and behavior' (Barthes, 1979: 166)

THE LANDSCAPES OF FOOD

The impetus that drives the approach to text within this project is ultimately a desire to defamiliarise the familiar, thereby enabling students to see things afresh and to critically read dominant political, social or cultural narratives - in this case those surrounding what, how and where we eat - and the ways these are situated and understood. In his essay 'Popularity and Realism' (1938) Brecht argues that realist literature should be a means of:

> ...discovering the causal complexes of society / unmasking the prevailing view of things as the view of those who are in power / writing from the standpoint of the class which offers the broadest solutions for the pressing difficulties in which human society is caught up / emphasizing the element of development / making possible the concrete, and making possible abstraction from it. (1938: 82)

I would argue that this process of 'unmaking' is also at the heart of education, but that the familiar settings, props and approaches we use to educate often work against this taking place. In the same essay Brecht acknowledges that 'methods become exhausted; stimuli no longer work' (ibid.). 'Doing' text does not only offer the opportunity to explore new methods, it insists upon it, since the organising framework through which we locate teaching and learning (the curriculum) is dissolved and reconfigured. Louis Rice (2009) expresses this in relation to 'playful learning':

> Playful modes of learning transcend the realm of academia and are transplanted into the 'outside' world. Ideas and concepts become hybridised between theory and practice through the use of play. (2009: 95)

The active agency suggested by the verb 'doing' coupled with the process of 'making strange' are key elements of the related notions of psychogeography, dérive and play. In his preface to the 2013 Barbican cinema season, *Urban Wandering*, Will Self describes psychogeography as, 'an examination – through creative praxis – of the free psychic interplay between the human mind and place' (2013: 8). The concept derives in part from the work of Guy Debord. Writing in the 1950s Debord defines psychogeography as, 'the study of the precise laws and specific effects of the geographical environment, consciously organized or not, on the emotions and behaviour of individuals' (1955: 5). Similarly, Michel de Certeau (1984) conceptualises the patterns, repetitions and coincidences established in seemingly unpurposeful and undirected walking in the city as 'a symbolic order of the unconscious'. Through 'escaping the imaginary totalizations produced by the eye' the everyday achieves 'a certain strangeness that does not surface, or whose surface is only its upper limit, outlining itself against the visible' (1984: 93).

Each of these definitions suggests that psychogeography aligns experience gained through sensation and mobility with the understanding and analysis achieved through reflection. Bolton (2005) argues that genuine reflective practice, 'lays open to question anything that is taken for granted' (2005: 6). This degree of cultural reflection constitutes a critical responsiveness to the contexts wherein a person carries out his or her everyday life. Appignanesi and Garratt (2005) define reflexivity as 'an immediate critical consciousness of what one is doing, thinking or writing' (2005: 73).

Psychogeography, as explored here, then, is the active search for, and privileging of, alternative ways of experiencing and reading the familiar. Meanings are not predetermined but are formed out of an individual and collective reflection upon the coincidences, intersections, patterns and repetitions directly experienced as the participants move through a physical environment. Therefore, while the dérive is, by its nature, unpurposeful at least on one level, it is, on another, full of purpose. It necessitates that students are informed and active pedestrians, moving in a manner aware and alert to meanings. Rather than being propelled by destination, oblivious to their surroundings, they become forensic observers capable of critically interrogating what they experience. Abrami et al (2008) define critical thinking as, 'the ability to engage in purposeful, self-regulatory judgement' and go on to argue that:

> This includes not only thinking about important problems within disciplinary areas… but also thinking about the social, political, and ethical challenges of everyday life in a multifaceted and increasingly complex world. (2008: 1102)

Reflexivity and critical thinking necessitate the broadening of students' awareness of the world and, specifically, their engagement with education beyond the limits of self-concern and entitlement. Being both reflexive and critically reflective means asking questions that further deep learning rather than merely assist clarification. Such questions should revolve around the ways in which our actions and perceptions reflect broader social conditions, ideas and political relationships. 'Where are we located within this multifarious and complex thing called human culture? In working towards a deeper understanding of our 'location', we also further appreciation for our cultural subjectivity – the person we think we are' (Prescott-Steed, 2013: 86).

The following experiment in learning outside the curriculum starts at that point of intersection where food as text brings into focus the interface between the social, the political and the ethical and, arguably, all other academic disciplines. Furthermore, food offers not only a site of study and exploration, but also an act of communication, as Cindy Spurlock (2009) suggests in her observation that 'because of their ability to signify, mediate, contest, and represent 'nature' and 'culture,' foodways are deeply rhetorical and performative' (2009: 6). Similarly, Sara Littlejohn highlights the potential of food as a signifier of human experience, stating that 'it is the narrative qualities—captured in discourse and behavior—that contribute to its meaning making, thus persuasive, properties' (2008: 1).

As suggested earlier, far from being a learning strategy which seeks to complement or extend existing approaches, this socio-cultural experiment deliberately seeks to challenge and disrupt normative practices within education and, more importantly, the assumptions that underpin them. The vision of education proposed by Paulo Freire advocates democratic learning environments in which teachers could also learn and students teach, an approach that would make possible an active learning community.

Democratic learning environments bring into question the very notion of pedagogy and the extent to which our theoretical understanding and practical implementations are shaped by the physical and cultural context in which this pedagogy is situated. The conventional learning environment – the classroom – encourages a view of pedagogy which has, at its heart, a predetermined curriculum and a subject to be imparted. Brian V. Street (2014) has argued that,

> When we participate in the language of an institution, whether as speakers, listeners, writers, or readers, we become positioned by that language; in that moment of assent, myriad relationships of power, authority, status are implied and reaffirmed. At the heart of this language in contemporary society, there is a relentless commitment to instruction. (2014: 127)

Encouraging learning outside the classroom has the potential to challenge the power dynamic often implicit in the understanding of pedagogy. However, if we continue to employ the discourse of the classroom even within non-traditional learning environments, we will perpetuate an experience of location that is similarly constraining and hierarchical. The experiment in learning described here is predicated on the belief that pre-selected texts deemed appropriate for academic study also position the student in ways which often devalue their own sense of identity as reader and critic. Texts and discourses that exist outside the mainstream are often negated or marginalised. Thus the literacy practices of those students whose ethnic, social, cultural and economic contexts place them on the margins may be regarded as inappropriate or problematic. Cazden et al (1996) highlight this when they assert that:

> Literacy pedagogy has traditionally meant teaching and learning to read and write in page-bound, official, standard forms of the national language. Literacy pedagogy, in other words, has been a carefully restricted project -- restricted to formalized, monolingual, monocultural, and rule-governed forms of language. (1996: 60)

In order to enable self-efficacy we must legitimise students' understanding of self and the literacies through which they understand and express that self. To do this we must develop, 'a pedagogy that views language and other modes of representation as dynamic and constantly being remade by meaning-makers in changing and varied contexts' (Cazden et al, 1996: 62). Moje and Luke (2009) suggest that identities inform, and are informed by, the texts that individuals both author and read, and that a theoretical focus on identity 'is crucial, not to control the identities that students produce, construct, form, or enact but to avoid controlling identities' (2009: 433).

Literacy and language act as forms of 'capital' that advantage those who possess it and disadvantage those who do not. Pierre Bourdieu argues that discourse embodies 'relations of symbolic power in which the power relations between speakers or their respective groups are actualized' (1991: 37). Achievement within an educational context derives from the ability to engage in valued language and discourse practices. In imposing texts 'worthy' of study and insisting upon formal academic literacy we are, as educators, in danger of not only ignoring the value of alternative discourses but also denying access to students who lack the required 'capital'. Cope et al make this point when they argue that,

> ... in a system that still values vastly disparate social outcomes, there will never be enough room 'at the top.' An authentically democratic view of schools must include a vision of meaningful success for all, a vision of success that is not defined exclusively in economic terms and that has embedded within it a critique of hierarchy and economic injustice. (1996: 12)

Working beyond the confines of traditional curriculum, freeing students from the constraints of hierarchical linguistic codes and positioning the teacher outside the role of the bestower of expert knowledge, we allow for the emergence of a learning community characterised by self-determination, intentionality, creativity and evaluation. Such an educational framework promotes the agency of students, equipping them with the capacity for critical and independent thought, rather than training them for assessment. Freire referred to this affirmation and empowerment of students as the process by which we nurture 'subjects of decision':

> People acquire autonomy through self-conscious reflection. Taking others into account when practising vision empowers them to question themselves, to critique social structures, and to image new realities. People learn best by doing; visioning creates autonomy. The practice of social criticism through vision is emancipatory. It dares the imagination, challenges assumptions, and declares its independence from tradition. Visioning is not for the nervous. Problematising the present through vision erases the security that springs from the taken-for-granted. (Schultz, 1995: 2)

The means to achieving this kind of self-conscious reflection is, according to Friere, through a method of problem-posing. However, as he points out, there is a danger that what actually occurs is a pseudo-dialectic, which merely provides the illusion that students and teachers are 'discovering' knowledge collaboratively, whereas in fact the teacher has already determined the 'right answer' before posing the question. The alternative is a genuine dialectic: the teacher poses a question or introduces an idea or concept with no preconceived outcome.

It is for this reason that Friere's method requires a degree of risk-taking since genuine problem-posing challenges traditional classroom hierarchy. Such an approach accords with Lawrence Stenhouse's 'process' rather than an 'aims and objectives' model of curriculum. Stenhouse advocated interdisciplinary learning that would challenge students through an exposure to 'the nature and structure of certain complex value issues of universal human concern' (1975: 12). This approach necessitates not only the provision of a wealth of resources which interconnect disciplines through cross-cutting themes, but also the development of skills that will enable student to articulate, express and represent their own critical responses in an equally multi layered way. Outcomes may take the form of creative and imaginative projects or more formal academic writing, but the teacher's role is one of 'procedural neutrality', and there are no pre-determined objectives. Stenhouse acknowledged that his process model 'is far more demanding on teachers and thus far more difficult to implement in practice but it offers a higher degree of personal and professional development' (1975: 96-7).

SEEKING A TRUE DIALECTIC: PLAYING WITH FOOD

> Information about food must be gathered wherever it can be found: by direct observation in the economy, in techniques, usages and advertising; and by indirect observation in the mental life of a given society. (Barthes, 1979: 172)

This particular experiment began with freeing students and teachers from any curriculum constraints. Over a two week period students were invited to 'play' with food with the only predetermined outcome being that they would provide – in whatever medium they chose – a reading of food.

On the basis that, 'students who pose their own problems are better motivated to solve them than if they are imposed from without – through texts or teachers' (Brown and Walter, 2014: xiv) there was no intervention by teachers: we merely observed and responded to direct questions. A group discussion led to two sub-groups forming. Some students began to investigate the contradictions surrounding our relationship with food: culturally and individually. This line of enquiry centred on obesity versus starvations; the enjoyment of food and the fear of it; food as a necessity and food as luxury. Students then began to identify the implications of these issue in relation to historical, socio-economic and political contexts. At the same time, others began to explore how food is represented: an area which invited a similarly interdisciplinary approach. This group compiled a range of texts derived from literature, song, film, adverts, menus and recipes; they explored alternative readings of these individually, and in terms of the relationships between them.

A sharing of preliminary work across the two groups led them to identify areas of overlap and interface between their different approaches and the outcomes of their research. Dominant themes that emerged at this stage were an interest in the relationship between food and locale and the meanings of food in terms of gender, race, class and ethnicity. In order to unpack these themes further students developed points for observational enquiry, designed to provoke an active reading of the everyday. In the first instance they agreed to record all of their interactions with food, documenting:

- What they ate;
- When they ate;
- With whom they ate;
- Who provided the food;
- Who prepared the food;
- Who cleared up after the meal;
- How much the food cost;
- The cultural influences on what, where and how they eat.

And also:

- Any adverts for food products that they saw;
- Any places they went to that sold food;
- Any food wrappings they saw.

No set format was agreed as to how they would document these interactions, although the following were discussed:

- A diary for the period in question;
- Photographs;
- Video recordings;
- Blogs or vlogs;
- Drawings.

In this way students identified the starting point for their own fieldwork – a literal point of departure and a touch-paper for preliminary ideas. For those wishing to undertake a similar experiment, I would suggest providing students with a starting point that has the scope to open up multiple divergent paths. Depending on the context: your geographical location, which disciplinary threads you wish to weave and the age range of the students you are working with (to name but three) – it could be anything that allows for problem-posing as a genuine dialectic and that encourages an exploration of space and the capacity to play. Our starting point, as described above, led students to want to investigate further their own immediate contexts through deconstructing the landscapes of food in the East London borough where they live. The dominant cultural narratives through which Waltham Forest is both represented and read, frequently evoke its ethnic diversity and high levels of economic deprivation. Both these factors are of significance in terms of how food is experienced by the local population and how these experiences might be read when juxtaposed with the meanings of food available within other locations in close proximity, i.e. central London. We started to collect other texts (such as photographs, menus, advertisements) that support these narratives: students interrogated them, positing questions and identifying patterns and parallels emerging from juxtapositions and repetitions.

The next stage was to build narrative possibilities out of the agreed starting point. In small, reconfigured groups students began to experiment with different ways of constructing narrative threads around the local texts that they had collected and explored ways to represent and articulate them. Through presentation and discussion they identified a means of visualising local hubs where many of the activities surrounding food are experienced (producing, purchasing, preparing, consuming, disposing). These physical locations were configured as a reworking of the London underground map, but with the college as the central point of the nexus.

From here students decided to explore these narrative threads and contest the found texts they had collected through an excursion where the only planned element was the starting point. As a whole group we marked out the parameters of our 'reconstituted landscape' through which we moved without a predetermined route or any rules regarding how much distance would be travelled or whether paths could be returned to or retraced. Students chose how and what to record – audio recordings, photographs, maps, drawings, descriptions, thoughts, found artefacts and so on.

The final stage was to compile, organise and sequence individual recordings. Through the act of composition, we found that a number of competing and complementary paradigms emerged, some anticipated and others unexpected. Student work was varied but was mainly demonstrated in the following ways:

- Through an exhibition – this took the form of various maps of East London with strings attached, leading to plastic wallets containing menus, narrative fragments, photos;
- Readings that juxtaposed found texts and re-creative responses;
- Autobiographical writings based on memories of food and offering reflections on identity.

The time-bound nature of this project meant that there were many areas of enquiry that were not pursued. In particular, students wanted further opportunity to engage in more sustained and substantive dialogue within their home and their immediate local contexts in order to develop the narratives of food they had begun to construct. With more time we would have further developed a 'Funds of Knowledge' approach which advocates utilising familial and community resources – 'historically accumulated and culturally developed bodies of knowledge and skills' (Moll et al, 2004: 72-3) to inform learning and literacy.

CONCLUSION

The educational legitimacy of a multi-disciplinary approach, the academic value of lived experience, and the belief that the development of critical thinking is a social endeavour are at the heart of this chapter. In challenging traditional notions of the curriculum we are also questioning the very nature of what knowledge within the context of education is or should be. James A. Beane states that 'Curriculum integration is not simply an organisational device requiring cosmetic changes or realignments in lesson plans across various subject areas. Rather it is a way of thinking about what schools are for, about the sources of curriculum, and about the uses of knowledge' (Beane 1995: 616). He goes so far as to say that 'the central focus of curriculum integration is the search for self- and social meaning'.

Exploring the limitations and opportunities of the formal curriculum and working creatively around it requires us to rethink how and to what end we are educating young people, and the extent to which the knowledge and discourses that we ask them to engage with are ultimately empowering. Knowledge does not exist outside the subjectivity of the individual but the means by which it is mediated and represented influence its significance and how it is interpreted by others.

The sociological concept of the hidden curriculum suggests that our cognitive experience within an educational context extends far beyond what we are explicitly and knowingly taught. Our knowledge contains the tacit and subconsciously received, as well as the consciously imparted. While we may have our own individual schemata, this is heavily influenced by those with authority and power. As teachers we can significantly shape the learning capabilities of students but we must endeavour to do so in ways that are not detrimental to their intellectual development or that do not negate their own enriching contexts. Hough and Duncan (1970) have argued that, 'The act of teaching is a complex process that is influenced by a field of forces of which teachers can only be in part aware and which the teacher can only partially control' (1970: 6).

This project recognises this complexity and asserts that we should continue to embrace and encourage those elements of learning which are beyond our control, accepting that education is a collective human activity. Ultimately the experiment described here was not merely a means of enabling a group of students to collaboratively, creatively and critically contest the meanings of food. More significantly, it was an attempt to explore a new pedagogy that has, at its core, a belief that now, more than ever, young people need to be able to make informed, well-reasoned and independent judgements. The exposure to almost limitless sources of knowledge through new technologies means that they need to be equipped to evaluate and interpret accurately information, views and ideas, constructed, filtered and circulated by the media and social networks emphasising ideology and image over substance and reason. For, as David Perkins (1989) points out:

> … the beliefs we hold, and consequently the inferences we later make and attitudes we later assume, depend in part on our reasoning about the grounds for those beliefs. Accepting beliefs wisely serves the ultimate end of later sound conduct as well as the more immediate end of sound belief itself. (1989: 175)

REFERENCES

1. Entitlement funding for activities such as tutorials, enrichment activities and additional courses was reduced from 114 hours per year to 30 hours in 2010. Sixth form colleges alone have seen an overall reduction in funding of around 10 per cent to date due to this cut. See James Kewin (2012), *Sixth Form Colleges and Funding: Summary for Stakeholders v2* London: Sixth Form Colleges Forum, page 2.
2. Ricoeur, P. (1977) *The Rule of Metaphor*, London: Routledge

WORKS CITED

Abrami, P. C., Bernard, R. M., Borokhovski, E., Wade, A., Surkes, M. A., Tamim, R., and Zhang, D. (2008) 'Instructional interventions affecting critical thinking skills and dispositions: A stage 1 meta-analysis'. *Review of Educational Research*, 78(4).

Appignanesi, R. and Garratt, C. (1999) *Introducing Postmodernism*. Royston: Totem Books.

Barthes, R. (1979) 'Toward a Psychosociology of Food Consumption', in Robert Forster, R. and Ranum, O. (eds) *Food and Drink in History*. Baltimore, MD: Johns Hopkins University Press

Beane, James. A (1995) 'Curriculum Integration and the Disciplines of Knowledge', in *The Phi Delta Kappan*, 76 (8).

Berger, R. (2003) *An Ethic of Excellence: Building a Culture of Craftsmanship with Students*. London & New York Heinemann.

Bolton, G. (2005) *Reflective practice: Writing and professional development*. London: SAGE.

Brecht, B. (1938) 'Popularity and Realism', in Bloch, E. (1980) *Aesthetics and Politics*, London: Verso.

Brown, Sl. and Walter, MI (2014) *Problem Posing: Reflections and Applications*. New York: Psychology Press.

Cazden, C., Cope, B., Fairclough, N., Gee, J. et al (1996) 'A pedagogy of multiliteracies: Designing social futures'. *Harvard Educational Review*; Spring; 66, 1; Research Library.

Christodoulou, D. (2014) *Seven Myths About Education*. London: Routledge.

Cope, B and New London Group (2000) *Multiliteracies: Literacy Learning and the Design of Social Futures*. London: Psychology Press.

DeBord, G. (1955) 'An introduction to a critique of urban geography', in Engel-Di Mauro, S. (2008) *Critical Geographies: a collection of readings*. Praxis ePress.

De Certeau, M. (1984) *The Practice of Everyday Life*. London: University of California Press.

Freire, P. (2008) 'The "Banking" Concept of Education', in *Ways of Reading* 8th ed. Bartholomae, D. and Petrosky, A. Boston: Bedford- St. Martin's.

Fullan, M. & Langworthy, M. (2014) *A Rich Seam: How New Pedagogies Find Deep Learning*. London: Pearson.

Giard, L. 'Doing Cooking' in Highmore, B. (ed.) (2002) *The Everyday Life Reader* London & New York: Routledge.

Hattie, J. (2011) *Visible Learning for Teachers*. Abingdon: Routledge.

Hough, J.B. and Duncan, J.K. (1970) *Teaching: Description and Analysis*. London: Addison-Wesley.

Key, P. (2013) 'The Overlooked: Landscapes Artistry and Teaching', in McIntosh P. and Warren, D. (eds) *Creativity in the Classroom: case studies in using the arts in teaching and learning in higher education*. Bristol: Intellect.

Kewin, J. (2012) *Sixth Form Colleges and Funding:Summary for Stakeholders v2*. London: Sixth Form Colleges Forum.

Lenk, H, (2009) 'Towards a technology-and action-oriented methodology of constructive realism', In Leidlmar, K. (ed.). *After Cognitivism: A Reassessment of Cognitive Science and Philosophy*. New York: Springer.

Littlejohn, S.J. (2008) *The Rhetoric of Food Narratives: Ideology and Influence in American Culture*. The University of North Carolina at Greensboro.

Mansell, W., James, M. and the Assessment Reform Group (2009) *Assessment in schools, Fit for purpose? A Commentary by the Teaching and Learning Research Programme*. London: Economic and Social Research Council, Teaching and Learning Research Programme.

Moje, E. B. and Luke, A. (2009) 'Literacy and identity: A review of perspectives on identity and their impact on literacy studies'. *Reading Research Quarterly*, 44 (4).

Moll, L., Amanti, C., Neff, D., Gonzalez, N. (2004) 'Funds of knowledge for teaching: Using a qualitative approach to connect homes and classrooms', in N. Gonzalez, L. Moll, & C. Amanti (eds), *Funds of Knowledge: Theorizing practices in households, communities and classrooms*. London: Routledge. pp. 71–88.

Moran, J, (2005) *Reading the Everday*. London & New York: Routledge.

Morin, E. (2001) *Seven complex lessons in education for the future*. Paris: UNESCO Publishing.

Nyirenda, JE. (1996) 'The Relevance of Paulo Friere's Contributions to Education and Development in Present Day Africa', *Africa Media Review*, 10 (1).

Perkins, D. N. (1989) 'Reasoning as it is and could be: An empirical perspective' in D. M. Topping, D. S. Cromwell, & V. N. Kobayaski (eds) *Thinking across cultures: Third international conference on thinking*. New York: Routledge. pp. 175-194.

Prescott-Steed, D. (2013) *The Psychogeography of Urban Architecture*. Florida: Brown Walker Press.

Repko, A. F. (2008) *Interdisciplinary Research: Process and Theory*. London: SAGE.

Rice, L. (2009) 'Playful learning'. *The Journal for Education in the Built Environment*, 4 (2).

Ricoeur, P. (1977) *The Rule of Metaphor*. London: Routledge.

Ritchhart, R. (2002) *Intellectual Character: What It Is, Why it Matters, and How to Get It*. San Francisco: Jossey-Bass.

Schultz W. L. (1995) 'Sidling into our Futures: provocation as a path to critical futures fluency', in *Futures Fluency: explorations in leadership, vision, and creativity*, University of Hawaii.

Spurlock, C. (2009) *Performing and Sustaining (Agri)Culture and Place: The Cultivation of Environmental Subjectivity on the Piedmont Tour* Text and Performance Quarterly Vol. 29, No. 1, January.

Stenhouse, L. (1975) *An Introduction to Curriculum Research and Development*. London: Heinemann.

Street, B.V. (2014) *Social Literacies: Critical Approaches to Literacy in Development, Ethnography and Education*. Abingdon: Routledge.

Winne, P. H., & Butler, D. L. (1994) 'Student cognition in learning from teaching', in T. Husen & T. Postlewaite (eds) *International encyclopaedia of education* (2nd ed.). Oxford: Pergamon. pp. 5738–5745.

Walters, E., 'Death of the Teacher?' *You Tube* (2009): https://www.youtube.com/watch?v=gql0nhgFsQQ&index=38&list=UU_fwBdOUwB29JA8mB7R-etQ (accessed 27 April 2015).

Wolf, A. (2011) 'Review of Vocational Education – The Wolf Report' *GOV.UK*: https://www.gov.uk/government/publications/review-of-vocational-education-the-wolf-report (accessed 20 April 2015).

10: AFTER THE SUBJECT: TOWARDS A REAL REFORM

Pete Bennett

> The multiple must be made.
>
> (Deleuze & Guattari 2004: 8)
>
> To miss the march of this retreating world
>
> Into vain citadels that are not walled.
>
> (Wilfrid Owen, *Strange Meeting*)

DISCIPLINE POLICIES

When this project was conceived in 2013, this chapter, always tentatively entitled *After the Subject: Towards a Real Reform*, was imagined very differently. Firstly, it was until quite recently going to be the opening salvo in a speculative assault on the curricular *status quo*, a manifesto of sorts, a set of principles to inspire a range of teacherly folk to imagine a life (and curriculum) beyond the confines of subjects. It was also, though, largely unwittingly, focused on the secondary and tertiary curricula and the provenance/ redundancy of subjects *per* se at the very moment that 'academic subjects' were being given their most substantial post-mortal revalidation since the Second World War in a programme of reform bizarrely oblivious to the world pupils and students now inhabit. The design principles of the reforms of GCSE and A level have sought to reduce the number of subjects offered by outlawing 'overlap' between subjects, in other words the very interdisciplinarity that we were seeking to inspire and support. Though, like Clifford Geertz, they recognise we are living in an age of 'blurred genres', a 'jumbling of varieties of discourse', they seem determined at least to weed this garden (cited in Moran, 2002: 18).

In England now, with the EBacc and 'new' A levels defined by content rather than concepts, our arguments suddenly find themselves fighting 'hand-to-hand' with government policy. And though as we will show, these reactionary outbursts, which NASUWT leader Chris Keates claimed were "entirely driven by political ideology rather than a genuine desire…reform the examination system in the best interests of children and young people' (Keates, 2012), represent a rejection of pretty much all of the philosophical movements of the last fifty years, ironically there is a darkly quirky postmodernism in the conception of these 'reforms'. They, to an extent, exemplify Baudrillard's account of the degradation of meaning in his account of the 'precession of the simulacra' whereby in our contemporary reality we are moving from 'signs that dissimulate something to signs which dissimulate that there is nothing' (Baudrilliard, 1998: 354).

As far as the English Baccalaureate (EBacc) is concerned this process feels somewhere between stages two ('It masks and perverts a basic reality') and three ('It masks the absence of a basic reality') in Baudrillard's 'precession' since what appears to be a qualification (and consciously so invoking the French Baccalaureate and International Baccalaureate) is in fact a school performance indicator, a contrivance of sorts. Critics might also argue that the 'new' reformed linear A levels with their 'back to the fifties' vibe ironically epitomise the postmodern condition since, for Baudrillard, 'when the real is no longer what it used to be, nostalgia assumes its full meaning' (ibid.). They are simulations of nostalgic ideas rather than representations of current educational needs. And in their persistent search for the lost heart (art?) of education we can only be reminded where Baudrillard goes next: 'There is a proliferation of myths of origin and signs of reality of second hand truths, objectivity and authenticity' (Storey [ed.], 2009: 412).

Place this into a context wherein the subject Media Studies, the tenth most popular A level had been shown the instruments of torture and it might have been easier to 'recant'. Indeed, the degree to which this popular and largely and inevitably contemporary subject was endangered is evident in David Buckingham's comment in February 2016: 'Last summer there was a moment when there were concerns that media studies might be deleted' (cited in Rustin, 2016). Buckingham is credited, with Natalie Fenton with brokering a deal to ensure that Media Studies has a future in English schools. Susannah Rustin (2016) summarises the changes as follows: 'a reduction in coursework and much greater emphasis on theory' including, according to Buckingham 'some theorists (Judith Butler, Baudrillard)' who are 'incredibly difficult'. The point is that in a world regularly described as 'media-saturated' an argument was engaged that suggested that this was the time to stop addressing 'media' in schools and colleges. At that point, as one of our eight authors pointed out, 'using text after the subject' was feeling remarkably prescient as if events were moving to make things ever more relevant and at the same time mournful. As if, in fact, Media Studies was asserting itself at last progressively as 'the subject' (in both senses) but only partly aware of the consequences: belatedly lighting up as if it had a choice.

EMBRACING THE GENTLE APOCALYPSE

However, the *Doing Text* project also emerged out of a longer term commitment which began with *After the Media* and continued, if obliquely, through our reboot of Barthes' *Mythologies* (2012) which was meant – as with this volume - to offer practical attempts to negotiate the arguments about theory and practice that *After the Media* proposes. Though circumstances may mean this is partly unavoidable, like Rancière in *The Distribution of the Sensible* (2006), a key text for our work, we would want to assert that 'These pages do not have their origin in a desire to take a polemical stance' (Rancière, 2006: 10). Rather, like Rancière's reformulated aesthetics, they are 'inscribed in a long-term project that aims at re-establishing a debate's conditions of intelligibility (ibid.). The 'long-term project' implies both investigation and reflection, of listening to current debates about contemporary reality and identifying the mismatch between what is professed politically and what can be convincingly argued. It is a realisation that the philosophical dispensation Peim calls 'post-structuralism' 'renders it impossible to claim that any signifying events, texts or practices can guarantee or fix their own meanings on their own' (Peim, 1993: 1). This echoes Barthes, who traversed the various collectives of late twentieth century thought at full tilt and addressed the operation of myth more than fifty years ago in this way: 'it organizes a world which is without contradictions because it is without depth, a world wide open and wallowing in the evident, it establishes a blissful clarity: things appear to mean something by themselves' (Barthes, 1972: 143).

Our authors rather offer contingencies and connections, contexts and concentration offering both variously and as a whole a new dispensation, incorrigibly plural. But beyond the range and verve of these interventions is also a remorseless logic that denies reactionary attempts to restore a canon nearly forty years after 'The removal of the Author', which is 'not merely an historical fact or an act of writing; it utterly transforms the modern text' (Barthes, 1977: 145). This is surely not the time for 'an approach predicated on notions of the independent and illustrious individual, whom Callon describes as 'a temporarily workable fiction created at the time of the enlightenment' (Bennett, Kendall and McDougall, 2011: 208). Rather, we call for Peim's 'completely decentring and deconstructive manner'(Peim, 1993: 1). This 'method' knows it is a fiction, this 'language about languages' is fully aware, as Barthes ultimately was, that 'every relation of exteriority of one language to another is, *in the long run*, untenable' (Sontag [ed.], 1993: 472). In such circumstances we must embrace Barthes' 'moment of gentle apocalypse' (Sonntag [ed.], 1993: 471):

There is an age at which we teach what we know. Then comes another age at which we teach what we do not know; this is called research. Now perhaps comes the age of another experience; that of **unlearning**, of yielding to the unforeseeable change which forgetting imposes on the sedimentation of the knowledges, cultures and beliefs we have traversed (Sontag [Ed.], 1993: 478).

This 'yielding to the unforeseeable change' is central to the approach we are advocating and ever more relevant in a context which asks teachers to prepare generic 'learners' for a world and work that potentially does not yet exist. And all this within the 'stereotyping' 'one size fits all' national curriculum and prescribed standardised tests where the' 'canonical, constraining form of the signifier' and at worst becomes 'the present path of truth' (Barthes, 1975: 42). Twenty years earlier Barthes had proposed the study of 'how a society produces stereotypes', which he famously defined as 'the word repeated without any magic as if it were natural'' (Barthes, 1975: 42). Now enthusiastically supported by the self-appointed Campaign for Real Education, the reforms system declares these areas of significant dispute 'unsuitable for study'. Peim identifies a myth of 'proper' education with all that entails using 'a language which does not want to die', rather it turns the meanings it feeds on into 'speaking corpses' (Barthes, 1972: 132).

A COMPREHENSIVE EDUCATION

Speaking in 2002 at the FORUM Memorial Lecture, Tim Brighouse reminded his audience of the high ideals of the hitherto much maligned 'Comprehensive school system but also of the reality of teaching before 'centralisation': 'Prior to the central prescription of the curriculum and tests, the curriculum offered varied too according to the ideas of the staff of the school'. Moreover, it was 'also in line with the positive assertion that secondary schools should reflect the communities within which they happened to be located' (Brighouse, 2002: 4). That we can insist that education in Scarborough and Weston-Super-Mare will be undertaken according to the same guidelines and will thus be necessarily unresponsive to their local contexts is ultimately as reassuring as finding they both have an identical retail park consisting of similarly liveried hangers. One of the ambitions of this volume is to refocus energy spent organising somebody else's content so it can be used to negotiate tests in order to address some version of another of Brighouse's 'comprehensive' ambitions 'to give equal value to all sorts of human potential and activity within certain moral limits and principles' (Brighouse, 2002: 3).

Our eight authors have struggled gainfully to address our criteria and realise Rosa Luxemburg's formulation that 'Freedom is freedom for those who think differently' (Luxemburg, 1918). They are beset on all sides but also 'inside' by their 'education' and training as teachers, 'each in the prison dreaming of the key'. In his Barthesian reading of contemporary education, Nick Peim asks provocatively 'what if there is no 'real' education beyond the enclosures of instrumental rationality?' and then further 'What if there is no pure and uncontaminated, 'proper' education that exists outside of or beyond the contingencies of its present historical configuration?' (Peim in Bennett & McDougall, 2014: 39). One of the obvious manifestations of this instrumental rationality is the almost fetishisation of English and Maths GCSE as *sine qua non* qualifications such that the necessarily unsuccessful 40% of the year cohort are to be made to stay on to pursue these universal panaceas, like it or not. And just to make it interesting this coincides with the creation of new, apparently more rigorous, versions (some even compare them to O Level as if it were a compliment). Actually all that happened to, for example, English, is that it has become more 'academic', 'excessively concerned with intellectual matters and lacking experience of practical affairs' (collinsdictionary.com) and therefore more conducive to one set of 'learners' (and here I'm using the term relevantly) rather than another. It is also now assessed merely by a couple of tests, aggrandised as 'exams' and a compulsory speaking and listening assessment which adds nothing to the student's overall score (the ability to effectively converse in the language is literally worth 0%), thus largely advantaging the same group of learners.

This remains a two-year course in a key subject (the most key!) and much is being made of its 'rigour' expressed in some quarters by a strange satisfaction in the fact that fewer children will succeed. The truth is, of course, that selling the validity of a two-year English course predicated on a couple of old fashioned tests is untenable not least because most teachers could prepare most of their students who are ultimately going to pass the sacred C barrier (and deliver what the system spuriously calls 'achievement') in a couple of weeks. In fact, many would reach this barrier without tuition of any kind since this version of English is predicated much more on social and cultural capital than enlightened instruction. Moreover and unequivocally for the record, the need for GCSE English is classically a 'false need', manufactured to the requirements of our increasingly standardised and pseudo-individualised society: a clutch of GCSEs is now the equivalent of your 'papers' allowing you reasonable access to a social world. Sixteen year-olds don't then need 'their English', they need to be more confident readers and writers and not of poems and plays any more than anything else. Peim's devastating indictment of *Subject English* written in 1993 suggested that 'It works against the majority of its students' and of 'systematic discrimination...most crudely realised in exam procedures' (Peim, 1993: 5). It seems, sadly that the womb it sprang from is going strong. And it is not just English, whatever critique Peim is offering 'about the identity and functioning of English in the secondary school curriculum' (Peim, 1993: 1) reads as an indictment also of much of this broader subject-confined curriculum. Even in the 1990s the General Editor of the Teaching Secondary English series, Peter King, was concerned that there were 'political forces currently at work which appear to wish to de-skill the teaching profession, to reduce the teacher to a technician carrying out the commands of those who determine what is to be taught' (Peim, 1993: xiv). For King, 'Teachers who refuse to think about the nature of their subject will make it easy for those forces to overcome the profession' (ibid.).

Moreover, the critique on which this collection of speculations, formulations, strategies and ruses is predicated does indict 'the institutionalised practices of teaching about popular culture' (aka 'the media studies project') for precisely 'failing to make these competing discourses a central object of study (Bennett et al., 2011: 17). And it is without any sense of pleasure or satisfaction that we point out that is precisely this failure to live up even to Peim's millennial hopes for *Subject English*'s 'more radical cousin' that has left the subject pleading for its life. Peim had merely hoped it might, with its 'Theories of popular culture and audience-oriented work', challenge 'cherished beliefs and practices about text and language according to the alternative perspective that Media Studies powerfully offers' (Peim, 2000: 173). In fact, a worst case scenario might conclude, with Peim, that 'English has incorporated Media Studies into itself entirely on its own terms' (ibid.) but that Media has provided so little resistance that it is now relegated to either pallid extension of *Subject English* with a newly bizarre canon of award-winning documentaries or an obsolescence based on having offered too little to counter the accusation that it offers areas 'unsuitable for study'.

We have argued repeatedly that Media Studies has often sought validation problematically: our three 'myths for media teachers' sum up 'much that is both questionable and 'common sense' about media studies as a subject

- That students need to be 'aware of' and be media-literate in an 'incredibly important and powerful media';
- That critically analysing 'popular' and 'accessible' texts employs critical tools identical or at least comparable to those studying, say, a Shakespeare play;
- That the economic power of the 'creative industries' in itself provides justification for academic study. (McDougall, 2004)

We wrote then of a subject which 'like Kafka's Josef K, it has been convicted in its absence of an unspecified crime' (Bennett et al, 2014: 16). Rather than taking for granted, as Bolas does, that 'the media' is an unquestionably legitimate object of study, we argue that such assumptions are symptomatic of the way 'a deeply conservative practice has been masquerading as inclusive, progressive education' (Bennett et al, 2014: 7). Thus Media Studies is still immersed in a way of thinking about the world wherein 'the media' is given agency to send 'messages' to 'the audience' within the workings of 'ideology'. The interventions in this volume are conscious of this critique:

> …we observe, even within such hybridity, the preservation of an unhelpful set of precepts for media education which we call *subject media*. These consist of the construction of 'the media' as a 'Big Other' (Žižek, 1999) to be at once looked at 'critically' and desired as a destination (for employment); the sovereign nature of the text – inherited from the socio-cultural framing of English teaching and the confining of empirical engagement with people (in their situated weaving of media activity into their everyday lives and the performance of identities) and the maintenance of a modernist conception of representation that ultimately serves to undermine the 'emancipatory' spirit of the (ideal) subject. The incomplete project we must press on with requires the removal of 'the media' from the equation. (Bennett et al, 2011: 2)

Of course, our notion of removing 'the media' is not here sympathetic to the job that the reform process seemed for a long time to be intent upon, but the susceptibility of the subject to such an unsophisticated attack is noteworthy. Moreover, we can but continue to challenge 'the institutionalised practices of teaching about popular culture' over their framing of 'specific reading and writing practices, particular ways of making meaning and understanding the world which are far from neutral' (Bennett et al, 2011: 4) which are, in fact, suspect and self-regarding.

Thus in its darkest hour *subject media* has little or no recourse to a discourse of its own, to our notion of an agenda predicated on 'what people do with culture, how they interact with identities, how they engage with the public sphere unevenly, increasingly with the use of digital tools for "being with others" while "the media" as an object of study is always-already compromised by the regarding of its own idea' (Bennett et al, 2011: 6). Potentially the failure to address the 'conditions of possibility' of contemporary cultural exchange, however construed, in terms of opportunities to think about culture and identity in new ways, is the most serious issue and one which our authors embrace without recourse to notions of 'the media'. This remains the central task: to seek 'resources' to employ in what Rancière has called a '"factory of the sensible"… the formation of a shared sensible world, a common habitat, by the weaving together of a plurality of human activities' (Rancière, 2006 :39). This is a very different to seeking 'media texts' and risking 'the institutional, and we argue deeply conservative, framing of the social practices brought together in the formal study of media in schools, colleges and – in many cases but not all – universities' (Bennett et al, 2011: 6). What this collection provides, and to an extent exemplifies, are pedagogic strategies that we hope might inform learning, teaching and research.

DISRUPTIVE EPISTEMOLOGIES

In describing Subject Media as 'a technology and a discourse constructed from and framed by its entire history', we were siting it within broader understandings of the multiple contexts, undercurrents and 'epistemological disruptions' (Bachelard, 2002) that accompany the transition from one way of knowing to another. Foucault called these historically-situated ways of knowing 'epistemes', explaining that 'I would define the episteme retrospectively as the strategic apparatus which permits a separating out from among all the statements which are possible those that will be acceptable within, I won't say a scientific theory, but a field of scientificity, and which it is possible to say are true or false' (Foucault in Gordon [ed.], 1980: 197). Though the 'scienticity' may seem a little tenuous in our case, it will be seen (and remembered) that a particular 'science of signs' has had a significant influence on the character and status of work with media and popular cultural texts, including our own reboot of Barthes!

In both **After** the Media and again here 'Using Media **after** the Subject' we are setting aside a problematic in order to encourage more radical thinking about Media Studies and 'Critical Studies' respectively, as if previous dominant ideas about 'the media' and academic disciplines had temporarily collapsed under the weight of their own contradictions. The notion of the temporal shift is ongoing, not decisive. It would, though, be disingenuous to deny that both books derive a little polemical punch from the suggestion of just such a decisive moment. And this is equally true of two other significant explorations of the contemporary episteme: Vlem Flusser's *What is the Future of Writing?* and Jacques Rancière's *The Future of the Image*. In each case also there is a psychological, even emotional, element to their epistemological speculations, a kind of alarm just as Bachelard argued with relation to epistemologies of science. Bachelard identifies 'epistemological obstacles', mind-sets which constitute an unwillingness to think in certain ways and make a lot of sense in terms of the inherent difficulty of creating new knowledge and approaches within both Media Studies and, more broadly, education (Bachelard, 2002).

Key to the psycho-emotional baggage visited on any consideration of culture in all of its expressions is a mournful nostalgia for lost things and the way things were, often masquerading as discussion about standards and 'quality texts'. These essentially reactionary impulses, which are blowing 'as wildly as the wind' at the moment in English education are quickly set aside by Rancière in his examination of 'how a certain idea of fate and a certain idea of image are tied up in the apocalyptic discourses of today's cultural climate' (Rancière, 2007:1). He goes on to expose the spurious nature of arguments that want to deem the cinematic image implicitly superior to the televisual image, a prompt so pertinent that the project which spurned this book had 'flattened hierarchies' as a guiding principle at the very moment that Ofqual were declaring whole areas of the media 'unsuitable for study'. In doing so Rancière also 'exposes' the real issues of representation, 'primarily operations, relations between the sayable and the visible, ways of playing with the before and after, cause and effect' (Rancière, 2007: 6): its conditions of intelligibility. It's why, despite the textual categories, this project is not about texts but rather relationships, approaches and 'excursions'.

TOWARDS A HISTORY OF THE PRESENT

And yet the image insinuates itself as text, clarified by the Barthes of *Camera Lucida* as *punctum* ('its immediate pathetic effect') plus *studium* (the 'information it transmits and meanings it receives') as a compound of 'hyper-resemblance' ('the alterity our contemporaries demand') and 'decoding' (Rancière, 2007: 10). Rancière writes of 'the senseless materiality of the visible' which is 'demanded by the contemporary celebration of the image or its nostalgic evocation' (Rancière, 2007: 9). Ironically by this process the mythologist returns a natural image 'constituted by the loss of the historical quality of things', 'it gives them the simplicity of essences' (Barthes, 1972: 143). Thankfully Rancière has depths of his own and a deep sense of historical context and is able to put these to work to provide the kind of Foucaultian 'history of the present' that we attempted in *After the Media*.

Here the point is to use history 'as a way of diagnosing the present' rather than to explain 'how the present has emerged from the past', 'to use it, to deform it, to make it groan and protest' (Foucault in Gordon [ed.], 1980: 54). Looking for contingencies rather than causes, Rancière takes the long view. He suggests that the 'regime of images' whose impact and aftershock we are still negotiating, was created at 'the point in the nineteenth century' which was 'the moment of this new exchange between artistic images and commerce in social imagery' and 'the moment when Marx teaches us to decipher the hieroglyphs written on the seemingly a-historical body of the commodity and to penetrate the productive hell concealed by the words of economics' (Rancière, 2007: 16). He writes of 'a solidarity forged between the operations of art, the forms of imagery and the discursiveness of symptoms' in other words in the heat of a struggle for social 'purchase' (Rancière, 2007: 17). Thus the history of the image in this respect is 'the fate of this logical paradoxical intertwining between the operations of art, the modes of circulation of imagery and the critical discourse that refers the operations of the one and the forms of the other to their hidden truth' (Rancière, 2007: 17-18). And to fail to get beyond this is to share its fate.

Ultimately, like our calling time on the unitary concept 'the media', 'the end of images is not some mediatic or mediumistic catastrophe' (Rancière, 2007: 18) to be remedied by some unspecified transcendence embedded in some process of chemical reproduction or return to celluloid. Rather they are both 'long gone': 'the end of images is a historical project that lies behind us…' (ibid.)

> At the start of the twentieth century, the media disappeared from the Western world. (Bennett et al, 2011: 3).

Thus any project which is interested in thinking about images or media or both of these, in exploring 'the intertwining of art and non-art, of art commodities and discourse' (Rancière, 2007: 19) is necessarily predicated on a sense of loss, an epistemological disruption. And partly this mourning is channeled through certain kinds of critical thinking which proved adept at tracking 'the messages of commodities and power hidden in the innocence of media and advertising imagery' (ibid.). Central to this 'transition' is what Rancière calls the loss of semiology (semiotics) 'as illustrated in exemplary fashion by the Barthes of *Mythologies*" (Rancière, 2007: 18). Though Rancière is appreciative of Barthes' work, it is very clear that he sees this 'phase' of the argument over and is sceptical about the long term achievements of structuralist semiotics.

We, of course, view Barthes as much more of a transitional figure and are keen not to saddle him with every limitation of every lightly taken position. If *Mythologies* remains his most influential and ground-breaking work, it is interesting to note that by the early seventies he understood it as a form which belonged to the past. In fact in his original preface (published in English in 1957) he claims only 'to live to the full the contradiction of my time, which may well make sarcasm the condition of truth' (Barthes, 1972: 11). It is a commitment that he spent the rest of his life fulfilling: 'I can only repeat to myself the words which end Sartre's *No Exit*: Let's go on' (Barthes, 1977: 136). Barthes cannot be held responsible for all of the imagined 'sins' of semiotics, but we must acknowledge the degree to which a certain kind of analysis has proved unhelpful to our hopes of an emancipated and emancipatory Media Studies.

Having written once of new territories often requiring not only new maps, but new cartographies, it is disappointing to record how often in our area old maps seem to 'do'. Too often a sophisticated critical system appears to provide justification enough and semiotics as such a system has no peer. Its contribution to a Media Studies fighting for its life, on the other hand is at least problematic. David Gauntlett's critique in 2007 of the 'traditional approach to Media Studies, which is still dominant in a lot (but not all) of school and university teaching, and textbooks' begins with 'A tendency to fetishise 'experts', whose readings of popular culture are seen as more significant than those of other audience members (with corresponding faith in faux-expert non-procedures such as semiotics)' (cited in Bennett & McDougall, 2014: 10). He clearly also has semiotics in mind when he writes ironically of the development of 'a wonderful set of tools, over 50 years, for understanding the media': in 2007 50 years was precisely the age of *Mythologies*. Nor is this criticism isolated or unwarranted, even the 'semiotician' Daniel Chandler concedes: 'At worst, what passes for 'semiotic analysis' is little more than a pretentious form of literary criticism applied beyond the bounds of literature and based merely on subjective interpretation and grand assertions' (Chandler, 2002). And far worse for our egalitarian and enabling educational project is the accusation that 'in some cases, semiotic analysis seems little more than an excuse for interpreters to display the appearance of mastery through the use of jargon which excludes most people from participation' (ibid.). Thus paradoxically the theoretical content that should put clear blue water between its critical actions and those of a 'theory-shy' literary criticism 'In giving priority to the determining power of the system…can be seen as fundamentally conservative' (ibid.). Moreover the focus is heavily on individual text analysis which 'does not address processes of production, audience interpretation or even authorial intentions' (ibid.). It is more often synchronic rather than diachronic in its analysis. Though prompted by Barthes who explicitly 'resented seeing Nature and History confused at every turn' (Barthes, 1972: 10), too much semiotic analysis over the last 50 years in a range of contexts has been progressively emptied of its historical character.

Chandler points to Judith Williamson's book *Decoding Advertisements* published in 1978, as emblematic of a certain kind of approach in which the task 'is to unveil through analysis what she calls the 'real' meaning of the words and images of an ad, and the 'real world' to which the 'unreal' images of the ad refer (Williamson, 1978: 47). Chandler questions the absence of a critical framework to address 'a clear assumption that 'reality' is not only quite distinct from 'fiction' but also morally superior' and suggests that 'a drawback of the approach is its hasty satisfaction that such equivalences constitute a complete analysis' (Chandler, 2002).

BRINGING IT ALL BACK HOME

If Media Studies has strayed, had its head turned by what Gauntlett calls 'an independently fascinating set of texts and technologies' now is the time to bring it home when in Nick Burbridge's memorable phrase 'the fear of being lost collides with the fear of being found' (Burbridge, 2003: *Asylum*). And this is not about the opportunity to return to its silo but to offer up its services to a new configuration which will be 'using' media irrespective of what the government wants or the future holds. It is predicated rather on Peim's agenda for English which now encompasses a range of critical and creative 'takes' and 'turns' and if it wasn't massively contradictory might be collectively called 'Text'. For Peim, and for us, the 'reconstruction' has a particular focus: 'addressing issues of inequality and cultural identity: it also means addressing more fully and more centrally issues of race class and gender…' (Peim, 1993: 8). It entails a commitment to courses rather than curriculum and courses that understand the need to be responsive, reactive and respectful of the 'landscapes' they travel through, principally our students. And in accepting Barthes' notion of 'the inevitability' of power informing the discursive forms of our teaching, we also accept his solution for 'loosening, baffling or at the very least of lightening that power': 'if one writes, fragmentation, and, if one teaches, digression, or, to put it in a preciously ambiguous word, *excursion*' (Barthes in Sontag [ed.], 1993: 476).

But these must not be heritage trails, merely organised trips to see the famous sights, or even 'sites'. This is a project motivated and engaged, following Matt Hills suggestion that elitist objectivity might be replaced with what we previously described as 'an amplification of 'passionate engagement' with texts that transcends fan culture and at the same time orthodox 'textual analysis'; that cultural theory makes political its observations, and that it situates culture – what matters and how it comes to matter – as a site of struggle' (Bennett et al, 2011: 8). Thus students serving their apprenticeships in our critical dispensation are apprentices in theorising their culture and the curricular space that Media Studies might have, and might still occupy is a place 'to facilitate 'mastery' in a meta-language which gives voice to reflexive negotiation of identity – a kind of 'culture literacy'' (Bennett et al, 2011: 13).

In all of this, 'text' remains an unwanted problematic, even the elephant in the room since traditionally all of our schooled critical instincts gravitate toward it and even the project of this book offers at some level basically a set of lists of texts. What is clear is that the integrity of the term is increasingly uncertain under the pressure of what Hills calls 'textualisation'. Hills is calling for a realisation that contemporary culture 'is created through how producers and consumers do different things with texts, including breaking the world in to certain textual, symbolic bits in the first instance' (Hills, 2005: 27). Certainly there can be no justification for endlessly classifying texts until we have interrogated the feasibility of the concept and entertaining the notion that these two activities may be intimately connected. Even as I write I am negotiating an identity for this 'text' which may paradoxically be more important (valuable) than the identities of any of those involved in its creation: readers or writers. I have been here before:

> What are we making and why does it matter? Abstract? Paper? Talk? Teach? Session? Lesson? Telling? Text? Something woven! This is the issue in Derrida's beguiling 'defence speech'/critical essay, The Law of Genre, an oft quoted but little explored 'essay'. The 'generic' is exactly that which stalks 'anticipation' and requires every act to meet our need to identify it. Derrida calls genre a 'principle of contamination…a law of impurity', insisting that 'Madness is law, the law is madness'. It is here in this 'paper thing' (in both senses) and in our attempts to define a context for discussion. (Bennett, 2012: 3)

Whether or not we need a notion of 'the text', we certainly need a renegotiation of its function within our new dispensation: shorn of its authority it might reinvent itself as a genuine resource. We consciously asked our contributors to try to fold in a literary or otherwise high cultural text for this reason and almost inevitably it proved the most problematic requirement. Peim juxtaposes Donne and Madonna and Verona and *Summer Bay* to expose the brittleness of arguments about 'distinction' and 'quality' but the inability of most of our authors to comfortably accommodate established literary work shows the damage still being done by and to this otherwise potentially useful set of selected texts. And perhaps the greatest pity is that a text like *Romeo and Juliet* which might be usefully employed by folks in conversations about who they are and what they need is effectively disabled by its 'weight', its literary status. And in simple terms this is because nobody remotely knows how to use it without reference to Shakespeare so it largely remains unpalatable and to some degree unreadable.

READING AS TRAVELLING

This is why in order to go forward we need to go back to reading, not as a basic skill or educational 'tool' (or God forbid a GCSE) but as on De Certeau's terms 'only one aspect of consumption, but a fundamental one' (De Certeau, 1988: 167). De Certeau is the poet of everyday life but we must do more than merely revel in his metaphors. Like Barthes for De Certeau 'Words are no longer conceived illusively as simple instruments, they are cast as projections, explosions, vibrations, devices' (Barthes in Sontag [ed.], 1993: 464). But the rest belongs to the reader, 'like a Robinson Crusoe discovering an island…

"possessed" by his own fooling and jesting…like a hunter in the forest, he spots the written quarry, follows a trail, laughs, plays tricks, or else like a gambler, lets himself be taken in by it' (De Certeau, 1988: 173). And we must do more than take these Robinson Crusoes on packaged tours abroad. When De Certeau writes that 'readers are travelers; they move across lands belonging to someone else, like nomads poaching their way across fields they did not write, despoiling the wealth of Egypt to enjoy it themselves' (De Certeau, 1988: 174) he was certainly not imagining a phalanx of literary or cultural critics armed with the *International Handbook of Semiotics*. There is rather an immediacy and genuine engagement in 'Reading takes no measures against the erosion of time (one forgets oneself and also forgets), it does not keep what it acquires' (ibid.). The reader is 'simultaneously inside and outside, dis-solving both by mixing them together, associating texts like funerary statues that he awakens and hosts, but never owns' (ibid.). And that for De Certeau is the path of emancipation: 'In that way, he also escapes from the law of each text in particular, and from that of the social milieu' (ibid.).

But this is not just the case for speculative 'foreign' theory. David Stevens writing *A guided reader for secondary English: pedagogy and practice* in the teeth of the current reforms is also keen to address our theme: 'My own aim is to move away from a conception of the critical reader, beholder, or commentator — away that is, from a position of insight which provides the ability to produce analytic critique, as the central goal of a humanistic education' (Stevens, 2012: 10). He writes of the need to support young people to be 'confident in the face of difference — cultural, linguistic, ethnic, ethical — and confident in the everyday experience of change; able to see change and difference as entirely usual conditions of cultural and social life; and to see them as essential productive resources' (ibid.). His model of a new 'English Curriculum' is closer than ever to our subject-less speculation as 'the curriculum of communication and of representation, among others, and in its treatment of the practices of communication, as of the practices of representation, the texts, the visions we make, and how we make them, it holds, implicitly, the most decisive power for the making of working futures.' (Stevens 2012: 11). Stevens also deplores '…the hegemonic impulses behind a National Curriculum which declares certain literary texts worthy (and by extension, others less worthy) of inclusion in the schooled experience of the nation's young people' (Stevens, 2012: 11). However he is most interesting and useful when he addresses the centrality of 'reading':

> Whether or not they are conscious of it, however, teachers at all levels are always teaching their students how to read. The different ways students are asked to read imply particular values and beliefs about the nature of texts, the nature of readers as subjects of texts and as subjects in the world, and about meaning and language itself. Yet the dominant ideological signification of reading often works against students' developing the capacity to think 'critically' about what they read, as many national assessments have demonstrated. As one possible solution to this apparent absence

of 'critical reading', students need to learn to locate the texts they read, as well as themselves as reading subjects, within larger social contexts; in short, they need to be able to inquire into and understand the interconnectedness of social conditions and the reading and writing practices of a culture. (Stevens 2012: 60)

De Certeau is predictably more dramatic: 'Today, the text is society itself. It takes urbanistic, industrial, commercial, or televised forms' (De Cereau, 1988: 167). Lyotard implores us to 'work without rules, in order to establish the rules for what will have been' and to 'produce new presentations – not to take pleasure in them but to better produce the feeling that there is something representable' (cited in Bennett et al., 2011: 14). For Barthes in the end 'The semiologist is, in short, an artist (the word as I use it, neither glorifies nor disdains)' (Sontag [ed.], 1993: 475) and 'this semiology… is not a hermeneutics: it paints more than it digs' (ibid.). In simple terms 'Writing makes knowledge festive' (1993: 464), it is 'in no way an instrument for communication, it is not an open route'. (Barthes 1967: 25). This is the 'creation' that Deleuze and Guattari call for, their resistance to the present' since 'A multiplicity has neither subject nor object… (Deleuze & Guattari 1988: 9). Sontag's final judgment on Barthes the teacher is pertinent too: 'the point is not to teach us something in particular', but rather 'to make us bold, agile, subtle, intelligent, detached' (Sontag [ed.], 1993: xvii).

The attempts made in this book are merely a starting point. As this chapter's pre-quote insists 'the multiple must be made', especially now when social media proliferates communities of practice predicated on all manner of interests and commitments. This veritable 'matrix' requires new models, new 'cartographies' rather than new maps or perhaps a principled attempt once again to apply cultural theory to the projects of learning. Dave Cormier finds just such a model in Deleuze and Gauattari's notion of the rhizome and though he is addressing online education his arguments remain pertinent. He argues that 'The rhizome metaphor, which represents a critical leap in coping with the loss of a canon against which to compare, judge, and value knowledge, may be particularly apt as a model for disciplines on the bleeding edge where the canon is fluid and knowledge is a moving target' (Cormier, 2008). He proposes, somewhat propitiously, 'The Rhizomatic Model of Education' and it has much to recommend it:

> In the rhizomatic model of learning, curriculum is not driven by predefined inputs from experts; it is constructed and negotiated in real time by the contributions of those engaged in the learning process. This community acts as the curriculum, spontaneously shaping, constructing, and reconstructing itself and the subject of its learning in the same way that the rhizome responds to changing environmental conditions. (Cormier 2008)

As Deleuze and Guattari point out, 'The rhizome operates by variation, expansion, conquest, capture, offshoots' and 'pertains to a map that must be produced, constructed, a map that is always detachable, connectible, reversible, modifiable, and has multiple entryways and exits and its own lines of flight' (Deleuze & Guattari, 1987: 21). Cormier's wish is that 'a community can construct a model of education flexible enough for the way knowledge develops and changes today by producing a map of contextual knowledge' (Cormier 2008) . He also cites Tella on our more pertinent focus: 'If the world of media education is thought of as a rhizome, as a library à la Eco [in The Name of the Rose], then we need to construct our own connections through this space in order to appropriate it. However, instead of that solitary groping made by Brother William, we see as our goal the co-construction of those secret connections as a collaborative effort' (cited in Cormier 2008). He offers examples which are comparable to Chris Waugh's students participating in *Edutronic* and allocates the teacher the role of offering 'not just a window, but an entry point into an existing learning community'. Cormier also claims that 'the rhizomatic viewpoint returns the concept of knowledge to its earliest roots' since it 'can allow a community of people to legitimize the work they are doing among themselves and for each member of the group' (ibid.).

In *After the Media* we proposed 'a pedagogy of the inexpert', 'intended as neither a tidy nor a literal concept, but more as a rhetorical provocation to the traditional model of the teacher as 'subject expert' and expressed our desire 'to sketch alternative possible subject positions for teachers and students engaged in text-conscious work that are predicated on the kinds of models of post-structuralist educational practice' (Bennett et al, 2011:231). Here is such a subject position fulfilling Peim's desire for 'a multi-directional thing, a mobile theory of texts, language, the subject, subjectivity' (Peim, 1993: 3). Hence Cormier's conclusion states that 'Through involvement in multiple communities where new information is being assimilated and tested, educators can begin to apprehend the moving target that is knowledge in the modern learning environment' (Cormier 2008).

However to return this experiment to its first principles I would like to re-visit the Tim Brighouse speech quoted earlier and given as the first memorial lecture in honour of Brian Simon and Caroline Benn described as 'the founding heroes of comprehensive education' because above all these interventions are attempts to defend, maintain and revive what FORUM Chairperson Michael Armstrong dubbed 'Two great beliefs':

> The first – that all children, however diverse, are alike in their capacity to reason and to imagine, to criticize and to create, to examine and to make, to interpret and to construct, to participate and to innovate in every aspect of culture.
>
> The second – that all children, however diverse, learn best when they learn together, sharing each other's insight and experience, absorbing knowledge and recreating knowledge as they collaborate, in the company of their teachers, in a common pursuit. (Brighouse, 2002: 4).

Armstrong quotes Keats in a letter arguing that arguing that originality is a common human possession rather than the privilege of a few, an argument we have found needs continually to be renewed:

> But the Minds of Mortals are so different and bent on such diverse Journeys that it may at first appear impossible for any common taste and fellowship to exist between two or three under these suppositions – It is however quite the contrary – Minds would leave each other in contrary directions, traverse each other in Numberless points, and at last greet each other at the Journey's End. (Armstrong, 2010: 33)

But the last words must be Tim Brighouse's, recalling a speech he made as Birmingham's education chief, expressing his hopes for 'what a full educational offer to all our children' would look like:

> We must all work to make this world worthy of its children. Because they are 100% of its future. Let this be the beginning of a wish for every Birmingham child: that we would want them to be people with a strong sense of themselves and their own humanity, with an awareness of their thoughts and feelings, with a capacity to feel and express love and joy and to recognise tragedy and feel deep grief. We would want them to be people who, with a strong and realistic sense of their own worth, are able to relate with others, to co-operate effectively toward common ends and to view humankind as one, while respecting diversity and difference. We will want them to be people, who even while very young, somehow sense that they have the capacity for lifelong spiritual and intellectual growth. (Brighouse, 2002)

Well, we're still working.

> I sincerely believe that at the origin of teaching such as this we must always locate a fantasy. (Sontag [ed.], 1993: 477)

> They never taught us nor allowed us to say our multiplicity. That would have been improper speech. (Irigaray, 1992: 207)

WORKS CITED

Armstrong, M. (2010) *What Children Know: essays on children's literacy and visual* at lulu.com.

Bachelard, G. (2002) *Formation of the Scientific Mind*. Clinamen Press.

Baudrillard, J. (1998) *Selected Writings*. M. Poster (ed.). Cambridge: Polity Press.

Baudrillard, J. (2009) 'The precession of the simulacra', in J. Storey (ed.) *Cultural Theory and Popular Culture: A Reader*, 4th edn. London: Pearson. pp. 409–15.

Barthes, R. (1972) *Mythologies*. London: Jonathan Cape.

Barthes, R. (1975) *The Pleasure of the Text*. New York: Farrar, Straus and Giroux.

Barthes, R. (1977) *Image, Music, Text*. London: Fontana.

Bennett, P. (2012) 'Songs of Sisyphus: of gestures and genres, trying and dying.' Paper presented at Extending Gesture Colloquium, University of Edinburgh, October.

Bennett, P., Kendall, A. and McDougall, J. (2011) *After The Media*. Abingdon: Routledge.

Bennett, P. and McDougall, J. (eds) (2014) *Barthes' Mythologies Today*. New York: Routledge.

Brighouse, T. (2003) 'Comprehensive Schools Then, Now and in the Future: is it time to draw a line in the sand and create a new ideal?' In FORUM, Volume 45, No. 1: http://www.theguardian.com/education/2002/sep/26/secondaryschools (accessed 13 February 2016).

Burbridge, N. (2003) *Claws and Wings* recorded by McDermott's 2 Hours v. Levellers on Hag records. B00008VFE4.

Chandler, D. (2002) *Semiotics for Beginners*: http://visual-memory.co.uk/daniel/Documents/S4B/ (accessed 13 February 2016).

Cormier, D. (2008) 'Rhizomatic education : Community as curriculum'. *Innovate* 4 (5): http://davecormier.com/edblog/2008/06/03/rhizomatic-education-community-as-curriculum (accessed 13 February 2016).

De Certeau, M. (1988) *The Practice of Everyday Life*. Berkeley, California: University of California Press.

Deleuze, G. and Guattari, F. (2004) *A Thousand Plateaus*. London: Continuum.

Gordon, C. (ed.) (1980) *Michel Foucault: Power/Knowledge: Selected Interviews and other writings 1972–1977*. Brighton. Harvester.

Hills, M. (2005) *How to Do Things with Cultural Theory*. London: Hodder Arnold.

Irigaray, L. (1992) 'When our lips speak together', in M. Humm (ed.) *Feminisms: A Reader*. London: Harvester Wheatsheaf.

Keates, C. (2012): http://www.itv.com/news/story/2012-09-16/gove-to-announce-exams-overhaul/?page=2 (accessed 13 February 2016).

Luxemburg, R. (1918): https://www.marxists.org/archive/luxemburg/1918/russian-revolution/index.htmt (accessed 13 February 2016).

McDougall, J. (2004) 'Subject media: the socio-cultural framing of discourse', University of Birmingham: http://etheses.bham.ac.uk/556/ (accessed on 14 May 2010).

Moran, J. (2002) *Interdisciplinarity*. Abingdon: Routledge.

Peim, N. (1993) *Critical Theory and the English Teacher*. London: Routledge.

Peim, N. (2000) 'The Cultural Politics of English Teaching' in *Issues in English Teaching*. London: Routledge.

Rancière, J. (2006) *The Politics of Aesthetics*, London: Continuum.

Rancière, J. (2007) *The Future of the Image*, trans. Gregory Elliott. Verso: London.

Rustin, S. (2016) *Media studies: why does the subject get such a bad press?*: http://www.theguardian.com/education/2016/feb/08/media-studies-bad-press-alevel-soft-option (accessed 13 February 2016).

Sontag, S. (ed.) (1993) *A Roland Barthes Reader*. London: Vintage.

Stevens, D. (2012) *A guided reader for secondary English: pedagogy and practice*. Abingdon. Routledge.

Storey, J. (ed.) (2009) *Cultural Theory and Popular Culture: A reader*, 4th edn. Harlow: Pearson.

Žižek, S. (1999) 'The spectre of ideology', in E. Wright and E. Wright (eds) *The Žižek Reader*. Oxford: Blackwell.

INDEX

After the Media 2–5, 7, 10, 13, 37–8, 95, 164, 169, 171, 177

Agency 6, 11, 37, 42, 55–6, 77–8, 83, 131–, 152, 154, 168

A Level 38, 68, 89, 93, 121, 145, 149, 163–4

Art 12, 18–19, 21, 26–30, 33, 41–2, 46–7, 51, 87–8, 102, 106, 108, 126, 164, 171

Audience 4–5, 8, 17–33, 54, 56, 66, 69, 86–8, 115–16, 119, 121, 123–7, 131, 134–5, 137, 140, 142, 166–8, 172

Autoethnography 59, 93–5, 98–9, 102

Autonomy 97, 104, 107, 135–7, 147, 155

Bakhtin, Michail 100

Bartlett, Man 12, 127

Barthes, Roland .... ix, 151, 155, 164–6, 169–74, 176

Baudrillard, Jean 163–4

Be Kind, Rewind (2008) 12, 84

Benefits Street (2014) 11

Blogging 12, 29, 51, 84–5, 98, 108–9, 124, 131, 134–6, 140, 157

Bourdieu, Pierre 5

Brecht, Bertolt 11, 22, 151

Bricolage 12, 97, 110

Bricoleur 93

Brighouse, Tim 166, 177–8

Buckingham, David 8–9

Camera Lucida 170

Canon .... xi, 5, 38, 136, 138, 165, 168

Cassette Boy 12, 86

Centre for Contemporary Cultural Studies 1, 101

Character 11, 39, 42, 51–2, 56, 61–3, 67–8, 70, 79, 105, 107–9, 115–17, 119–21, 125–6, 131, 139, 169, 172

Cinema 38, 88

Creativity 3, 41–2, 51, 54, 56, 65, 71, 86–7, 95, 125–6, 148–9, 154

Cultural Studies .... ix, x, 2, 8, 105

Curriculum .... xi, 1, 3, 6, 11, 38, 55, 64, 75–7, 87, 95, 98, 102, 114, 136, 142, 149–51, 153–5, 158–9, 163, 165–7, 173, 175–6

Debord, Guy 152

de Certeau, Michel 151, 174–6

Deleuze, Giles 6, 10, 163, 176–7

Democracy 39–40, 70

Derrida, Jacques .... ix, xi, 98, 174

Diegetic / Non-Diegetic 64, 79, 117

Discourse .... ix, 12, 18, 59–60, 64–6, 69–71, 82, 95, 97, 99–101, 106, 140–2, 146–8, 150–1, 153–4, 158, 163, 167, 169–71

Disney Infinity 12, 120–4

Distribution of the Sensible, The (2006) 165

Doctor Martens 11, 44, 50

Doctor Who (1963–) 86

Documentary 22, 29, 106

Douglas, Stan 12, 127–8

Drama 9, 24–6, 77, 105, 113, 115–16, 118, 121, 145

Educating Essex (2011) 105, 108

Edutronic, The 12, 131–2, 134, 137, 139, 141, 177

EHRC 96

'Eight Learning Events Model' (8LEM) 96

Elder Scrolls 60–1, 71

Engagement .... xi, 2, 6, 9, 11, 20–1, 23, 25–6, 29–30, 59, 64–5, 77, 88, 90, 94, 102, 110, 122–3, 138, 152, 168, 173, 175

English .... x–xi, 1–5, 8, 12–13, 37, 60, 70, 105, 113, 115, 131–2, 145–8, 141–2, 166–9, 173, 175

English Baccalaureate (EBacc) 164

Environment 1, 22–4, 31–3, 59, 74, 81–3, 89, 113, 124, 152, 177

INDEX

Epistemology 2, 4–6, 8, 10, 93, 97, 105, 146, 169–71

Ethnography 8–9

Everyday life 1, 3, 5, 11, 39–40, 47, 71, 80–4, 105, 107, 145, 152, 174

Expertise 3–6, 27, 60, 62, 67, 80, 99, 138

Feedback 59, 64, 76, 104, 107, 109, 133, 138, 140, 149

Feminism .... x, 52, 56

Film Studies 37–8, 60, 79, 81, 93, 115

Freire, Paulo 12, 94–5, 103–4, 148, 153–4

Fenton, Natalie 4, 101, 164

Flusser, Vlem 170

Foucault, Michel .... ix, 41, 99, 106, 169–70

'Funds of Knowledge' 13, 158

Gage, Zack 12, 82

Game of Thrones (2011–) 11, 20

Gameplay 11, 24, 30–2, 51, 59, 167–71, 121

Gauntlett, David 8, 93–4, 172–3

GCSE .... x, 77, 93, 149, 163, 166–7, 174

Gender 6, 41–2, 52, 61, 68, 80, 96, 156, 173

Genre 17, 37, 48, 84, 108, 116, 119, 124, 138, 163, 174

Goffman, Irving 80, 114–15, 121–4

Grand Theft Auto 11, 51, 53–4, 81

Guattari, Felix 6, 10, 163, 176–7

Hall, Stuart 2, 11, 40, 54

Hashtagging 82

Hegemony .... x, 2, 6–7, 39, 175

Hoggart, Richard 1–2

Identity .... x, 2, 5, 7–8, 11, 19–20, 26, 28, 37, 39–41, 43–6, 51–6, 59, 66, 95–6, 104, 106, 108–10, 121, 123, 135, 146, 154, 158, 167, 169, 173–4

Instagram 12, 81–2

Intertextuality .... ix, 11, 88

It Felt Like a Kiss (2009) 22–5

It Happened One Night (1934) 119

Jenkins, Henry 8, 122, 125

Juxtaposition 13, 22, 46, 157–8, 174

Lego Serious Play 94

Levi-Strauss, Claude 93

Literacy 1–2, 5–9, 11, 59, 105, 136, 141, 168, 173

Literature .... ix–xi, 2–3, 7, 9, 12, 18, 37, 41–2, 46, 51, 94, 113, 115, 117–19, 138, 148, 151, 154, 156, 172

The Long Revolution 1, 8, 13

Masks 11, 24–6, 31, 49, 164

Mass Media 3–4, 41, 46, 51, 84–6, 123–4, 125

Mean Streets 11, 79

Media Studies .... ix–xi, 4–5, 7–8, 10, 13, 19, 37–42, 55, 60, 114, 120–2, 128, 164, 167–70, 172–3

Mediated / Mediation 1, 4–7, 37, 39, 52–3, 56, 81, 117, 120, 124, 126, 128, 135, 148, 153, 159

Meme 11, 53, 55

Mise-en-scène 11, 42, 64, 79, 87, 116, 118

Mods / Modding (of games) 65–7

Macbeth 12, 133–4

Much Ado About Nothing 12, 117–21, 125, 128

Narrative 8, 11, 13, 21–4, 29, 31–2, 51, 54, 64, 70, 77–8, 93–4, 98, 101–4, 108, 117, 120–1, 123, 138, 143, 151, 153, 157–9,

Neo-liberal 2

Occulus Rift 7–11, 30–3

Ofqual 170

Paratextual 11

Parkour 12

Pedagogy .... 2, 4, 59–60, 63–7, 69–70, 89–90, 93, 95, 97, 113, 145, 147–8, 150, 153–4, 159, 169, 175, 177 'pedagogy of the inexpert'.............. 2, 6, 8–9, 12, 95, 177

Peim, Nick........................ 5, 9, 12–13, 165–8, 173–4, 177

Performance 12, 21–6, 32–3, 37, 41, 87, 105, 108, 113–29, 138, 147–8, 164, 168

Perry, Grayson 9, 11, 28–9

Pink, Sarah 95, 99, 107

Pinterest 11, 42, 46, 50–1, 53

Play 3, 5–7, 12, 21, 32, 60–2, 64, 66, 68, 71, 73–91, 94, 107, 121–3, 151, 155, 157

PlayStation Network (PSN) 12, 123–4

Popular Culture .... x–xi, 1, 7, 13, 59, 71, 104, 125, 167, 169, 172

Postmodern 11, 163–4

Power 5–7, 13, 18, 40–1, 49, 62, 66–9, 76, 101, 118, 135, 141, 151, 153–5, 159, 168, 171–3, 175

Presentation of Self in Everyday Life 115

Prosumers 17

Psychogeography 12, 152

Punchdrunk Theatre 11, 22–4, 26, 31

Quests 59–64, 68–70

Rancière, Jacques 4, 6, 165, 169–71

Rankin 11, 28–9

Rear Window 12, 85

Reading 2–4, 7, 10, 12–13, 17–33, 37, 40–1, 43, 45, 54, 65, 71, 77, 84, 98, 109, 126, 136–7, 145–8, 152, 155–6, 158, 169, 172, 174–8

Reception Theory 19, 27, 54, 148

Reflection 81, 109, 131

Reforms 38, 100, 147, 149, 163–79

Ricoeur, Paul 151

Representation 12, 23–5, 31, 37, 39–40, 42–3, 52, 55–6, 94, 99, 101, 105–6, 108–9, 116–17, 122, 146–7, 154, 164, 168, 170, 175

Rhizome 6–7, 11–13, 176–7

Ritzer, George 103

Romeo and Juliet 12, 132, 137, 174

Sartre, Jean-Paul 95, 98, 100, 105–6, 172

Scary Mary (2006) 12, 126

Self, Will 12

Selfie 1, 39–44, 46, 50–1, 53–4, 56

Sherman, Cindy 11, 79, 87

Spectatorship 24

Ska, Tom 12, 87

Skills 6–7, 17–19, 62, 76, 86–8, 96–7, 99, 104, 113–14, 116, 118, 123, 125, 133, 136, 145, 147, 149, 155, 158

Simpsons, The 11, 53

Squidverse 12

subject media 2–3, 42, 168–9

Suspiria 12, 127–8

A Streetcar Named Desire 11, 22

Social Media 3–4, 16, 19–21, 25, 31–2, 47, 50–1, 59, 81–2, 127, 136, 176

Skyrim 11, 60–71

Students 7–13, 17–21, 23–6, 29, 32–3, 37–44, 48–56, 60–71, 73, 76–82, 86–9, 93–7, 99–101, 103–10, 113–15, 117–22, 124–8, 131–9, 142–3, 145–9, 163, 167–8, 173, 175–7

The Drowned Man 22, 24–5

'Teaching by Phenomena' 113–14

Technology 8–9, 13, 19, 21, 31–3, 39, 85–6, 89, 127, 131, 169, 173

Television 3, 11, 23, 25–9, 49, 70, 77, 80, 86, 93, 109, 118

Textual / Textuality .... ix–xi, 1–13, 37–8, 41–3, 46, 48, 50, 59, 78, 80–4, 88, 93, 95–7, 99, 101–8, 110, 142, 170, 173–4

Theatre 3, 11, 19, 21–6, 30, 115, 117–18, 120

Third Space 6, 10

Toca Nature 88

Unesco 6

Urban Wandering 152

Uses and Gratifications 121–2

Video games 3, 41, 51, 55, 59–72, 84, 88–9, 120–4, 128,

Virtual Reality 31–2

WhatsApp 1, 39–43, 50

Wiki 11, 51, 59–60, 64–5, 70–1

Williams, Raymond 1, 7–8, 11, 13

Wolf Report 96

Wright Mills, C 95–7, 104

Writing 2–3, 8, 10–13, 26, 38–9, 50, 59–72, 74, 84, 93, 98, 105, 114, 132–9, 141, 146, 151–2, 155, 158, 169–70, 175–6

YouTube 5, 31–2, 39, 84, 86

Žižek, Slavoj 7, 168

Zoella 12, 87

www.ingramcontent.com/pod-product-compliance
Lightning Source LLC
Chambersburg PA
CBHW062044220426
43662CB00010B/1641